From Infrastructure to Services

Praise for this book

'The quest for sustainable water and sanitation services in many developing countries is ongoing, and the challenges to deliver such services in an equitable manner are immense. Policy makers and practitioners thus need to continue to find solutions that are appropriate and are adequately resourced. Evidence of what works and what does not (and why), supported by critical insights and interpretation is absolutely essential. This book rightly highlights the need for robust monitoring and makes a strong case based on practical examples – a must-read compendium for anyone who seeks to transform the manner in which water and sanitation services are delivered.'
Girish Menon, Director of International Programmes and Deputy Chief Executive, WaterAid

'If the human right to water and sanitation is to be realized for all in a sustainable manner, then monitoring advances and possible slippages in access is fundamental. *From Infrastructure to Services* brings us up to date on important new advances in monitoring water and sanitation services being implemented on the ground. It is essential reading for all those working to achieve and maintain water, sanitation and hygiene services for all and forever.'
Catarina de Albuquerque, First United Nations Special Rapporteur on the Human Right to Water and Sanitation (2008-2014), Vice-Chair of Sanitation and Water for All

'A timely assessment of the potential of WASH sector monitoring approaches to support the achievement of universal access to sustainable services post-2015.'
Tom Slaymaker, WHO/UNICEF Joint Monitoring Programme on Water Supply and Sanitation

'*From Infrastructure to Services* provides crucial insights, experiences and practical ways to marry monitoring and learning with programming for real change in water and sanitation services delivery. Written by some of the WASH sector's finest thinkers and practitioners, this book may prove a critical piece in the WASH community's growing arsenal of assets needed to actually solve the global water and sanitation crisis.'
Ned Breslin, Chief Executive Officer, Water For People

'*From Infrastructure to Services* provides an updated picture of today's monitoring achievements and drawbacks, opportunities and challenges from a practitioner point of view and in accessible language. It is a must, not only for M&E specialists working in the water, sanitation and hygiene sector in developing countries, but also for all decision-makers and senior managers in governments, development organizations and NGOs who are asked to create sustainable M&E systems, and to make use of the data for lasting development results.'
Fabio B. Losa, Senior Monitoring and Evaluation Specialist, Water and Sanitation Department, African Development Bank Group

From Infrastructure to Services

Trends in monitoring sustainable water, sanitation, and hygiene services

Edited by
Ton Schouten and Stef Smits

Practical Action Publishing Ltd
The Schumacher Centre
Bourton on Dunsmore, Rugby,
Warwickshire CV23 9QZ, UK
www.practicalactionpublishing.org

© IRC International Water and Sanitation Centre, 2015

ISBN 978-1-85339-813-1 Hardback
ISBN 978-1-85339-814-8 Paperback
ISBN 978-1-78044-813-8 Library Ebook
ISBN 978-1-78044-814-5 Ebook

All rights reserved. No part of this publication may be reprinted or reproduced or utilized in any form or by any electronic, mechanical, or other means, now known or hereafter invented, including photocopying and recording, or in any information storage or retrieval system, without the written permission of the publishers.

A catalogue record for this book is available from the British Library.

The contributors have asserted their rights under the Copyright Designs and Patents Act 1988 to be identified as authors of their respective contributions.

Schouten, T., and Smits, S., (eds) (2015) *From Infrastructure to Services: Trends in monitoring sustainable water, sanitation, and hygiene services,*
Rugby, UK: Practical Action Publishing,
<http://dx.doi.org/10.3362/9781780448138>

Since 1974, Practical Action Publishing has published and disseminated books and information in support of international development work throughout the world. Practical Action Publishing is a trading name of Practical Action Publishing Ltd (Company Reg. No. 1159018), the wholly owned publishing company of Practical Action. Practical Action Publishing trades only in support of its parent charity objectives and any profits are covenanted back to Practical Action (Charity Reg. No. 247257, Group VAT Registration No. 880 9924 76).

Cover design by Mercer Design
Indexed by Sandy Aitken
Typeset by eGIANTS
Printed by Standartu Spaustive, www.stanadrd.lt,
Vilnius, Lithuania

Contents

Tables	vi
Figures	vii
Boxes	ix
Preface	xi
Acknowledgements	xiii

1 Know the problem, find the solution! Monitoring sustainable WASH service delivery: opportunities and challenges
Stef Smits and Ton Schouten — 1

2 Making the invisible visible: monitoring the costs and finance needed for sustainable WASH service delivery
Catarina Fonseca — 21

3 Messy, varied, and growing: country-led monitoring of rural water supplies
Kerstin Danert — 39

4 Transforming accountability and project monitoring for stronger national WASH sectors
Harold Lockwood — 63

5 Technology, data, and people: opportunities and pitfalls of using ICT to monitor sustainable WASH service delivery
Joseph Pearce, Nicolas Dickinson, and Katharina Welle — 85

6 Behaviour, sustainability, and inclusion: trends, themes, and lessons in monitoring sanitation and hygiene
Carolien van der Voorden and Ingeborg Krukkert — 109

7 Small steps towards building national–regional–global coherence in monitoring WASH
Piers Cross — 137

8 Setting the priorities
Ton Schouten and Stef Smits — 157

http://dx.doi.org/10.3362/9781780448138.000

Tables

3.1	Indicators relevant for rural water supplies in Uganda, Malawi, and Timor-Leste	46
3.2	Different water supply monitoring systems in South Africa	53
4.1	Typology of potential strategies for NGOs to support sector monitoring	75
5.1	ICT within the flow of monitoring information	88
5.2	Methodologies for ICT-based data collection in WASH	89
5.3	Some applications that support data management or visualization 'out of the box'	92
5.4	Some automatic technologies for data collection	93
6.1	Example of a block planning sheet	121
6.2	The 15 headline indicators used by WASH II	127

Figures

1.1	Areas of monitoring	7
1.2	Four scenarios of monitoring as a function of the degree of inter-institutional cooperation and complexity	9
1.3	Typical monitoring cycle	11
2.1	Financing sources and recurrent costs for sustainable service delivery	23
2.2	Components of lifecycle costs	25
2.3	TrackFin: conceptual financing flows for the water and sanitation sector at a national level	27
2.4	Fontes Foundation: tracking financing flows in Uganda	28
2.5	WaterAid Ethiopia: the financing gap for operational and minor maintenance	29
3.1	Typical messiness of monitoring	41
3.2	Countries with annual or biennial reviews of rural drinking water	43
3.3	Data sources, information flows, and analysis: sector performance monitoring in Uganda	44
3.4	Comparison of water point functionality of water systems over time in Timor-Leste	54
4.1	Central themes and challenges to integrating project monitoring with national frameworks	68
4.2	The development partner's dilemma – the vicious cycle of accountability	69
4.3	The three-tier approach of OWAS's monitoring and evaluation (M&E) strategy	70
4.4	WASH in Schools monitoring and evaluation 'integration' ladder	77
5.1	Water point data transmitter, sending data periodically by SMS, attached to an India Mark II handpump	94
5.2	A framework for updating water point data in Liberia	96
6.1	The shift in the focus of sanitation services as sanitation coverage increases	111
6.2	Example of baseline and endline assessments for rural sanitation in Himachal Pradesh and Madhya Pradesh in India, Indonesia, and Tanzania	115

6.3 ODF population in the West and Central Africa region, mid-2012 118
6.4 An ODF protocol 119
6.5 Summarized hygiene effectiveness ladder 123
7.1 Average number of indicators identified across all data sources in Uganda and Kenya 140
7.2 Key factors influencing monitoring systems 141
7.3 Convergence in Ethiopia's rural water coverage figures 142
7.4 Roles in WASH monitoring 150

Boxes

3.1	Joint sector reviews	43
3.2	Proxy indicators and definitions of coverage, access, and use	47
3.3	Clarifying and aligning indicator definitions in Madagascar	48
4.1	USAID Water and Development Strategy	72
4.2	Bridging the financing gap for monitoring at district level in Malawi	73
4.3	Sustainability check tool – Mozambique	78
4.4	Scaled-up database for rural water and sanitation – Indonesia	78
4.5	Service delivery indicators – Ghana	78
4.6	SIASAR initiative – Honduras, Nicaragua, and Panama	79
5.1	Mobile and internet penetration worldwide and in developing countries	86
6.1	Monitoring hand-washing behaviour change	116
6.2	Block system planning and monitoring in Malawi	121
6.3	The human right to water and sanitation: what to measure?	125

Preface

Ton Schouten and Stef Smits

Monitoring is an essential building block to make water, sanitation, and hygiene (WASH) services sustainable. In particular, monitoring at local level is a prerequisite for taking action to maintain water systems, to repair them, to expand or upgrade the system, and to plan and budget for full coverage. Reliable national data enables national government to adapt its policies and regulation, to target finance, to instruct service providers to increase their performance, and to support local government. Development partners need data to be accountable to their home constituencies and to support government. Financiers and entrepreneurs need data to justify and plan investments in water and sanitation.

There is growing momentum to improve monitoring. Governments and development partners realize that, without monitoring, investments put into water and sanitation infrastructure over the last decades will be wasted; data is needed to know what is working and what is not, and what needs corrective action to protect such investments.

New information and communication technology (ICT) offers great opportunities for more effective and cheaper monitoring, but there are big challenges too. Despite the commitment to decentralization, local government is often under-resourced; capacities for data collection, analysis, and use are not well developed; budgets for monitoring are non-existent; and there is a whole lot of monitoring conducted in parallel projects and not coordinated to support local government in leading on the delivery of water and sanitation services. The problem is not always a lack of data – too often, data is there but is not used, or it is not relevant or lacks ownership and purpose. The WASH sector is ready to tackle these challenges and to strengthen monitoring systems in order to make these services truly sustainable.

This book describes the state of the art in monitoring – which countries have made progress in monitoring and how; what opportunities are offered by new ICT; what kinds of monitoring are needed for sanitation now that the focus is shifting from counting toilets to monitoring 'open defecation free' status; how can project monitoring support country-led monitoring; how to monitor the costs of service delivery; what will be the effect on monitoring of the endorsement by the United Nations of the human right to water and sanitation; and how to make data fit for purpose. This book offers case studies, opinions, models, new technologies, and the current debate on monitoring. It is not a handbook but a book to inspire sector professionals to make progress in monitoring and make it contribute to lasting WASH services for all.

Acknowledgements

This book is the outcome of the Monitoring Sustainable WASH Service Delivery symposium that took place in Addis Ababa, Ethiopia, in April 2013. The book is a reflection of the topics discussed during the symposium and the content inputs provided in symposium papers and presentations. Our gratitude therefore goes to the 410 participants of the symposium, the authors of papers, the presenters, and all those who actively participated in plenary and topic session discussions. These inputs were brought together by the six topic leaders of the symposium and the main authors of the chapters in this book: Kerstin Danert, Catarina Fonseca, Carolien van der Voorden, Piers Cross, Harold Lockwood, and Joseph Pearce. We thank them and their co-authors Ingeborg Krukkert, Nicolas Dickinson, and Katharina Welle for writing such content-rich chapters and providing state-of-the-art knowledge in their fields of expertise.

The symposium was hosted by the government of Ethiopia and was organized by IRC in partnership with the African Ministers' Council on Water (AMCOW), WaterAid, Water and Sanitation for Africa (WSA), the Rural Water Supply Network (RWSN), the Water Supply and Sanitation Collaborative Council (WSSCC), and Water For People. We thank them all for their support.

Finally, the symposium could not have been such a success and this book could not have been written without the professional and dedicated support of colleagues in IRC: Anjani Abella, Vera van der Grift, Petra Brussee, Tettje van Daalen, Cor Dietvorst, Marion Giese, Angelica de Jesus, Sangeeta Mangal, and Audrey van Soest. A special thanks goes to Inge Klaassen of Quest for working from content to logistics and back. It was a pleasure working with you all. Thank you!

Ton Schouten and Stef Smits (editors)

CHAPTER 1

Know the problem, find the solution! Monitoring sustainable WASH service delivery: opportunities and challenges

Stef Smits and Ton Schouten

Monitoring water, sanitation, and hygiene (WASH) services is a broad topic, often understood differently by different people depending on the purposes, methods, and approaches of their monitoring initiatives. This introductory chapter provides a background to the topic. It identifies key trends and developments and the opportunities and challenges that go with them. This is followed by a presentation of the main concepts and terminologies used, and specific examples and experiences with monitoring in the WASH sub-sectors are captured in the subsequent chapters. This book has been written from the perspective of strengthening local government monitoring systems for WASH because, ultimately, these systems need to be in place to improve the sustainability of WASH service delivery. Every chapter of this book, every sub-sector dealt with and every initiative described will come back to the following question: is this contributing to strengthening monitoring systems at local government level?

Keywords: monitoring, local government, service delivery, indicators, sustainability

Introduction

Trends and developments in monitoring water, sanitation, and hygiene services

Monitoring is not new in the water, sanitation, and hygiene (WASH) sector, but the way in which it is done is changing rapidly. Bostoen and Luyendijk (2013) show how monitoring the sector has evolved over the last 50 years. Over these years, United Nations (UN) bodies and other international organizations have led global monitoring efforts. Monitoring has also become an integrated part of many WASH projects. Data collection has often been a bottleneck, limiting regular updating of information after an initial assessment. Also, much of what was labelled as monitoring stopped at the level of reporting, with little action taken as a result of the monitoring. The last decade has seen a number of trends and developments that are affecting the scope of WASH monitoring and the way in which this is done.

Monitoring access to WASH has become standard practice almost everywhere. The UN Joint Monitoring Programme (JMP) has set the standards for monitoring access to water and sanitation globally. In addition, various countries have started undertaking nationwide inventories of access to water and, to a lesser extent, sanitation facilities, referred to as water point or sanitation mapping (Pearce, 2012).

Increasingly, **other service delivery indicators** are also being monitored; access only tells part of the story of progress in WASH. For example, progress towards the achievement of the millennium development goals (MDGs) would be significantly lower if water quality was taken into account (Bain et al., 2012; Onda et al., 2012). Recent monitoring initiatives seek to include indicators such as water quantity, quality, and reliability, and even the performance of the service provider. This is reinforced by the need to monitor progress towards the realization of the human right to water and sanitation (De Albuquerque, 2013).

Increased attention is being paid to the **monitoring of 'inputs'**, such as finance flows and policies and legislation for WASH services. There are initiatives to monitor these at global level, through the two-yearly GLAAS (Global Analysis and Assessment of Sanitation and Drinking-Water) process, as well as at country level, for example through budget tracking.

The changes in what is being monitored are accompanied by changes in **who monitors**. Monitoring was often the domain of implementing organizations, reporting on numbers of new facilities built. At best, these results fed into national asset inventories, but more often they remained internal reports for funders. With a changing focus on monitoring service delivery, local and national governments in particular are getting involved, as they are ultimately responsible for delivery.

Monitoring is also getting more prominence due to the **increased demand for accountability**. Users of water and sanitation services seek to hold service providers to account over the services they receive. The aid effectiveness framework, as reflected in the Paris Declaration on Aid Effectiveness, highlights mutual accountability between recipient governments and donors as one of its key principles (OECD, 2005). And, as a result of a more critical attitude of taxpayers in the North with regard to the use of aid, donors seek to provide accountability for the impact of aid. Much effort has therefore gone into operationalizing the accountability relations between donors, governments, and users, for which monitoring of service delivery is a prerequisite.

Lastly, developments in **information and communication technology** (ICT) have significantly reduced the costs and time needed for data collection, processing, and visualization, and have provided opportunities for more stakeholders to collect and access data.

Vision

Driven by these trends, we see an emerging shared vision for the role of monitoring in the WASH sector: one where **strong national sector monitoring systems enable the planning and sustainability of WASH services**. Strong monitoring systems involve various elements:

- Monitoring must be engrained in the national sector institutions that have the mandate to carry out monitoring, act upon the results, and be accountable for them.
- Strong monitoring systems imply having clear institutional arrangements, with dedicated financial and human resource capacity. This also often means having arrangements to share the costs of monitoring between sector institutions and having the mechanisms to create an intrinsic motivation for carrying out that monitoring, including, for example, mandates and incentives.
- It implies having information systems, including indicator sets, surveys, and new ICT that collects and stores data.

Achieving this vision is not straightforward: it requires capitalizing on the trends and opportunities outlined above. It also means dealing with challenges such as finding a balance between the complexity of indicators and their ease and cost-effectiveness of use; and making the most of the parallel monitoring systems of national governments, projects, and international organizations.

Scope of the book

We have identified six topics of 'where the heat is' in monitoring – that is, where the trends and developments manifest themselves most strongly, and where sector stakeholders are getting to grips with the opportunities and challenges of monitoring. Together, these six topics cover the main issues in the contemporary monitoring debate.

The focus of this book is on monitoring WASH in rural areas and small towns, which have been lagging behind urban settings as far as monitoring is concerned.

In Chapter 2, on **monitoring the finance**, Fonseca (2014) discusses the approaches and methodologies for monitoring investments made in the sector and whether these are delivering value for money.

For monitoring to be effective, it needs to be firmly embedded in the national institutions that are mandated with service delivery. Chapter 3, by Danert (2014), elaborates on the experiences of countries that are developing their **national monitoring systems**.

For the next 10 to 15 years, while aid remains a major driver of WASH sector development, **project monitoring** is likely to be a continuing feature of the sector. In Chapter 4, Lockwood (2014) explores how project monitoring can be positive by creating innovations that can support national government systems, but often is negative due to misaligned accountability, parallel project-monitoring systems and the counterproductive use of scarce resources.

In Chapter 5, on new **information and communication technology**, Pearce, Dickinson, and Welle (2014) elaborate on the opportunities that ICT developments are bringing to monitoring and the factors that lie behind the successful design and implementation of ICT systems, but they also reflect critically on the problems of these innovations in monitoring service delivery.

Van der Voorden and Krukkert (2014) consolidate trends in **monitoring sanitation and hygiene** in Chapter 6, focusing on the complexities of monitoring community-led total sanitation, open defecation-free (ODF) status, sanitation markets, and hygiene practices, among other issues.

Global and regional monitoring efforts have made a significant contribution to national monitoring systems. However, differences in data and definitions between these levels are often a source of confusion. Cross (2014) discusses the challenges of **building coherence in global, regional, and national monitoring** in Chapter 7.

Conceptual framework for monitoring WASH service delivery

In this section we propose definitions and key concepts, going through the **why**, **what**, **who**, **how**, and **how much** questions for monitoring. While not aiming to be exhaustive, we intend to cover the most common forms of monitoring in the WASH sector, and the ways in which terminology and concepts are understood.

Why? – Purposes for monitoring

The *Oxford English Dictionary* defines monitoring as the observation and checking of progress or quality of 'something' over a period of time, or keeping it under systematic review. The implicit assumption behind this is that monitoring is done recurrently to see whether an expected result is achieved, and to take action if what is observed deviates from what was expected.

The purposes of monitoring WASH service delivery are manifold, as different stakeholders have different information needs. A user of a water point in Ethiopia may want to check the books of the water committee to make sure that the tariff they pay is used to maintain the pump; the water committee member may want to monitor the income from those tariffs to see whether the costs of all necessary repairs can be covered; the *woreda* (district) official wants to monitor which pumps in the area are non-functional so that they can send a handpump mechanic to help with repairs; a person in the Ministry of Water and Energy monitors functionality rates of handpump throughout the country to see whether national targets are met and to analyse whether the operation and maintenance framework is leading to results; a Dutch government official monitors expenditure on WASH in Ethiopia in relation to the data of the JMP to assess whether its funding to the WASH sector makes a difference; and, yet another step removed, a member of parliament in the Netherlands monitors expenditure reports of Dutch funding to WASH in Ethiopia to see whether they can explain to their constituency that Dutch tax money is being spent effectively to keep water supplies in poor countries flowing.

The list could easily be expanded beyond these examples. The number of possible purposes is almost as large as the number of stakeholders in the sector. In this book, we focus on the most common types and purposes of monitoring in the WASH sector.

- *Project cycle monitoring.* This refers to monitoring progress in infrastructure development projects with the purpose of achieving timely and efficient implementation of the project, according to specifications. It entails activities such as checking the quality of the construction, monitoring stocks of building materials, keeping track of expenditures and time spent on the project, and supervising contractors and builders. This type of monitoring is typically done by the entity responsible for implementation of the project (e.g. an international non-governmental organization (NGO) or contractor), but also the overseeing authority will want to know if the implementer is delivering according to the contract.

- *Project or programme result monitoring.* This concerns the monitoring of final outputs of the implementation, specifically in relation to the number of assets developed and the number of people who gained access to water and sanitation. Its purpose is to provide accountability for the results obtained from funds that were spent. An interesting recent development is to express results not only in terms of new WASH systems constructed or people covered, but also to include the level of services delivered in terms of water quantity, quality, reliability, and accessibility, and to monitor the strength of the enabling environment. Examples include the sustainability check used by UNICEF in Mozambique (Godfrey et al., 2009) and the proposed sustainability clause that DGIS (Directorate General for International Cooperation of the Government of the Netherlands) uses in the projects it funds (DGIS, 2012). Further details on this type of monitoring are elaborated by Lockwood in this book.

- *Inventories for asset management.* This refers to the regular updating of an inventory or register of all assets in an area to provide information on which systems have become dysfunctional and which ones have been repaired. Unlike the previous types of monitoring, this is not limited to a specific project or programme, but should cover an entire administrative area (e.g. a district, region, or country) and is therefore the responsibility of the relevant local or national authorities. The purpose of these inventories is one of asset management in its broadest sense: planning infrastructure development and major repairs and replacement. 'Water point mapping' is the term often referred to for the initial development of the inventory (see Pearce, 2012, for an overview; Welle, 2005; Rabbani, 2009), but regular updating of the inventory is also needed. Examples of sanitation mapping exist (Roma et al., 2012), but they are less well developed, not least because of the amount of data that would be involved (Pearce, 2012).

- *Service delivery monitoring.* This entails the monitoring of characteristics of the service provided (water quality, quantity, reliability, accessibility, affordability) and the performance of service providers in their roles of operation, maintenance, and administration. The purpose is to identify weaknesses or lack of compliance with national standards and norms and to define corrective action. Service delivery is often done at different levels: users monitor the service they receive on a day-to-day basis and monitor their service providers' performance; service providers typically carry out many routine monitoring tasks such as making monthly accounts of income and expenditure, or regular water quality tests; service authorities monitor the performance of the service providers in their areas, ideally against predefined service delivery indicators; and national regulators may also carry out monitoring, for example to assess whether service providers meet performance standards.

- *Monitoring the enabling environment.* This refers to the tracking of what AMCOW (2011) calls the service delivery pathway, or the conditions in the financial, institutional, policy, and planning environment for service delivery. The purpose is to inform decision-making processes (often at the highest policy and strategy levels) by identifying gaps and bottlenecks in the enabling environment that need to be resolved. It entails tracking whether certain policy or strategy decisions have been put into practice, but also an analysis of the impact of such decisions on actual service delivery. This type of monitoring is typically done as a joint effort by entities operating at national level, such as relevant ministries, the regulator, and development partners, sometimes in the form of joint sector reviews. It may go beyond the WASH sector and include institutions such as the Ministry of Finance. This type of monitoring has also been given new impetus by international and regional initiatives, including country status overviews (CSOs) in various countries in Africa (AMCOW, 2011), MAPAS (Monitoreo de los Avances del País en Agua Potable y Saneamiento or Monitoring of Country Progress in Drinking Water and Sanitation) in Central America, and UNICEF's Bottleneck Analysis Tool (BAT) (Hutton et al., 2013).

What? – Scope of monitoring WASH service delivery

Having described the most common purposes of monitoring, the following aspects of WASH services can be differentiated in terms of what can be monitored, following the broad service delivery pathway shown in Figure 1.1.

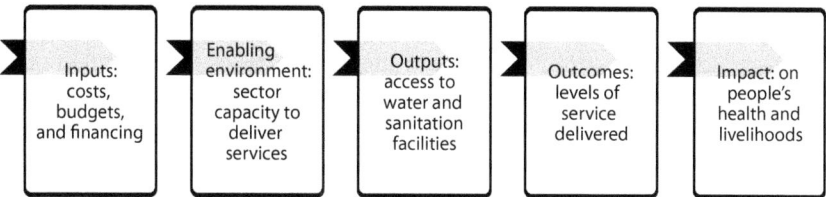

Figure 1.1 Areas of monitoring

- **Inputs** are the costs, budgets, and financing of WASH services. At a global level, the GLAAS reports compile data on financial inputs from a large number of countries (WHO, 2012), while countries such as Uganda track unit costs and financing flows as part of their sector performance monitoring (Ssozi and Danert, 2012). These are complemented by studies, such as budget tracking (see, for example, Van Ginneken et al., 2012) and lifecycle cost analysis (Burr and Fonseca, 2013), that have high potential to become monitoring tools. For example, a study on costs of point source development in Mozambique by WASHCost led to a regular review to identify changes in unit costs and use them for budgeting and planning (Zita and Naafs, 2011).

- The **enabling environment** monitors the capacity of the WASH sector to use the inputs to deliver WASH services. It includes aspects such as the development of plans and policies, institutional and human resources capacity, and the performance of sector stakeholders. For example, the GLAAS report and CSOs track progress in policy and strategy development and institutional capacity at international and national level. At country level, it is common to have indicators monitoring the performance of service providers and authorities. For sanitation, this includes factors such as the market conditions for sanitation (see Sparkman, 2012).

- **Outputs** refer to access to water and sanitation facilities. This has been the focus of most monitoring efforts so far. Key indicators typically monitored are the number of assets that meet the criteria for being 'improved' according to the definition of the JMP (UNICEF and WHO, 2012) or other country-specific definitions.

- **Outcomes** refer to the levels of services that are actually delivered. Even though most countries have norms or standards for services, such as water quality or minimum quantities to be supplied, few countries are actually monitoring these. For water, this would refer to indicators for services delivered in terms of water quality, quantity, reliability, and accessibility, often captured in the form of a water ladder (see Moriarty et al., 2010). The functionality status of water infrastructure and service downtime or response time could also be part of this. Potter et al. (2011a) propose a service ladder for sanitation that monitors indicators such as accessibility, safe use, operation and maintenance, and environmental protection. Kvarnström et al. (2009) suggest functions to be fulfilled such as containment of faecal matter. ODF status is another outcome that is often monitored. Hygiene outcomes to be monitored could include hygienic behaviour practices in relation to faecal containment, latrine use, hand washing with soap (or substitutes), and the management of drinking water in the household (Potter et al., 2011b).

- **Impact** is the eventual change that access to WASH services has on people's health and livelihoods: for example, reduced morbidity and mortality due to water-borne diseases, reduced drudgery, and increased incomes. As these impacts are costly to monitor and difficult to attribute to WASH services only, they are often not monitored on a routine basis but through one-off evaluations or assessments. Alternatively, global reference data sources are used for measuring impact, as described in the work of Hutton and Haller (2004) and Hutton et al. (2007).

Whether all these aspects need to be monitored in a given context, and at what level of detail, depends on the information demands of stakeholders and on available capacities.

Who? – Institutional responsibilities and incentives in monitoring

While there is a multiplicity of purposes for monitoring, there is an even larger number of stakeholders with an interest in collecting information.

It is important to differentiate between stakeholders needing to obtain information and stakeholders providing the information. Sometimes they are one and the same: for example, a service provider might need to have information for its financial balances and to collect data on revenue and expenditure. In other cases, the organization needing to know information might differ from the one providing that information. For example, a regulator would want to acquire information on the financial performance of service providers and would collect that information from all the service providers in the country. In this case – where the organizations needing to have information and those providing it are not the same – there may be a limited incentive for the latter to provide that information or to provide it accurately.

A first type of disconnect may occur between institutional levels; the level collecting the data might not directly use the data itself but needs to satisfy the need for information of higher institutional levels. This is, for example, the case where a district official provides data from the district to update the national asset inventory in order to justify the national investment plan and to obtain funds to improve WASH assets. If the two are not linked, this could easily become an exercise in reporting data rather than in monitoring for action. Such a situation may also lead to perverse incentives. If the amount of

KNOW THE PROBLEM, FIND THE SOLUTION! 9

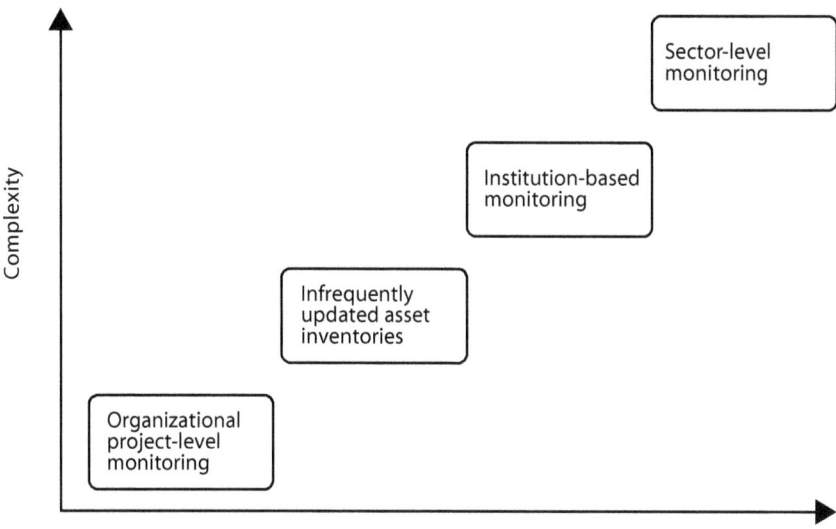

Figure 1.2 Four scenarios of monitoring as a function of the degree of inter-institutional cooperation and complexity

funding to the district depends on national asset inventories, there may be a perverse incentive to alter the data to obtain more funds.

A second type of disconnect in monitoring purposes is when a national agency updating its asset inventory depends on the inputs of project monitoring by implementers. Often there is no incentive for the latter to feed information into a national inventory. This is common in places where infrastructure is provided by a large number of NGOs or development partners, or where government agencies responsible for implementation operate in isolation from those responsible for planning and regulation.

In situations of disconnect, it is important to standardize indicators and monitoring methods to (dis)aggregate information. This requires a high degree of institutional collaboration at sector level. In practice, the standardization and aggregation of data for monitoring at different levels does not often take place. Dickinson and Bostoen (2013) present different scenarios of data management, ranging from a complete lack of structured data collection to open access data on WASH. Four scenarios for the degree of institutional collaboration in monitoring can be identified, as shown in Figure 1.2.

- *Organizational project-level monitoring.* This refers to scenarios where monitoring is done by individual organizations and only for the projects they implement. Sector collaboration for monitoring is not existent and it is impossible to aggregate data for national WASH inventories and macro-level planning.

- *Infrequently updated asset inventories or service delivery information systems.* In this case, besides project cycle monitoring, monitoring systems exist with the potential to compile information on WASH assets in a specific geographic area. Such systems are often only partially updated and information collected remains largely underused. This is typical for intensive, often externally funded, asset inventories where there is no clear institutional responsibility for updating the databases and no incentives or capacities for using the data (as Scott, 2012 identifies for Malawi).

- *Institution-based monitoring.* This refers to the situation in which monitoring is done by a mandated sector institution, such as a ministry or regulator. Data is collected regularly and used by that institution for analysis and for taking action. Since WASH sector institutions are often spread between different government agencies, there is a risk of duplication of effort and conflict over the legitimacy of data.

- *Sector-level monitoring.* This scenario occurs where there is a common monitoring framework for the sector as a whole, to which most of the sector organizations contribute. Under such a scenario, data from different sources are combined. Institutions at different levels contribute to updating data, and the data can be accessed openly. Data analysis and interpretation take place with the involvement of all stakeholders on a regular basis. In line with the principles of what is called country-led monitoring (Segone, 2009), a dedicated government institution has the lead. It coordinates regular updating, ensures processes of aggregation and disaggregation, and encourages use of the data by all. Segone (2009) emphasizes that civil society should be included so that it can evaluate public services. Donors may still play a role in sector-level monitoring but the coordination and leadership lies with the country stakeholders. Uganda's joint performance monitoring would be an example of such a scenario, where the government, through its Ministry of Water and Environment, has the lead role, but with clear involvement of civil society organizations, local government and donors (see Ssozi and Danert, 2012); they all contribute to data collection and, above all, to joint analysis and reflection.

Combinations of these four basic scenarios may occur: in a country with a relatively well-established sector monitoring system, organizations may still be monitoring their own projects but not contributing to the sector monitoring system.

The scenario of sector-level monitoring does not necessarily imply having one single information system. It is often more feasible to have different monitoring systems for different purposes – for example, one for budget tracking and one for asset management – as long as the results are combined eventually and the monitoring systems are compatible. A drawback of a single

KNOW THE PROBLEM, FIND THE SOLUTION! 11

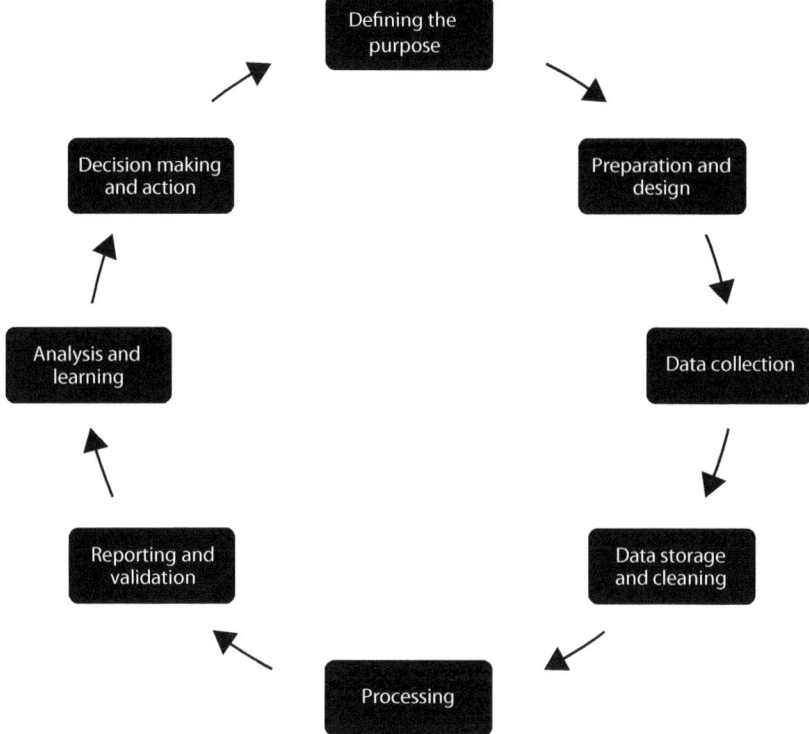

Figure 1.3 Typical monitoring cycle

system may be the credibility of data. A consumer organization may want to collect data through its own system, independently from a government database, so that it is able to contest government statistics.

The most important features of monitoring contributing to sustainable WASH service delivery are that it is country-led or country-based; that it reflects the needs of citizens, government, and service providers for information; and that the information is used for planning and regulatory purposes, but also for reflection and debate and for holding all country stakeholders to account.

How? – Steps and phases in monitoring

As noted by Pearce (2012), many mapping initiatives put the emphasis on data collection rather than on data analysis and use. This is due to the fact that data collection is often the most costly and intensive part of monitoring. However, many data collection initiatives are one-off external projects with limited ownership over the use of data. It is therefore important to clarify the full extent of a monitoring cycle. Figure 1.3 shows all the steps that are essential for monitoring sustainable WASH service delivery.

- *Defining the purpose.* What do we absolutely need to know, for example to provide services efficiently, to regulate service providers, or to hold government to account? What would be nice to know? What is the absolute minimum amount of data required? Where and how would data feed into decision-making processes?
- *Preparation and design.* This step includes defining the indicators and the corresponding data to be collected. It involves the design of a methodology to collect, analyse, and use the data, including the sampling framework, surveys, and the tools for data collection. It also includes logistical preparation, coordination with relevant stakeholders, and training.
- *Data collection.* All required primary and secondary data needs to be collected in a systematic and cost-efficient manner.
- *Data storage and cleaning.* This is where data is transferred from the data collection tool (a mobile phone or piece of paper, for example) to a database. This includes a review of data to check for outliers, errors, and inconsistencies.
- *Processing.* Data is processed and prepared for analysis; this step often involves algorithms, a number of indicators, and possibly the (dis) aggregation of data.
- *Reporting and validation.* The raw and processed data is published either in hard copy or online, and are shared with stakeholders for validation. Reports must be designed for appropriate use by different stakeholders – reports with headlines and summaries for policy makers, and reports with data details for asset managers.
- *Analysis and learning.* This is when sense is made of the results obtained in relation to certain standards or benchmarks. The most striking results – either positive or negative – are identified and root causes analysed.
- *Decision making and action.* The type of decisions depends on the purpose identified in the first step: if a water quality test has failed, a simple decision can be made by a service provider to adjust the dose of chlorination; if an asset inventory shows that 30 per cent of the handpump are not functional, a decision can be made to revise operation and maintenance strategies. This step also includes defining responsibilities and allocating resources for taking actions.

The most important part of the monitoring process is doing something with the results before the next round of data collection and analysis takes place. That may sound obvious, but if local government does not have the finance to repair the pumps, if capacity to operate and maintain the water system is non-existent, and if chlorination is not available on the market, monitoring risks becoming superfluous.

How? – Information systems

An information system consists of three components: 1) definitions of parameters and indicators; 2) algorithms to process data; 3) information and communication technologies. Each of these is elaborated below.

What are we measuring? The terms 'criteria', 'parameters', and 'indicators' are often used interchangeably. We differentiate them as follows:

- A criterion is the broad category of what you want to monitor.
- An indicator is the state or level of that broad category.
- A parameter is the measurable factor (or factors) that makes up the indicator.

For example, if the criterion to be monitored is the financial performance of the service provider, then one of the indicators is the accounting balance. To assess this indicator, you need to measure various parameters such as revenues and expenditures.

The criteria, indicators, and parameters to be used depend on the purpose and scope of monitoring, the reliability of data, and the costs of collecting and managing the data. A compromise is needed between accuracy (expensive) and broad results (less expensive, but less precise). The compromise also applies to scale: there is often a tension between the need to have comprehensive data that provides a full picture of service delivery (i.e. a census) and the costs and efforts to collect data. Even if the criteria are limited, one can easily end up with a large number of parameters.

Measuring service delivery in Colombia was done by looking at five criteria for service levels; the three criteria for service provider performance required 21 indicators. In total, data for some 75 parameters was collected (Smits et al., 2012). Uganda has a limited set of 11 'golden' indicators that are actually criteria (Ssozi and Danert, 2012). Each criterion still needs two or three parameters. In the joint performance report, the data sets are then disaggregated by various categories (such as rural and urban). So, although the number of 'golden' indicators is limited, the number of parameters to be collected is high.

Algorithms for aggregation, indices, and scoring. The way in which the value of an indicator is expressed also depends on the purpose. Sometimes the absolute value of an indicator is of interest; for example, a service provider might need to know the volume of water sold or the revenue collected. In many cases, the relative value is of more interest; a local authority could want to know which providers in the area meet the standards for service delivery and which ones don't, or which providers perform better and which ones worse than average. In other cases, there is an interest in more aggregated data; for example, a national authority might want to know on which parameters service providers in the country score poorly so that it can adapt its regulations.

Monitoring systems use indices or scores. An index is a mathematical combination of a set of indicators without a common meaningful unit of measurement and weighting (Nardo et al., 2008). A score is the quantitative value attached to a specific situational statement. Franceys and Fonseca (2012) provide an overview of commonly used scoring systems and indices in the sector. Scores are often used in WASH monitoring systems, such as the scorecards used for monitoring the sustainability of the WASH sector in CSOs (AMCOW, 2011). An example of scores used in a national monitoring system is the SIASAR (Sistema de Información de Agua y Saneamiento Rural) in Central America. SIASAR classifies all water systems on a scale from A to D (with A being the highest performance and D the lowest), based on the scores for a number of indicators (World Bank, 2013).

In order to aggregate data and to convert absolute values into relative ones and assign scores, a set of algorithms, or data-processing rules, is needed. For example, an algorithm may take the absolute values obtained for each of the service-level parameters of a specific water system and assign a score to that system based on the number of parameters that meet the national norms. An information system therefore contains a series of algorithms to process the data and convert these into scores and indices, and to provide both absolute and relative values.

Information and communication technologies. WASH service monitoring is undergoing rapid changes as a result of developments in ICT and the ever-decreasing costs of tools. The use of mobile phone technology (as summarized by Hutchings et al., 2012) for data collection is one of the most striking manifestations of these changes. Monitoring systems using mobile phone technology include 'top-down' systems where trained enumerators or district staff regularly monitor the service delivery characteristics of water points – examples include FLOW (Field Level Operations Watch) and SIASAR. In 'bottom-up' systems, users report breakdowns using SMS, as in Uganda's Mobile For Water (M4W) system (Abisa et al., 2013). Thomson et al. (2012a) provide a case study of mobile phones being used to measure the number of strokes on handpump in order to transmit estimates of water use. The latter application has the potential to increase the amount of data, and also the speed at which such data can be collected, even making real-time monitoring possible. This should then facilitate rapid decision making and response. However, Thomson et al. (2012b) warn that there can be data bias, particularly in relation to crowd-sourced data.

Dickinson and Bostoen (2013) describe the types of ICT tools available for each step in the monitoring process: from data collection to storage, processing, and visualization. These tools can contribute to more effective monitoring by reducing the time needed to validate and process data and by improving accessibility of the information. In particular, online data sharing makes it possible for all interested stakeholders to access data and use it for their own purposes.

The extent to which effectiveness and efficiency in monitoring are improved in practice also depends on the institutional capacity to respond to the results of monitoring, as argued by Thomson et al. (2012b) and Dickinson and Bostoen (2013). Pearce (2012) notes in the summary of an e-discussion on water point mapping that much of the emphasis is still on the data collection and visualization stages, but that the use of data is still not well understood. So, whereas ICT tools can increase the collection, processing, and visualization of data, the final step of analysis and use will continue to depend on the capacities of the individuals and organizations that need to use and act upon the data.

How much does it cost to monitor?

There is a growing body of evidence on the costs of WASH monitoring. Pearce (2012) compiles cost data based on figures quoted in a recent e-discussion on water point mapping, while Smits et al. (2013) provide costs of monitoring in Latin America. Both note that different countries estimate costs in different ways: by including or excluding certain cost items, by expressing costs in different units (e.g. US$ per water point or local currency per person), or by referring only to the costs of data collection and processing but not to the costs of the analysis – which is like 'comparing apples to oranges' (Smits, 2012). After correcting for the differences, evidence shows that the costs of monitoring are in the order of US$0.10 to US$0.20 per person per round of monitoring.

As Pearce (2012) indicates, there is a need to have a better understanding of the costs involved in the different steps in the monitoring process. One way of doing this is by itemizing costs and accounting for them in a standardized manner, and breaking these down for each of the steps in monitoring, so that a better analysis and comparison can be made of what is included and what is not.

Opportunities and challenges

There is a lot going on in the area of monitoring WASH service delivery, and much of it aims to strengthen monitoring at local government level. There is a shift to **monitoring of outcomes** besides outputs, such as access to infrastructure. The adoption of the human right to water and sanitation implies the monitoring of service levels, and asset inventories increasingly include data on services provided. There is growing awareness of the necessary shift from project- and institution-based monitoring to **sector-level monitoring**. **Global and regional initiatives**, such as the JMP, the UN-Water GLAAS initiative, CSOs, and BATs, have given strong impetus to WASH monitoring and have provided relevant standards, tools, and methods.

The review of the JMP within the post-2015 MDG framework provides an opportunity to make it more supportive of country-led monitoring (JMP, 2012). The final opportunity to move towards the vision of strong country-led monitoring, particularly at local government level, is the development of **ICT applications** that can make monitoring cheaper, faster, and more inclusive.

There is still a lot to be done and overcome. The monitoring of services implies an increase in the number of parameters; some data is not easy or cheap to collect; and more complex scoring systems or indices may be required. In addition, the focus on service delivery means that the inputs and enabling environment need to be monitored. The biggest challenge is the **governance of monitoring**; this includes improving coordination and aligning aid-driven project-monitoring systems with the monitoring systems of government agencies and with global monitoring efforts (Brocklehurst, 2012). Another challenge is creating **incentives** to continue collecting and using monitoring data. Another group of challenges relates to the **capacity for monitoring**; there is a risk that ICT-driven monitoring systems expand without there being the institutional capacity to use the data generated. A final challenge is the *cost* of data collection and use. If monitoring costs US$0.10 to US$0.20 per person, how much will be left to spend on acting upon the results?

Monitoring is a means to an end: to obtain information on WASH service delivery in order to be able to take corrective action. Good services will not be provided by having good monitoring systems only. However, monitoring can be an impetus for a greater effort to improve service delivery. Knowledge is a prerequisite for the motivation and engagement to do something. We believe that local government in particular needs to know the status of services and service delivery. In most cases, local government has the duty to deliver these services and the mandate to act on monitoring information. Information from local government level can be aggregated to support policy making and regulation at national level, and strong national-sector monitoring systems will make a significant contribution towards sustainable WASH service delivery. The next chapters consider how to achieve that vision, seizing the opportunities while dealing with the challenges.

References

Abisa, J., Magara, P. and Wakholi, P. (2013) 'Experiences with remote data collection: using mobile phones and PCs for monitoring delivery of rural water services in Uganda', paper presented at the IRC Symposium 2013: Monitoring WASH Services Delivery, Addis Ababa, Ethiopia, 9–11 April.

AMCOW (2011) *Pathways to Progress: Transitioning to Country-led Service Delivery Pathways to Meet Africa's Water Supply and Sanitation Targets. AMCOW's Country Status Overview Regional Synthesis Report*, Washington DC: Water and Sanitation Program of the World Bank.

Bain, R.E.S, Gundry, S.W., Wright, J.A., Yang, H., Pedley, S. and Bartram, J.K. (2012) 'Accounting for water quality in monitoring access to safe drinking-water as part of the Millennium Development Goals: lessons from five countries', *Bulletin of the World Health Organization* 90: 228–35.

Bostoen, K. and Luyendijk, R. (2013) 'Global monitoring's forgotten history: typewriter to smartphone in five decades', PowerPoint presentation at the IRC Symposium 2013: Monitoring WASH Services Delivery, Addis Ababa, Ethiopia, 9–11 April.

Brocklehurst, C. (2012) 'WASH sector monitoring: where will the future take us?', PowerPoint presentation at the Stockholm World Water Week 2012, Stockholm, Sweden, 26–31 August.

Burr, P. and Fonseca, C. (2013) *Applying a Life-cycle Costs Approach to Water: Costs and Service Levels in Rural and Small Town Areas in Andhra Pradesh (India), Burkina Faso, Ghana and Mozambique*, WASHCost Global Working Paper 8, The Hague: IRC.

Cross, P. (2014) 'Reasons for optimism: towards achieving coherence in global–regional–national monitoring', in T. Schouten and S. Smits (eds), *From Infrastructure to Services: Trends in Monitoring Sustainable Water, Sanitation and Hygiene Services*, pp. 137–157, Rugby: Practical Action Publishing.

Danert, K. (2014) 'Messy, varied and growing: country-led monitoring of rural water supplies', in T. Schouten and S. Smits (eds), *From Infrastructure to Services: Trends in Monitoring Sustainable Water, Sanitation and Hygiene Services*, pp. 39–62, Rugby: Practical Action Publishing.

De Albuquerque, C. (2013) 'Monitoring the human right to water and sanitation', keynote paper presented by Virginia Roaf at the IRC Symposium 2013: Monitoring WASH Services Delivery, Addis Ababa, Ethiopia, 9–11 April.

DGIS (2012) *Beleidsreactie op Beleidsdoorlichting van de Nederlandse bijdrage aan drinkwater en sanitaire voorzieningen (1990–2011)*, The Hague: Ministerie van Buitenlandse Zaken.

Dickinson, N. and Bostoen, K. (2013) *Using ICT for Monitoring Rural Water Services: From Data to Action*, Triple-S Working Paper 4, The Hague: IRC.

Fonseca, C. (2014) 'Making the invisible visible: monitoring the costs and finance needed for sustainable WASH service delivery', in T. Schouten and S. Smits (eds), *From Infrastructure to Services: Trends in Monitoring Sustainable Water, Sanitation and Hygiene Services*, pp. 21–38, Rugby: Practical Action Publishing.

Franceys, R. and Fonseca, C. (2012) *Exploratory Note on Benchmarking Progressive Improvements: Scenarios for Composite Indicators and Indexes*, The Hague: Post-2015 JMP Water Working Group.

Godfrey, S., Freitas, M., Muianga, A., Amaro, M., Fernandez, P. and Sousa Mosies, L. (2009) 'Sustainability check: A monitoring tool for the sustainability of rural water supplies', paper presented at the Water, Sanitation and Hygiene; Sustainable Development and Multi-sectoral Approaches, 34th WEDC International Conference, Addis Ababa, Ethiopia, 18–22 May.

Hutchings, M.T., Dev, A., Palaniappan, M., Srinivasan, V., Ramanathan, N. and Taylor, J. (2012) *mWASH: Mobile Phone Applications for the Water, Sanitation, and Hygiene Sector*, Oakland CA: Pacific Institute.

Hutton, G. and Haller, L. (2004) *Evaluation of the Costs and Benefits of Water and Sanitation Improvements at the Global Level*, Geneva: World Health Organization.

Hutton, G., Haller, L. and Bartram, J. (2007) *Economic and Health Effects of Increasing Coverage of Low Cost Household Drinking-water Supply and Sanitation Interventions to Countries Off-track to Meet MDG Target 10*, Geneva: World Health Organization.

Hutton, G., Trevett, A. and Harvey, P. (2013) 'The WASH Bottleneck Analysis Tool (BAT)', paper presented at the IRC Symposium 2013: Monitoring WASH Services Delivery, Addis Ababa, Ethiopia, 9–11 April.

JMP (2012) *Proposal for Consolidated Drinking Water, Sanitation and Hygiene Targets, Indicators and Definitions*, Geneva: Joint Monitoring Programme (JMP) of the World Health Organization (WHO) and UNICEF.

Kvarnström, E., McConville, J., Johansson, M., Bracken, P. and Fogde, M. (2009) 'The sanitation ladder – a need for a revamp?', paper presented at the IWA Development Congress, Mexico City, Mexico, 15–19 November.

Lockwood, H. (2014) 'Transforming accountability and project monitoring for stronger national WASH sectors', in T. Schouten and S. Smits (eds), *From Infrastructure to Services: Trends in Monitoring Sustainable Water, Sanitation and Hygiene Services*, pp. 63–84, Rugby: Practical Action Publishing.

Moriarty, P., Batchelor, C., Fonseca, C., Klutse, A., Naafs, A., Nyarko, A., Pezon, K., Potter, A., Reddy, R. and Snehalatha, M. (2010) *Ladders and Levels for Assessing and Costing Water Service Delivery*, WASHCost Global Working Paper 2, The Hague: IRC.

Nardo, M., Saisana, M., Saltelli, A., Tarantol, S., Hoffmann, A. and Giovannin, E. (2008) *Handbook on Constructing Composite Indicators: Methodology and User Guide*, Paris: Organisation for Economic Co-operation and Development (OECD) and European Commission Joint Research Centre.

OECD (2005) *The Paris Declaration on Aid Effectiveness and the Accra Agenda for Action*, Paris: Organisation for Economic Co-operation and Development (OECD).

Onda, K., LoBuglio, J. and Bartram, J. (2012) 'Global access to safe water: accounting for water quality and the resulting impact on MDG progress', *International Journal of Environmental Research and Public Health* 9 (3): 880–94.

Pearce, J. (2012) *RWSN Water Point Mapping Group: A Synthesis of Experiences and Lessons discussed in 2012*, St Gallen, Switzerland: Rural Water Supply Network.

Pearce, J., Dickinson, N. and Welle, K. (2014) 'Technology, data and people: opportunities and pitfalls of using ICT to monitor sustainable WASH service delivery', in T. Schouten and S. Smits (eds), *From Infrastructure to Services: Trends in Monitoring Sustainable Water, Sanitation and Hygiene Services*, pp. 85–108, Rugby: Practical Action Publishing.

Potter, A., Klutse, A., Snehalatha, M., Batchelor, C., Uandela, A., Naafs, A., Fonseca, C. and Moriarty, P. (2011a) *Assessing Sanitation Service Levels*, WASHCost Global Working Paper 3, 2nd edition, The Hague: IRC.

Potter, A., van de Reep, M., Burr, P., Dubé, A. and Krukkert, I. (2011b) *Assessing Hygiene Cost-effectiveness: A Methodology*, WASHCost Global Working Paper 7, The Hague: IRC.

Rabbani, E. (2009) *Water Point Monitoring System in Machinga District, Malawi: Design and Development*, Lilongwe: EWB and WaterAid.

Roma, E., Pearce, J., Brown, C. and Islam, S. (2012) 'Sanitation mapper: a tool for mapping and monitoring sanitation in low-income countries', *Waterlines* 31 (4): 309–13.

Scott, O. (2012) 'Supporting institutionalized monitoring systems for rural water supply and sanitation in Malawi', *Waterlines* 31 (4): 272–9.

Segone, M. (2009) *Country-led Monitoring and Evaluation Systems: Better Evidence, Better Policies, Better Development Results*, Evaluation Working Paper Series, Geneva: UNICEF Regional Office for Central and Eastern Europe and the Commonwealth of Independent States (CEE/CIS).

Smits, S. (2012) 'Apples and oranges: a comparative assessment in WASH' in Water Services that Last [blog] <http://waterservicesthatlast.wordpress.com/2012/11/23/apples-and-oranges-a-comparative-assessment-in-wash/> [accessed 3 October 2014].

Smits, S., Tamayo, S.P., Ibarra, V., Rojas, J., Benavidez, A. and Bey, V. (2012) *Gobernanza y sostenibilidad de los sistemas de agua potable y saneamiento rurales en Colombia*, Monograph IDB-MG-133, Washington DC: Inter-American Development Bank.

Smits, S., Uytewaal, E. and Sturzenegger, G. (2013) *¿Cómo institucionalizar sistemas de monitoreo del servicio de agua en zonas rurales? Lecciones de Honduras, El Salvador y Paraguay*, Washington DC: Inter-American Development Bank.

Sparkman, D. (2012) 'More than just counting toilets: the complexities of monitoring for sustainability in sanitation', *Waterlines* 31 (4): 260–71.

Ssozi, D. and Danert, K. (2012) *National Monitoring of Rural Water Supplies: How the Government of Uganda Did It and Lessons for Other Countries*, RWSN-IFAD Series 4, St Gallen, Switzerland: Rural Water Supply Network.

Thomson, P., Hope, R. and Foster, T. (2012a) 'GSM-enabled remote monitoring of rural handpumps: a proof-of-concept study', *Journal of Hydroinformatics* 14 (4): 829–39.

Thomson, P., Hope, R. and Foster, T. (2012b) 'Is silence golden? Of mobiles, monitoring, and rural water supplies', *Waterlines* 31 (4): 280–92.

UNICEF and WHO (2012) *Progress on Drinking Water and Sanitation: 2012 Update*. New York NY: UNICEF and World Health Organization (WHO).

van der Voorden, C. and Krukkert, I. (2014) 'Behaviour, sustainability, and inclusion: trends, themes, and lessons in monitoring sanitation and hygiene', in T. Schouten and S. Smits (eds), *From Infrastructure to Services: Trends in Monitoring Sustainable Water, Sanitation and Hygiene Services,* pp. 109–136, Rugby: Practical Action Publishing.

Van Ginneken, M., Netterstrom, U. and Bennett, A. (2012) *More, Better, or Different Spending? Trends in Public Expenditure on Water and Sanitation in Sub-Saharan Africa*, Water Papers, Washington DC: World Bank.

Welle, K. (2005) *Learning for Advocacy and Good Practice: WaterAid Water Point Mapping*, London: WaterAid and Overseas Development Institute.

WHO (2012) *UN-Water Global Annual Assessment of Sanitation and Drinking-Water (GLAAS) 2012 Report: The Challenge of Extending and Sustaining Services*, Geneva: World Health Organization (WHO).

— (2013) *The SIASAR Initiative: An Information System for More Sustainable Rural Water and Sanitation Services*, Briefing Note, Washington DC: Water Partnership Program of the World Bank.

Zita, J. and Naafs, A. (2011) *Costs of Rural Water Point Sources in Mozambique: Unit Costs Analysis of Contracts January up to June 2011*, WASHCost Mozambique Briefing Note C3A, Maputo: WASHCost Mozambique.

About the authors

Stef Smits is Senior Programme Officer and coordinator of IRC's Latin America Regional Programme. Stef Smits co-developed a methodology for monitoring the sustainability of rural water services in Latin America, and supported WASH monitoring in several countries in the region.

Ton Schouten is Senior Programme Officer in charge of IRC's monitoring work. Ton Schouten was responsible for organizing IRC's first international conference on monitoring (in Addis Ababa, 2013), an event replicated in Burkina Faso for Francophone Africa. Ton Schouten has been Chair of the Rural Water Supply Network since 2014.

CHAPTER 2

Making the invisible visible: monitoring the costs and finance needed for sustainable WASH service delivery

Catarina Fonseca

Only in the last couple of years, in low income countries, have governments and development partners recognized the need for reliable cost information for water and sanitation services. From a monitoring perspective, it is important to know who needs to monitor finance and for what purposes. Local government needs to know the costs of sustaining services in its jurisdiction, the systems that need replacement or repair, the costs of post-construction support, and the sources of finance required. Even when government financial systems are well developed, it is not easy to make cost data understandable and to relate these to service delivery outcomes. Infrastructure development is spread over different organizations, each one often using its own financial systems, and most of them designed to monitor the costs and finance for providing access to infrastructure and not for delivering services. Ultimately, financial monitoring will be useful only if governments lead in setting the service-level standards they want to deliver to citizens.

Keywords: finance, lifecycle costs, asset management, transfers, tariffs, taxes

Introduction

The vision for water, sanitation, and hygiene (WASH) in the post-2015 millennium development goal (MDG) era is to reach everyone by 2030. One of the priorities set in the technical proposal (UNICEF and WHO, 2012) is that WASH should be equitable and sustainable. Governments and donor agencies have responded to the ambitious targets by saying that it will be expensive to achieve them and that large injections of funds are needed.

In some low- and middle-income countries, financial requirements may indeed exceed the available funds, but in many other countries the funds are available but not used effectively or not used at all (WHO, 2012). Better tracking of finance can improve value for money, can provide costs and financing benchmarks for countries with different rates of development, can assist in better utilization of existing funds, and can enable the sector to begin finding structural solutions to problems related to absorptive capacity, the lack of asset management, and the lack of clarity on how to fund recurrent costs.

From a human right perspective to water and sanitation, the main reason for monitoring the finance is to target and shift financial resources to those who most need basic, safe access to a water supply, sanitation, and hygiene. By tracking finance, policy and implementation decisions will be properly informed so that realistic progress to a basic level of service can be made.

The key questions that this chapter address are:

- What is the relevance of tracking finance at global and national level? How does it feature in the post-2015 monitoring discussions?
- What has been the progress during the past three years on monitoring finance for WASH?
- What are some of the latest methodologies to monitor finance for WASH?
- What are the incentives for financial monitoring and how can financial data be used to improve service delivery?

Making the invisible visible: costs and finance

Monitoring finance in the WASH sector in low income countries is very limited. The most common approaches used to track financial flows are budget tracking, as applied by the GrassRootsAfrica Foundation (Amenga-Etego, 2011) and WaterAid (Mehta, 2008; WaterAid, 2010); public expenditure tracking surveys (PETSs) from the World Bank (Dorotinsky, 2004; Tolmie, 2010); and financial and institutional mapping, as carried out by the Water and Sanitation Program (WSP) of the World Bank (WSP 2003; 2004). Due to the fragmentation in the WASH sector, off-budget funds from donors and international non-governmental organizations (NGOs) are difficult to track.

These approaches are not straightforward and require additional methods and tools to provide a more complete and nuanced picture of funding flows. The most important limitation is that the expenditure for WASH, while important, is not in itself an indicator of the effectiveness, efficiency, or sustainability of investments (WSP, 2003). Tracking budgets and financing flows tells little about the actual services being provided to the population, and the impact of such expenditure is largely unknown (Moriarty et al., 2010).

The systematic collection and publication of unit costs for water and sanitation in lower-income countries, and specifically for rural and peri-urban areas that are not served by utilities, is relatively recent. There is little knowledge regarding how much is allocated by governments and donors and even less on how much households are contributing towards the construction or maintenance of the infrastructure (WHO, 2012).

In order to achieve sustainable services, all sources of funding (transfers, tariffs, and taxes; also called the 3Ts) (OECD, 2009; Hervé-Bazin, 2012), whether private or public, and all costs for providing services must be known (Figure 2.1). If they are not known, it will not be clear how much more finance

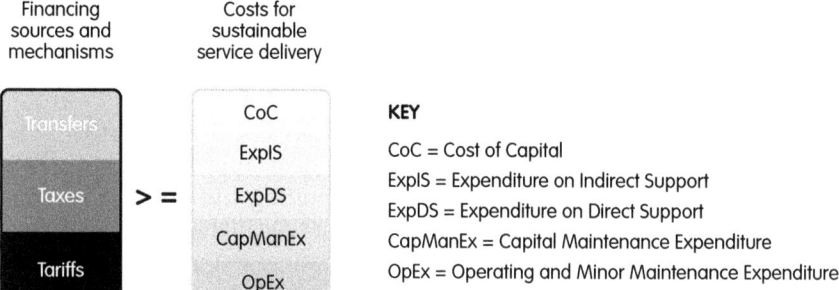

Figure 2.1 Financing sources and recurrent costs for sustainable service delivery
Source: Norman et al., 2012.

will be needed to reach universal and sustainable coverage by 2030 and who needs to contribute with what (WHO, 2012).

Taxes refer to funds originating from domestic taxes that are channelled to the sector via transfers from all levels of government (WHO, 2012). Such funds would typically be provided as subsidies for capital investment or operations. 'Hidden' forms of subsidies may include tax rebates, soft loans (i.e. loans at a subsidized interest rate), or subsidized services (such as subsidized electricity). Most lower-income countries do not collect enough taxes at decentralized levels of governance to finance infrastructure development (Norman et al., 2012). Most taxes in these countries are collected at national level and distributed to lower government levels according to an allocation formula; in general, allocations from the national budget for water and sanitation are very limited (WHO, 2012).

Transfers refer to funds from development banks, international donors, and charitable foundations including NGOs and decentralized cooperation and local civil society organizations, which typically originate in developed countries (WHO, 2012). Examples of transfers are grants, concessionary loans (i.e. loans that include a grant element in the form of a subsidized interest rate or a grace period), and guarantees. Transfer mechanisms include overseas development assistance (ODA) and direct transfers known as remittances. In many developing countries, transfers remain a major source of financing for sanitation and drinking-water, mostly for capital expenditure (WHO, 2012).

Tariffs are contributions made by users of WASH services (WHO, 2012). Users generally make payments to service providers for receiving access to and using the service. When the service is self-supplied – when a household builds and operates its own well or latrine, for example – the equity invested by the household in the form of cash, materials, or time also falls under the category of tariffs. In cases where households try to improve the service they receive by improving water quality or quantity, this is also considered to be a household contribution; they may do this by using filters or storage tanks and rainwater harvesting facilities. Tariffs may cover operating costs but are rarely enough to cover all other costs (OECD, 2009). The main constraint in tracking financial expenditure via tariffs is that contributions from households in developing countries – which are much higher than assumed – are not captured (Burr and Fonseca, 2012; Trémolet et al., 2010).

To capture and monitor the costs of WASH services, it is important to be aware of the different elements associated with delivering such services. IRC, through its WASHCost project, has been promoting the use of a lifecycle costs approach and a common terminology that facilitates a 'like with like' comparison. For instance, 'maintenance', 'operation and maintenance', and 'capital maintenance' are cost aggregations with different components within them. As in global accounting systems, a common cost standard is needed in the sector.

Lifecycle costs encompass the costs incurred during the different stages of service delivery, including both hardware and software, such as the costs for operation, maintenance, management, and replacement of infrastructure. The lifecycle costs approach adapts the regulatory accounting approach to aggregating costs and separating investment costs; for example, it separates capital expenditure from recurrent costs (Fonseca et al., 2011). Capital expenditure refers to the costs of providing a service where there was none before or of substantially increasing the scale or level of services. Recurrent expenditure refers to the maintenance expenditure associated with sustaining an existing service at its intended level. These costs are summarized in Figure 2.2.

The funding for the different cost categories can come from one of the 3Ts: tariffs, including householders' expenditure, taxes, and transfers. For services to be sustainable, Figure 2.1 illustrates how a combination of financing sources is required that is equal to or higher than the annual recurrent costs. Note that none of the figures is meant to represent the relative magnitude of recurrent costs.

Over the last five years, achievements have been made in monitoring finance. There is a shared language both for the 3Ts and for the different cost categories that define recurrent expenditure. More than a hundred organizations and governments are using lifecycle costs to measure and benchmark their investments (Cross et al., 2013). There is also an increased demand for simple methods and indicators to make financial assessments easier.

However, three key challenges remain for making financial information accessible:

- Most governments and donors struggle to submit disaggregated financial data, and little is reported on recurrent expenditures (WHO, 2012).
- When financial data is available in completion reports or studies, it is presented only in aggregated formats and the source data is not accessible.
- It is difficult to assess costs when financial data is accessible in spreadsheets that do not include proper documentation of any cost manipulations (such as currency converters and deflation converters, or the many possible units of calculation – per person, per household, per service area, per design, etc.).

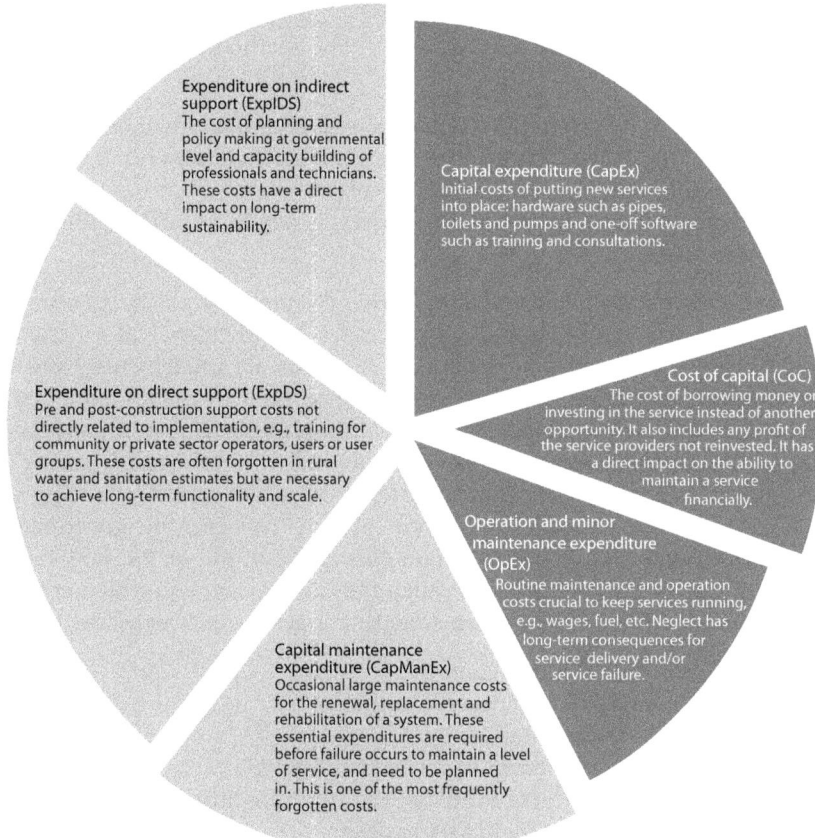

Figure 2.2 Components of lifecycle costs
Source: McIntyre et al., 2014: 99.

There are examples of how to make invisible finance more visible. In East-Timor, the government has started a programme of asset managing systems; the first step was to make an asset inventory using a simple Excel tool. Estimates of the real lifespan compared with the theoretical lifespan of some of the infrastructure were made to know when infrastructure components need major repairs and to plan the financing of related costs. In Ethiopia, a database was created that donors need to feed with information on what they are spending in the country. There are challenges with tracking the funds from NGOs because they often operate in parallel to government systems. This is being resolved through an annual joint review process to measure the performance of each NGO against how much they spent; however, expenditure reported by NGOs does not always reflect all the costs incurred.

The latest approaches and methodologies to monitor finance flows

Currently, there are three approaches to and methodologies for tracking financial flows:

- using the UN-Water GLAAS (Global Analysis and Assessment of Sanitation and Drinking-Water) TrackFin for international comparisons;
- mapping funding flows at national level;
- using the lifecycle cost approach to access expenditure, affordability, and service levels.

The UN-Water GLAAS TrackFin initiative (Trémolet et al., 2010) aims to define and test a global methodology to track WASH finance at a national level, in order to monitor whether commitments are implemented and to encourage good utilization of existing funds. The initiative is a response to the challenges with tracking financial flows identified in the GLAAS initiative and proposes to support countries to develop national WASH accounts, similar to the national health accounts that are used in the health sector.

TrackFin builds on the information already collected by government statistical services and identifies: total expenditure in the sector; how funds are distributed; who pays and how much they are paying; and which entities are channelling the funds. By implementing TrackFin, it is expected that it will be possible to:

- compare financial data between countries;
- benchmark financial data;
- compare outcomes in terms of access to funding;
- look at the distribution of funding (leading to accountability);
- identify who is paying for WASH services;
- coordinate donor expenditure and international transfers.

Four countries have expressed an interest in testing the methodology – Morocco, Brazil, Ghana, and Vietnam – and the results of the testing will be part of the 2014 GLAAS report. The next step is to have a revised methodology for GLAAS 2016 and to introduce national WASH accounts in more countries. The methodology allows expenditures from non-WASH agencies and ministries to be captured, but not those from NGOs, since these funds remain outside the formal government channels (Figure 2.3).

Biteete and van Lieshout applied a mapping scan that looked at cost data used for financial planning and budgeting in Uganda (Biteete and van Lieshout 2013). The scan mapped the expenditure flows of the entire rural water and sanitation sector in Uganda, including all the institutions and organizations involved in channelling funds. Figure 2.4 shows the capital expenditure and recurrent expenditure for piped water schemes only but provides a good overview of how complex the sector is and how difficult it can be to access value for money when both implementation and financial responsibilities are spread between too many agencies.

MAKING THE INVISIBLE VISIBLE 27

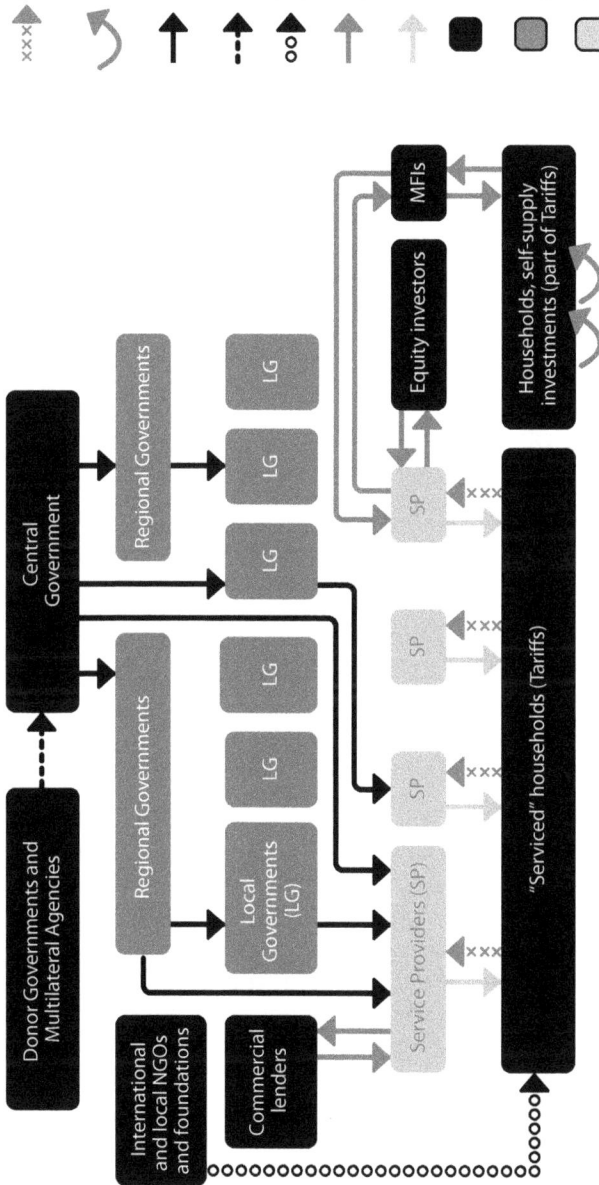

Figure 2.3 TrackFin: conceptual financing flows for the water and sanitation sector at a national level

Source: adapted from Trémolet and Rama, 2012.

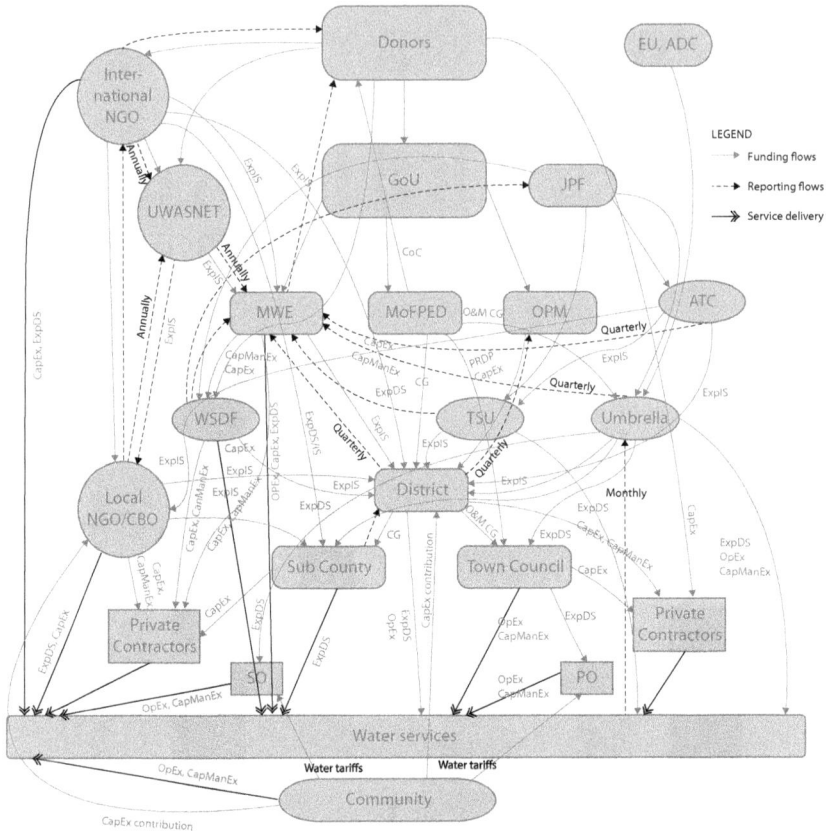

Figure 2.4 Fontes Foundation: tracking financing flows in Uganda
Source: Biteete et al., 2013.

Some of the key findings from the scan include the following:

- The institutional arrangements to finance capital maintenance expenditure are very complex and not clear, and therefore they are difficult to track. This contributes to the problems implementers face in financing capital maintenance expenditure and managing ageing infrastructure. Districts in Uganda receive only a small percentage (8 per cent) of the conditional grant for capital maintenance expenditure, which was equal to approximately US$1.6 million in 2011–2012, meaning that only US$14,300 was available for large maintenance and rehabilitation projects in a district (assuming that there were 112 districts, although this figure varies). Districts have between 200 and 400,000 consumers, and some districts need more funds for rehabilitation than for new sources.
- The institutional arrangements for operational expenditure are simpler, mainly taking place at community and service provider level. They are therefore easier to track.

- Significant amounts are being invested in initial software and post-construction support, yet the results are not felt on the ground and functionality is a challenge. A first estimate of the current spending on direct support costs in Uganda is approximately US$0.10 per person per year, while the WASHCost project identified a benchmark with a range of US$1 to US$3 per person per year, suggesting that increased expenditures on support services may be needed to achieve higher coverage and functionality.

National coverage in Uganda is not increasing, even though access to new water sources is established each year and population growth is low (less than 1.53 per cent). Some of the issues described above certainly contribute to this situation. The next step is to conduct a similar analysis at district level and to develop benchmarks for district budgeting and planning purposes.

WaterAid Ethiopia used the lifecycle costs approach to track expenditure and affordability in the Amhara and Oromia regions (Aboma, 2013). More than 900 household surveys were conducted in early 2013. Tracking finance and services at district level showed that most people were accessing very small quantities of water per day from a formal source and that service levels were generally low. Cost data was available for hand-dug wells, shallow wells, and protected springs.

The most critical finding from the WaterAid study was that there is an 83 per cent financing gap between the existing recurrent costs for maintenance and the required amounts (Figure 2.5). Tariffs are not even covering minor works and maintenance. Only 0.3 per cent of household income is currently spent on water services, which indicates that extremely low tariff levels are being collected. However, results from individual interviews indicated that even the existing level of tariff is not affordable for a typical poor household, meaning that many use water from both protected and unprotected sources.

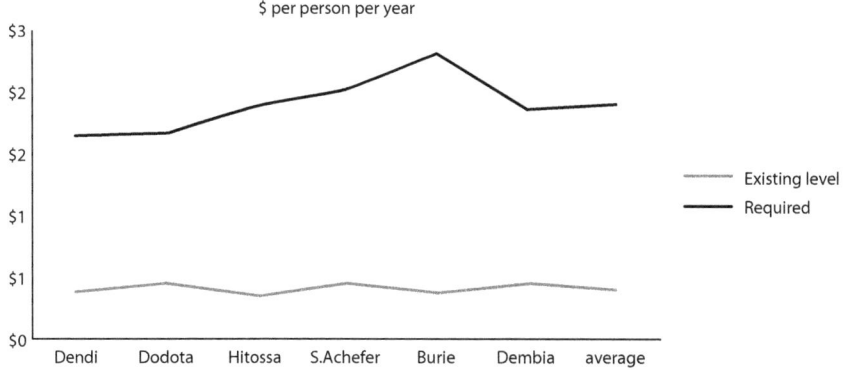

Figure 2.5 WaterAid Ethiopia: the financing gap for operational and minor maintenance

Source: Aboma, 2013: 14.

Considering the existing resources available to the *woredas* (districts) through block grants from the regions, it is not realistic to conclude that the financing of rural water services is affordable for households. With the current financing levels, reaching universal access to water may take an additional 45 years; alternatively, it requires local governments to allocate US$368 per person per year continuously for the coming 10 years.

Both the Fontes Foundation study in Uganda and the WaterAid study in Ethiopia showed that involving government officials in the design of the studies, the data collection, and the data analysis increased their understanding of the relevance of tracking finance. These studies can be done in countries at relatively low cost.

In Ethiopia, the WaterAid study in two regions cost about US$5,000; in Uganda, at the national level, the cost of the scan was about US$25,000. IRC's experience from rolling out the lifecycle cost approach in African countries showed that an in-depth detailed study at national level, including training several stakeholders, costs about US$100,000. Finance and cost tracking is most expensive the first time it is carried out; follow-up initiatives, which can be done on a case-study basis, are much cheaper to conduct.

Tracking finances and influencing decision making towards sustainable services

There is a leap of faith in thinking that, once financial data has been collected, it will influence decision making and ultimately have an impact on the services consumers receive. However, decision makers will need incentives to start tracking financial flows and use the data.

Julia Zita of WSP Mozambique and Arjen Naafs of WaterAid explain how capital expenditure data is influencing decision making in Mozambique and how the monitoring of cost data has helped improve transparency in the country. The research was done using the framework of the WASHCost project (Zita and Naafs, 2013). In Mozambique, the research focused on obtaining data on the unit costs of boreholes. This started as an action research programme, but is now part of the government's monitoring processes.

Over the past five years, a database has been generated with some 700 contracts representing data from more than 6,000 boreholes. The database provides information on the contract partners, the objectives of the contract, the number of boreholes, how much they have cost, and where they are located.

A key factor in the success of the research is the government of Mozambique's leadership and its willingness to collect cost data. A government department helped define what needed to be monitored and restricted the number of indicators that were analysed in order to keep financial tracking simple and meaningful. The data is now used to benchmark the costs of boreholes around the country and has become valuable in making borehole contracting more transparent. The information is used for value-for-money discussions, for instance when contracts have much higher costs than the regional average. The team has also investigated the cost drivers; an inflation rate of over 10 per cent per year turned out to be an important cost driver with severe budgetary implications.

Another study in the context of the WASHCost project has been undertaken by Dr Kwabena Nyarko from Kwame Nkrumah University of Science and Technology in Ghana. This demonstrates the different ways in which regional governments and NGOs can track and utilize the costs of annual recurrent expenditures for planning and budgeting (Nyarko and Dwumfour-Asare, 2013). Awareness of these costs has led to discussions with the responsible agency for rural water supply, the CWSA (Community Water and Sanitation Agency), and some district assemblies on how these costs should be financed (i.e. from taxes, tariffs, or transfers).

Rural water coverage in Ghana has increased, but there are concerns about the service levels achieved. Emerging work from the Triple-S project is throwing light on the high rates of breakdowns. Studies also found that data on the expenditure of direct support costs was not adequate because critical activities were not included, for example capacity building for monitoring, repairs, basic operation, and maintenance. These findings were discussed with the CWSA and the district assemblies and more realistic expenditure levels were applied in planning and budgeting exercises (Adank et al., 2013).

It is still too early to assess the impact of using the lifecycle costs approach on the services delivered in Ghana. This demands more than just a technical budget exercise; for example, recurrent support costs are included in the budgets but it requires a certain level of political will to actually spend these budgets at district level. For now, the most important result is that civil society and government know how much funding is needed to provide a decent level of service.

Further work has been conducted in Ghana on tracking and financing infrastructure assets by Peter Burr (Burr, 2013). Ghana is a success story because the government has been effective in mobilizing funds for infrastructure, but the breakdown rate of boreholes is very high and represents a loss of about US$2.1 million over the last couple of years.

Monitoring data from East Gonja, a district in the northern region of Ghana, showed that capital maintenance accounts are not being kept, that maintenance is very ad hoc, and that responsibility for maintenance is ill defined. As a result, service levels are low. The difficult question for the district assembly of East Gonja is who will pay for these costs. The information collected on the low level of services, the broken-down pumps, and the inadequate budget for area mechanics to repair infrastructure had an impact on the district assemblies. It is expected that this data will be taken into account in the next planning cycle.

Asset management is about monitoring the infrastructure to keep it working properly. In practice, it is very simple: local service providers need to know what is on the ground to be able to plan preventive or replacement maintenance. But what is considered an appropriate level of maintenance is different depending on the amount of risk the service provider is willing to take. It is not uncommon to repair boreholes with handpump after their failure, and local governments and NGOs plan for the finance needed only once the system collapses.

Dr Richard Franceys from Cranfield University investigated how the financial monitoring indicators used by service providers in the United Kingdom inform regulatory and operational decision making (Franceys, 2013). Very sophisticated financial monitoring has revealed previously hidden problems, such as the inefficiency of the public sector, and has contributed to holding the private sector accountable. Tracking finance is important and needs to be accessible and utilized if the monitoring system is to last – 'use it or lose it'. The UK has invested in monitoring systems; however, too much financial data is understood only by experts. It is not clear whether the data is being used to help customers get a better service. Making financial data available will not have an impact if very few can engage with the complexity of the financial monitoring information. To improve the situation, the UK regulator – Ofwat – has created a simple interactive webpage with key performance indicators for customers.

Other challenges for financial monitoring to be able to influence government decision making are of a more practical nature. There are increasing opportunities to collect data using mobile devices but this does not mean that government departments are ready to process and analyse the data. Financial data from different sources will make data validation and cleaning more complex.

In peri-urban areas the challenges are different. There are examples of politicians discouraging service providers from collecting financial data because the data could show budget deficiencies and the need to increase the tariffs. Raising tariffs, however, is often blocked politically. As Franceys says: 'Are we not being a bit naïve in thinking that there is a solution in monitoring and having the data, when it is all about politics?' (Franceys, 2013). This reinforces Franceys' finding that, if regulators are not strong, civil society not organized, and research not independent, monitoring will have no impact on decision making. According to Franceys: 'Our experience is that politicians will only listen if you have your facts right and after a long engagement process' (Franceys, 2013).

The key lesson for influencing decision makers lies in making the invisible financial data visible. Small-scale action research involving those who need to know is a good start in setting up financial monitoring systems. This has been done in several countries but financial data is yet to be embedded in budgeting cycles.

Financial sustainability and affordability indicators for global monitoring

There are two relevant financial indicators to be tracked at global level and compared between countries. The first indicator is the financial sustainability of WASH services: if these services cannot be maintained, money and resources invested in the assets will be wasted. The second critical indicator is affordability: if people cannot pay for the services, universal access will not be achieved. These two indicators are related and it will be critical to achieve the right balance between the financing (the 3Ts) and the affordability of services for different segments of the population and also for service providers.

Relevant work has been done by the UN Office for the High Commission on Human right and by the Joint Monitoring Programme Post-2015 Working Groups for Water, Sanitation and Hygiene (UNICEF and WHO, 2012). Two questions and related indicators for the global monitoring of financial sustainability have been proposed:

- Does revenue cover at least the recurrent costs? This indicator would be measured by the ratio of annual revenue to annual expenditure on operating expenditures, capital maintenance, and debt servicing.
- If revenue covers the recurrent costs, is the expenditure on recurrent costs in balance with the value of infrastructure assets? This indicator would be measured by the ratio of annual expenditure on operating expenditures, capital maintenance, and debt servicing to the annualized value of capital assets.

Measuring these indicators raises some additional questions: is it sensible and meaningful for countries to have this type of aggregated data beyond the level of service provision? And who needs to know and why? A second challenge relates to determining what constitutes an adequate ratio. A final problem is related to choosing financial indicators used by urban utilities to measure financial sustainability in rural areas. It was argued that if the sector needs national-level indicators for financial sustainability, then it would be better to start with very simple indicators that can become more complex for more developed countries.

For affordability, the proposed indicator is the percentage of the population in the poorest quintile whose financial expenditure on WASH is below 3 per cent of the national poverty line (rural and urban). The current focus of survey questions in the DHS (Demographic and Health Survey) and the MICS (Multiple Indicator Cluster Survey) makes it hard to collect this information in contexts where services are not networked. Also, measuring the expenditure on the service tells us what people actually pay but does not tell us anything about the service they receive. Services may be affordable but people might be receiving a minimum level of service, or services could be unaffordable but people get much more than the minimum. The threshold of 3 per cent may not be right for all contexts, and who is to judge? One could imagine that poor households might have a different threshold than non-poor households, for instance.

The relevance of the affordability indicator for the water sector needs to be questioned. If there are affordability problems, then the transfers required to improve access by the poorest should not necessarily come from the water sector, but from social security or from other parts of the national budget. Affordability, and monitoring whether the poorest can pay for their water, could be seen as an overall government responsibility that justifies a broader perspective on poverty instead of focusing solely on the water sector. Transfers from international partners – not necessarily to the WASH sector but for targeting the poorest and most disadvantaged households, even within middle-income countries – could play an important role. US$2.6 billion has been transferred as ODA in the last years to the Africa region alone. The question is whether these transfers should go directly to the WASH sector in order to allow that sector to correct affordability problems, or whether these transfers should go straight to the poorest layers of the population through social security or other poverty reduction mechanisms in state budgets.

All in all, there is a real need to target the poor. From a global perspective, there are limitations in defining who are the poor, but within a country or district this can be done more precisely. In India, despite great advances in water and sanitation coverage, the poorest quintiles have made very little progress. But in Bangladesh, where the poor have been targeted explicitly, progress in reducing inequalities in access to services has been made (WHO and UNICEF, 2013).

Overall, it is positive that these issues – financial sustainability and affordability – are prominent in the post-2015 technical proposal and have been translated into three sub-indicators, even though further research will be needed on thresholds, aggregation, and measurability.

Conclusions

The WASH sector has come a long way in establishing a more coherent discourse on finance. There is a more realistic idea of how much it costs per person per year to provide basic water and sanitation services and the need for national and global finance monitoring is widely recognized. More countries and donors are reporting on financing flows to the GLAAS report (WHO, 2012). There is a greater focus on sustainability, in part motivated by the availability of data on water system failures (Improve International, 2014), internal evaluation reports (European Court of Auditors, 2012; DGIS, 2012), and slippage data on sanitation programmes (WHO, 2012).

The financial discourse is largely influenced by the dominant model of community management, where communities are assumed to cover the costs of a sustainable water supply. The assumption that, after the ribbon has been cut, the community will take care of its handpump and make sure that the finance is there so that water will flow for ever has in many instances proven to be false. This assumption also contributes to the invisibility of all other costs required to provide services after the ribbon cutting, which makes it hard to plan financially for sustainable water service delivery.

There are promising initiatives at a global level, such as the UN-Water GLAAS TrackFin initiative and the financial sustainability and affordability indicators being proposed in the post-2015 process, but real change will happen only if there is political will at country level to collect and share financial data. None of the indicators and methodologies will be used if there are no incentives, if there is no regulation, and if there is no support at country level to report the data required. The challenge is to collect financial and cost data for the first time and to have incentives and a process in place to do it again. The examples seem to indicate that support from semi-independent research organizations or NGOs is a good trigger to kick-start financial monitoring.

Independently of the methodologies used, financial tracking tools cannot underestimate the complexity of current funding flows in the WASH sector or the need for some form of harmonization. With so many different funding flows in a country and so many different definitions of service levels and unit costs, it is hard to have national or even district overviews that can indeed inform national- and district-level decision making.

Gradually, financial data is becoming available, but so are reports of data overkill, a lack of opportunities to act on the basis of data, a lack of incentives to use data, data ignored by decision makers, and data not being reliable. However, in individual countries and internationally, the need for data is being recognized more and more, and more and more data is being used to challenge assumptions, policies, and practices. And that is a good thing!

References

Aboma, G. (2013) 'Life cycle costs and affordability of water services in Ethiopia', paper presented at the IRC Symposium 2013: Monitoring WASH Services Delivery, Addis Ababa, Ethiopia, 9–11 April.

Adank, M., Smits, S., Bey, V., Verhoeven, J. and Pezon, C. (2013) 'Development and use of service delivery indicators for monitoring rural water services in Ghana, Uganda, Burkina Faso, Colombia, Honduras, Paraguay, El Salvador', paper presented at the IRC Symposium 2013: Monitoring WASH Services Delivery, Addis Ababa, Ethiopia, 9–11 April.

Amenga-Etego, H.N. (2011) *Water and Sanitation Budget Tracking Report of Findings*, GrassRootsAfrica Foundation.

Biteete, L. and van Lieshout, R. (2013) 'Applying the life-cycle costs approach in Uganda for improved financial planning and budgeting', paper presented at the IRC Symposium 2013: Monitoring WASH Services Delivery, Addis Ababa, Ethiopia, 9–11 April.

Biteete, L., Jangeyanga, P. and Barigya, G.W. (2013) *Life-cycle Cost Analysis of Rural Water Supply in Uganda, Kabarole District*, Kampala and The Hague: Triple-S Uganda and IRC.

Burr, P. (2013) 'Linking financial monitoring with decision making: asset monitoring for sustainable services in rural Ghana', paper presented at the IRC Symposium 2013: Monitoring WASH Services Delivery, Addis Ababa, Ethiopia, 9–11 April.

Burr, P. and Fonseca, C. (2012) *Applying a Life-cycle Costs Approach to Water: Costs and Service Levels in Rural and Small Town Areas in Andhra Pradesh (India), Burkina Faso, Ghana and Mozambique*, WASHCost Global Working Paper 8, The Hague: IRC.

Cross, P., Frade, J., James, A.J. and Trémolet, S. (2013) *WASHCost End-of-project Evaluation*, The Hague: IRC.

DGIS (2012) *From Infrastructure to Sustainable Impact: Policy Review of the Dutch Contribution to Drinking Water and Sanitation (1990–2011)*, IOB Evaluation, The Hague: Ministry of Foreign Affairs of the Netherlands (DGIS).

Dorotinsky, B. (2004) 'Public expenditure accountability in Africa: progress, lessons and challenges', in S.J.K.B. Levy (ed.), *Building State Capacity in Africa: New Approaches, Emerging Lessons*, p. 377, Washington DC: World Bank Publications.

European Court of Auditors (2012) *European Union Development Assistance for Drinking-water Supply and Basic Sanitation in Sub-Saharan Countries*, Special Report 13/2012, Luxembourg: Publications Office of the European Union.

Fonseca, C., Franceys, R., Batchelor, C., McIntyre, P., Klutse, A., Komives, K., Moriarty, P., Naafs, A., Nyarko, K., Pezon, C., Potter, A., Reddy, R. and Snehalatha, M. (2011) *Life-cycle Costs Approach: Costing Sustainable Service*, The Hague: IRC.

Franceys, R. (2013) 'Financial monitoring high-income country WASH', paper presented at the IRC Symposium 2013: Monitoring WASH Services Delivery, Addis Ababa, Ethiopia, 9–11 April.

Hervé-Bazin, C. (2012) *'3Ts': Tariffs, Taxes And Transfers In The European Water Sector: Short Guide*. Brussels: EUREAU.

Improve International (2014) 'Statistics on water system failures' [website] <http://improveinternational.wordpress.com/handy-resources/sad-stats/> [accessed 4 October 2014].

McIntyre, P., Casella, D., Fonseca, C. and Burr, P. (2014) *Priceless! Uncovering the Real Costs of Water and Sanitation*, The Hague: IRC.

Mehta, M. (2008) *Financing Water and Sanitation at Local Levels: Synthesis Paper*, London: WaterAid.

Moriarty, P., Pezon, C., Fonseca, C., Uandela, A., Potter, A., Batchelor, C., Reddy, R. and Snehalatha, M. (2010) *WASHCost's Theory of Change: Reforms in the Water Sector and What They Mean for the Use of Unit Costs*, WASHCost Global Working Paper 1, The Hague: IRC.

Norman, G., Fonseca, C. and Jacimovic, R. (2012) *Financing Water and Sanitation for the Poor: Six Key Solutions. Water and Sanitation for the Urban Poor*, Discussion Paper 003, The Hague and London: IRC and Water and Sanitation for the Urban Poor (WSUP).

Nyarko, K. and Dwumfour-Asare, B. (2013) 'Tracking direct support and capital maintenance cost in rural water service delivery in Ghana', paper presented at the IRC Symposium 2013: Monitoring WASH Services Delivery, Addis Ababa, Ethiopia, 9–11 April.

OECD (2009) *Managing Water For All: An OECD Perspective On Pricing And Financing: Key Messages For Policy Makers*, Paris: Organisation for Economic Co-operation and Development (OECD).

Tolmie, C. (2010) *Using Public Expenditure Tracking Surveys (PETS) to Monitor Projects and Small-Scale Programs: A Guidebook*, Washington DC: World Bank Publications.

Trémolet, S. and Rama, M. (2012) *Tracking National Financial Flows into Sanitation, Hygiene and Drinking Water*, Geneva: World Health Organization.

Trémolet, S., Kolsky, P and Perez, E. (2010) *Financing On-site Sanitation for the Poor: A Six Country Comparative Review and Analysis*, Water and Sanitation Program Technical Paper, Washington DC: Water and Sanitation Program.

UNICEF and WHO (2012) *Progress on Drinking Water and Sanitation: 2012 Update*, New York NY: UNICEF and World Health Organization (WHO).

WaterAid (2010) *Governance and Transparency Fund Developing Southern Civil Society Advocacy in Water and Sanitation in Sub-Saharan Africa, South Asia and Central America (CN-010). Annual Report 2009/2010*, London: WaterAid.

WHO (2012) *UN-Water Global Annual Assessment of Sanitation and Drinking-Water (GLAAS) 2012 Report: The Challenge of Extending and Sustaining Services*, Geneva: World Health Organization (WHO).

WHO and UNICEF (2013) *Progress on Drinking Water and Sanitation: 2013 Update*, Geneva: World Health Organization (WHO).

WSP (2003) *Governance and Financing of Water Supply and Sanitation in Ethiopia, Kenya and South Africa: A Cross Country Synthesis*, Sector Finance Working Papers 5, Washington DC: Water and Sanitation Program (WSP).

WSP (2004) *Sector Finance and Resource Flows for Water Supply: A Pilot Application for Kenya*. Sector Finance Working Papers 7, Washington DC: Water and Sanitation Program (WSP).

Zita, J. and Naafs, A. (2013) 'Monitoring and sustaining services: lessons learned from WaterAid's post-implementation monitoring surveys and the use of information and communications technology (the Mozambique pilot)', paper presented at the IRC Symposium 2013: Monitoring WASH Services Delivery, Addis Ababa, Ethiopia, 9–11 April.

About the author

Catarina Fonseca leads the International and Innovation Programme of IRC and was Director of WASHCost, a programme known to have increased sector understanding of the real costs to sustain rural and peri-urban water and sanitation services in low-income countries. At present, Catarina Fonseca is involved in adapting WASHCost's lifecycle costing methodology and tools to monitor costs and services provided in schools and refugee contexts.

CHAPTER 3

Messy, varied, and growing: country-led monitoring of rural water supplies

Kerstin Danert

Country monitoring, led by governments, together with civil society and the private sector, is essential for decision making and action to realize and improve water supply services. However, in low- and middle-income countries, the lack of a voice for rural dwellers coupled with weak incentives for accountability, government resource constraints, fragmented funding, and donor dominance pose great challenges to country-led monitoring. Project- and donor-led reporting that overshadow country priorities exacerbate these difficulties. The result is a partial, messy, and fragmented monitoring landscape. Nevertheless, some governments are starting to undertake performance measurement and water services monitoring. There appears to be a resurgence of inventories, fuelled by technical innovations around water point mapping. Reflections on 12 country case studies show the diverse journeys taken by each, and provide an insight into the realities of developing comprehensive and systematic country-led monitoring processes. This takes years, has no blueprint, and has no guarantees to deliver expected results in the short term.

Keywords: joint sector reviews, country-led monitoring, monitoring culture, government leadership, water user perspectives

Introduction

The Paris Declaration on Aid Effectiveness (OECD, 2005; 2008), the Busan Partnership for Effective Co-operation (OECD, 2011), the New Deal (IDPS, 2011) and the Dili Consensus of the g7+ (2013) all emphasize ownership of development priorities by developing countries themselves. By extension, the mechanisms to monitor, evaluate, and learn about development should also be led by the countries themselves.

The term 'country-led' is in the title of this chapter. Some have argued that the term 'government-led' should have been used instead. However, 'country-led' has been chosen as it is considered to better reflect shared civil society, private sector, and government leadership roles in the process.

Ideally, country-led monitoring of water supplies in rural areas and small towns should systematically consolidate and analyse both quantitative and qualitative data about all water services in the country (or state or region). Monitoring should continue and evolve over decades, with the information generated used to support planning, decision making, and actions that improve service delivery over the long term. The information should inform the public. Conceptually, country-led monitoring is very different from funder-led and project-driven monitoring. These tend to be temporally and spatially piecemeal and are undertaken mainly for the foreign constituencies that provide aid rather than for the developing country's citizens and institutions.

In practice, systematic country-led monitoring of rural water supplies in low- and middle-income countries is difficult. Firstly, the rural dwellers (who are usually poor) have little voice in the political landscape. Thus their demands are unheard and their needs are often overlooked by country elites. Accountability of service providers to rural citizens is generally very weak, particularly for water supplies that are essentially gifts to the community and end up being managed by volunteers. Despite the proliferation of mobile phone technology, the mechanisms for information flows relating to drinking water services as well as the priorities and plans of government or other service providers are lacking. There are relatively few incentives. On the whole, there is very little regulation of those who fund, construct, operate, or manage water supply services in rural areas.

Rural water supply supplies in many low- and middle-income countries benefit and suffer from a proliferation of non-governmental organizations (NGOs) that tend to report only to their funders. Local governments have inadequate regular resources to visit and follow up communities. Unlike the health and agricultural sectors, rural water supply rarely has extension staff operating at community level. Even technicians and officers for water supply at district level may be few in number. Government staff may also face challenges with data analysis, or even simple tasks such as printing and photocopying materials. Rural water supply services in a given area tend to be provided by multiple projects, with the implementers all incentivized to report to their funders. Multiple reports with different information are rarely synthesized.

Nevertheless, there are examples where efforts are being made to develop systematic, country-led monitoring systems. In particular, there are encouraging examples of performance measurement, water services monitoring, and compliance monitoring. Several countries have recently undertaken baseline surveys and are using data from household surveys and activity reporting. This chapter summarizes these case studies and draws lessons from them.

The messiness of monitoring

Some countries (such as Liberia) have relatively little monitoring in place for rural and small town water supplies (Koroma, 2013). Ethiopia, for example, has just completed its first national baseline. Others (including South Africa) have multiple initiatives, not all of which are well integrated (De La Harpe et al., 2013). In some countries (notably Kenya), fairly robust monitoring mechanisms are in place for piped water supplies in some small towns, but rural populations with point sources are not monitored (WASREB, 2012). In the case of Thailand, data on drinking water sources and water quality is available and improving, while information on infrastructure costs or who is doing what is scattered.

Figure 3.1 illustrates the messiness of the monitoring landscape in most countries and shows the following problems:

- *Missing stages.*[1] A particular initiative may not include all of the stages of the monitoring process. Communication may be lacking or there may be little action taken on the findings. The donor baseline (Figure 3.1, right), which comprises only three stages (planning, data collection, and information), is illustrative of this.

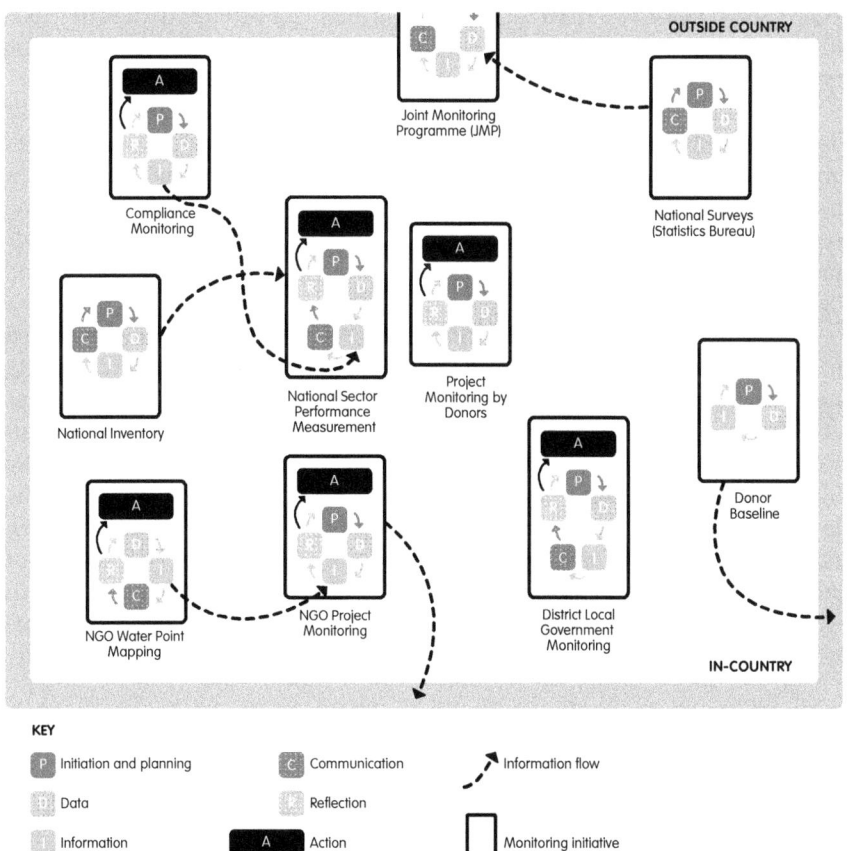

Figure 3.1 Typical messiness of monitoring

- *Processes overlooked.* There may be good monitoring processes in place but they may be completely overlooked by the national ministry responsible for rural water supplies. These can include local government monitoring (Figure 3.1, bottom right). Similarly, data generated from national surveys (Figure 3.1, top right) might feed into the Joint Monitoring Programme (JMP) but not into national reporting, despite the fact that they provide valuable information on drinking water used, collection times, and distances.
- *Findings leave the country.* Sometimes the information generated is communicated outside the country, particularly to generate external funding, but does not find its way into country processes. The donor baseline (Figure 3.1, right) and NGO project monitoring (Figure 3.1, bottom centre) are cases in point.

Key issues for country-led monitoring

Leadership

Who should **take the lead** for monitoring and thus determine the questions to be asked, the methods to be used, the analytical approach, and how the findings will be communicated and used?

Segone (2010) uses the term 'country-led monitoring', stressing that this does not imply exclusive central government responsibility. Local authorities and civil society are also involved and contribute, and may take on a particular leadership role, as may the private sector. However, not everybody is comfortable with the term 'country-led', arguing that the process needs to be explicitly 'government-led' – 'this is a matter of national sovereignty' (Ssozi, 2013).

Given that ensuring access to safe drinking water for all citizens is enshrined in many constitutions, national government has a leading role in making sure that progress is monitored. Ideally, it should monitor the effectiveness of policies, strategies, and implementation. Government-led monitoring thus seems to be a more appropriate title. However, the term 'country-led' may be more palatable to development partners working in developing countries. The capacity constraints of government, the fact that resources and power often remain in the hands of development partners and political elites, concerns about government accountability, and lack of trust in governments make the term 'government-led' hard to swallow for some. The joint sector review (Box 3.1) seems to be a response to the question of government versus country leadership.

Information flow

How can the **information flow** from NGOs and projects to government be ensured in order to provide an overview of what is happening in the country, and ultimately to support national and local processes of planning and resource allocation?

> **Box 3.1 Joint sector reviews**
>
> There appears to be a growing consensus around the need for recurring joint sector reviews that are led by national government and involve all major stakeholders. These events can enable project managers, technicians, and political leaders from national and local government as well as donors, civil society, and academia to come together. They can reflect on what has been achieved, and examine problems in an open and inclusive manner. At least 40 countries now hold annual or biennial reviews of rural drinking water performance (often combined with urban water and sanitation), and 13 countries are in the process of establishing such mechanisms (Figure 3.2).
>
> However, reliable information, in structured and understandable formats, is essential for such events. In 2013, national performance reports, containing information on rural water supplies, were available for many countries.

Figure 3.2 Countries with annual or biennial reviews of rural drinking water
Source: WHO, 2012: 19.

Underlying the concern about information flow is a question of accountability. Most donors and external implementation organizations report on the specifics of their project or programme to their board or their funders (Lockwood, 2013). Although projects may incorporate some monitoring (and evaluation), this rarely strengthens monitoring or governance in the country as a whole.

Uganda seems to have overcome the challenge of information flow (Ssozi and Danert, 2012). Figure 3.3 illustrates the flow of data from local governments and NGOs to central government. The Uganda case is an example of relative order compared with the messy 'spaghetti' diagram in Figure 3.1:

- Local government reports provide data to national government (the Ministry of Water and Environment) as an integral part of activity reporting. Local governments risk budget cuts if they do not report accordingly.
- Most of the NGOs in Uganda report to the Uganda Water and Sanitation NGO network (UWASNET), which provides a synthesis report to national

44 FROM INFRASTRUCTURE TO SERVICES

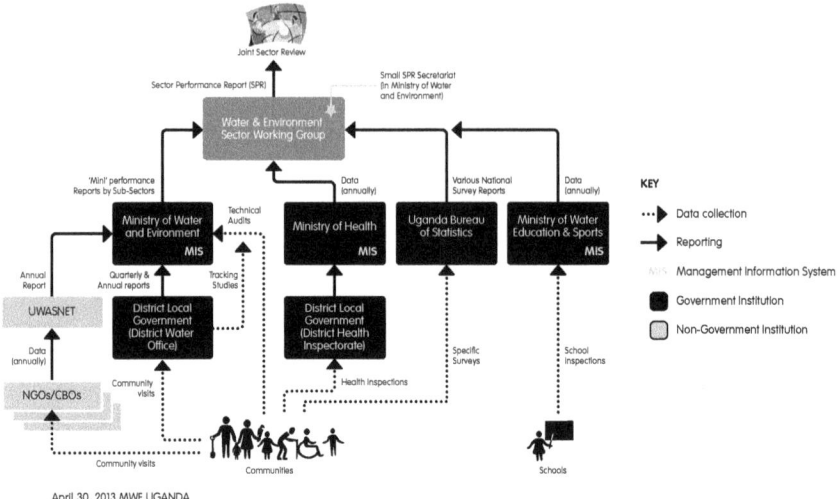

Figure 3.3 Data sources, information flows, and analysis: sector performance monitoring in Uganda

government. UWASNET is under pressure to provide this input for the joint sector review. It is part of the sector culture and is non-negotiable.
- Data from the Bureau of Statistics is drawn into an annual sector performance report and provides complementary information to that generated directly by the Ministry of Water and Environment.
- Information that is generated through processes under the auspices of the Ministry of Education is drawn into the national report.

Monitoring activities for water services that are undertaken in the West African countries of Benin, Burkina Faso, Chad, Mali, and Mauritania provide another perspective on information flow. An NGO, a local consulting firm, and/or a national agency collect and analyse technical and financial data on selective piped water supplies. They report the results back to all water service stakeholders on site, and prepare a written report for the water service authority and the minister in charge of water. This monitoring mechanism, which has been in place for as long as 15 years in some countries, is reported to have improved service management and reduced operation and maintenance costs of these systems (Désille et al., 2013). However, as in the case of Kenya, rural dwellers with small piped systems and point sources are not part of this monitoring mechanism (WASREB, 2012).

Perspectives of water users and community-led monitoring

As the framework for sustainable development (i.e. beyond the millennium development goals or MDGs) is debated, the international community currently stands at a crossroads. Will the new generation of indicators at international level properly take account of the **perspectives of water users** (Guzha, 2013)?

The concept of community-led monitoring has not featured in the post-MDG debate so far, which is more concerned about the links between national and international indicators and systems. However, there are some examples of community roles in monitoring:

- One of the encouraging aspects of water services monitoring in the West African countries of **Benin, Burkina Faso, Chad, Mali, and Mauritania** is that the reporting is also available to the water users (Désille et al., 2013). The NGO, local consulting firm, and/or national agency that collect and analyse technical and financial data on selective piped water supplies report the results back to all water service stakeholders on site.
- In **Thailand**, a national project is under way to ensure that water quality is monitored by over 1 million volunteers throughout the country. Local stakeholders have been trained and linked together into networks. Not only can they test key water quality parameters, but they also know about the importance of safe water for health. Thailand's model is highly participative, with the volunteers responsible for actively checking on water quality and feeding the information back within their village (Wongpiyachon, 2013).
- It is also worth noting that the water point mapping work in **Malawi** was triggered by community members asking WaterAid why they did not have improved supplies while their neighbours had many water sources.
- In **Uganda**, the Ministry of Water and Environment produces a popular version of the annual sector performance report, which is published in a national newspaper.
- Maluti GM in **South Africa** found out that it was much more effective to call water users to find out about services than to expect them to send an SMS.

Indicators

As the international community debates the next steps in terms of post-MDG indicators, will there be a proliferation of new indicators at global level that cannot be properly handled by the countries involved, thus undermining growing national monitoring efforts?

At national (and in some cases more local) level, numerical indicators, such as those in Table 3.1, are being used by governments to measure and report on performance. Malawi and Timor-Leste include data from national household surveys as headline indicators. In Uganda, the survey data augments the 'golden' indicator on access.

The numerical nature of an indicator gives the impression that it is completely objective. However, this is not always the case. Welle (2013) compares figures for water coverage for a lower-level local government (or

Table 3.1 Indicators relevant for rural water supplies in Uganda, Malawi, and Timor-Leste

	Uganda golden indicators (Ssozi and Danert, 2012)	Malawi headline indicators (Meek and Young, 2013)	Timor-Leste indicators (Willets, 2013
Access	Percentage of people within 1 km (rural) of an improved water source	Percentage of households within 500 m (rural) of an improved water source Percentage of people whose average total time to collect drinking water (from the main source) is less than 30 minutes	Number of households (served and unserved) Time taken to collect water
Functionality	Percentage of improved water sources that are functional at time of spot check	Percentage of improved water point sources that are functional at time of checks	Water system functioning status Adequate water supply (periods of the year with low flow rate/low level)
Value for money	Average cost per beneficiary of new water and sanitation schemes		
Quality	Percentage of water samples taken at the point of water collection and waste discharge point that comply with national standards		Water quality and level of water source protection
Equity	Mean parish deviation from the district average of the number of people per improved water point (for national purposes, mean sub-county difference from the national average in the number of people per water point is reported)	Standard deviation of districts' access to safe water	
Management	Percentage of water points with actively functioning water and sanitation committees (rural)		System management, including water user groups – funds collected, repairs undertaken, etc.
Gender	Percentage of water user committees/water boards with women holding a key position		Number of women in roles of responsibility (leader, technician, treasurer)

Note that Malawi also has headline indicators for water, sanitation, and hygiene (WASH) in schools, and both Malawi and Uganda also have sanitation and hygiene indicators, but these are beyond the scope of this chapter.

sub-district, known as the *kebele*) in Ethiopia and found that the 'percentage served' was 70 per cent or 94 per cent depending on the inputs into the calculation; for instance, different assumptions about the population made a huge difference to the figures.

It may seem obvious, but, for comparability, every aspect of an indicator needs to be fully defined, and for a proper analysis every aspect needs to be well understood. Take the indicator of the 'percentage of the population within a certain distance from an improved water supply' (e.g. 0.5 km or 1.5 km): this distance may never actually be measured but rather another proxy used (Box 3.2).

When it comes to indicators, nothing can be taken for granted. Different definitions mean that data can be misunderstood and misquoted, and can even cause friction. Ministries typically present provider-based data on outputs (defined as 'coverage' in Box 3.2), whereas national statistics agencies usually present user-based data on outcomes ('use' in Box 3.2).

Indicators can also create perverse incentives for organizations. As an example, an indicator for the percentage of enterprises with permits that comply with regulations contributed to enterprises not being encouraged to obtain such permits. This was because, without a permit, the poorly performing enterprises were not included in the statistics. In another case, the water access figures quoted by the local and regional water offices (for the same area) in Ethiopia differed by 20 to 30 percentage points. The *woreda* (district or local authority) water office used population data and calculation methods to arrive at a lower figure in order to justify more funding. Meanwhile, the regional bureau of water resources used a calculation method in line with federal guidelines, which represented a good level of performance in water access (Welle, 2013). Thus, politics and subjectivity, as well as the rationale of individuals, play a significant role when reporting on indicators.

Box 3.2 Proxy indicators and definitions of coverage, access, and use

The terms 'water supply access', 'coverage', and 'use' are quite distinct concepts, but are often used imprecisely in water supplies and WASH documentation:
- The term **coverage** refers to whether there is an improved water supply near a dwelling. In the case of rural areas, typically, countries have set standards for a maximum distance, such as 1 km or 1.5 km. However, there may be cases when a person or household has coverage but does not use the supply because they are excluded due to non-payment or for some other reason.
- Water supply **use** usually refers to whether a person or household actually utilizes a particular water supply. In general, household surveys ask questions about water use.
- Water supply **access** is a term often used in the phrasing of national targets. In some publications, the term 'access' is used interchangeably with the term 'coverage', while in others it is used interchangeably with the term 'use'. Within the human right discourse, the term 'access' has also been defined, alongside several other aspects of water supplies (De Albuquerque, 2012).
- '**Access coverage**' is referred to in Ethiopia's universal action plan.

Within country-led monitoring there is a **proliferation of indicators**. The international debate appears to be moving on from the binary 'improved/unimproved'[2] sources currently set out in the JMP towards something that is more nuanced and reflects levels of service. Examples of a more granular definition of indicators are as follows:

- From the human right framework, there is a drive to consider the 'normative criteria' of availability, quality, acceptability, accessibility, and affordability, as well as other aspects such as non-discrimination (De Albuquerque, 2012).
- Adank et al. (2013) recommend that quantity, quality, distance, and crowding indicators are combined into a water services ladder, thus providing a composite indicator. This idea is being tested (in Burkina Faso, Colombia, Ghana, and Uganda) and implemented at scale in Ghana.
- Flores Bacquero et al. (2013) define indicators that consider the human right criteria. Their research in Nicaragua revealed new insights into the availability and quality of water for self-providers compared with those served by community committees.
- South Africa's Blue Drop Certification Programme to monitor and encourage improvements in municipal drinking water quality incorporates water safety plans, process controls, water quality compliance, and asset management, among other factors, into a composite score (De La Harpe et al., 2013).

Before advocating for more nuanced and more complicated indicators, it is worth pausing to take stock of how the indicators currently used in various countries are actually supporting the monitoring process. Experiences from Uganda show that indicators considered good at the start can prove to be too complicated to measure or understand and thus need modification later (Ssozi and Danert, 2012).

Box 3.3 Clarifying and aligning indicator definitions in Madagascar

In 2001, Madagascar witnessed conflicting results from the household monitoring survey and sector monitoring. This triggered a series of round-table discussions between the statistics bureau, the line ministries (health and water), and key development partners (including WaterAid, UNICEF, and Diarano-WASH). It became clear that there was a need to clarify definitions of (un)improved water and sanitation facilities. Definitions were changed to reflect government policy and fulfil the needs of all parties. The household questionnaires used the new definitions in the 2004 and 2005 surveys. Subsequently, there was another round of changes.

In 2008, the government was embarrassed by huge differences in the coverage figures used by donors (from the JMP) and by national WASH professionals. While definitions had been harmonized within the country, there were still differences with the JMP. This was particularly problematic for planning and resource allocation at the highest levels. The process of 'data reconciliation' between the JMP and the Madagascar government has further sharpened definitions, and has influenced the design of the census questionnaire. A booklet that defines water and sanitation facilities for enumerators and interviewers has also been developed.

Source: Rasolofomanana, unpublished.

The process of aligning indicators within a country, as well as with international indicators, is a considerable undertaking. The data reconciliation process in Madagascar (Box 3.3) illustrates the detailed work and time needed.

In addition, not everything can be represented by indicators and numbers, which are merely an interpretation of reality. They provide a starting point for further questions and enquiry. This comes out particularly strongly in the Liberia case, where water point mapping triggered substantial discussion about the causes of the poor functionality rates, and what could be done about them (Koroma, 2013). Monitoring, after all, is a means to an end and not an end in itself.

Monitoring journeys and monitoring cultures

Monitoring is a process rather than a one-off event, and it takes time to mature (O'Brien, 2013). It takes time to learn what works and what does not. It also takes time for information generated to be used for planning and decision making, and there are no guarantees that information will be used at all! In Uganda, for example, there was a three-year lag between acknowledging that there were major inequities between districts to actually changing the allocation of funds to address the problem.

Some countries are undertaking journeys to establish and make use of country-led monitoring for drinking water supplies in rural areas (including small towns). There are examples where a 'monitoring culture' is taking root. The term 'culture' reflects a shared set of values and behaviours that enable a monitoring system (or set of systems) to function. A monitoring culture thus means that there is a genuine desire by most stakeholders to share, reflect, and learn from ongoing development efforts.

Many countries have taken steps to improve their monitoring systems: Ethiopia, Liberia, Malawi, South Africa, Thailand, Timor-Leste, and Uganda, as well as Benin, Burkina Faso, Chad, Mali, and Mauritania. Each country has started out on its own course and is adjusting and amending its systems over time. There does not seem to be a blueprint. The monitoring journey of each country depends on the country's history and policies, as well as the way in which the government, major development partners, NGOs, and private sector organizations work together.

There are different starting points for country-led monitoring; the process can kick off with a national inventory (e.g. Liberia and Ethiopia), grow out of a sector-wide approach (Uganda), initially be driven by NGOs (Malawi), be fostered by a major development partner (Timor-Leste), or evolve from the regulatory framework (Thailand, South Africa, Benin, Burkina Faso, Chad, Mali, and Mauritania). The sheer size of a country and the number of local governments make a difference too – compare the 13 districts of Timor-Leste (population 1.2 million) with the over 1,000 *woredas* of Ethiopia (population 85 million).

Uganda

In the case of Uganda, institutional reform together with a shift to a sector-wide approach to planning provided the foundation for the performance monitoring in place today (Ssozi and Danert, 2012). But this is not the whole story. In 2002, the UK Department for International Development (DFID) funded the development of a performance measurement framework for water and sanitation (MWLE, 2004). This was DFID's exit strategy from the sector (Swann, 2012). The funds paid for part-time consultancy over two years. A set of eight 'golden' indicators was initially defined (Table 3.1), chosen jointly by government, civil society, and development partners to enable the country to examine select outputs and outcomes. The indicators, coupled with a change from individual projects to a sector-wide approach, helped both to introduce and to consolidate a culture of country-led monitoring. Champions in the Ministry of Water and Environment ensured that the framework became the process that is now part of the sector's culture. The sector performance report is used for decision making, policy formulation, and planning. For example, it was used to change the resource allocation to district local governments and to introduce additional efforts to improve water point functionality. Uganda's journey was one in which capacity grew at individual and institutional levels over a period of about seven years, and continues today. It required very detailed work with individuals to gradually change the culture within the Ministry of Water and Environment from one in which only positive stories were told into one where problems and challenges could be shared, to look for solutions.

At an individual level, it meant building skills and confidence in data analysis, and presenting information in both graphical form and text. Two or three champions in particular played a tremendous role in motivating others to analyse and write, and quality assured their work. Shifting the culture so that it became the norm for individuals and departments to set out progress and challenges in an analytical manner took years.

At an institutional level, within the lead ministry it took several years for the sector performance report to be embedded in the annual joint sector review process and for the findings to be reflected upon. From one year to the next, the interest of senior management increased until the findings started to influence the planning and budget allocation processes. However, a tremendous amount of work is still undertaken every year to quality assure the data and analysis. Opportunities such as changes to local government reporting formats have been seized so that the data required for the 'golden' indicators can flow to the lead ministry. The release of significant funds to local governments for water supplies is tied to reporting (Figure 3.3), providing a major incentive for the flow of information.

Malawi

Malawi has witnessed several initiatives to improve the monitoring of rural water supplies over the years. The Ministry of Irrigation and Water Development has a performance measurement framework in place and has selected national headline indicators (Table 3.1). An indicator handbook has been published (MoWDI, 2010). The indicators inform the annual sector review, part of the sector-wide approach that is being established. The ministry has been producing a sector performance report since 2010, with data drawn from the national statistics office and the ministry itself (MoWDI, 2010).

It is worth noting that it was a question from community members in Salima district that triggered water point mapping work in 2002. The community asked WaterAid why they did not have improved water points while their neighbours had several (Welle, 2007). This prompted a research project within the district that showed significant inequities. The work subsequently led other development agencies in the country to take water point mapping to other parts of Malawi until it became a national exercise. In 2003, the WaterAid mapping team worked within the planning unit of the (then) Ministry of Water. However, this arrangement did not work well and the team was moved to the Malawi branch of the Water Supply and Sanitation Collaborative Council (WSSCC). In 2005, the water point mapping work was moved back to the ministry with support from UNICEF before being withdrawn again and becoming part of the UNICEF country office. Quite some journey!

District local governments in Malawi receive funding for water supplies from different sources, each with different reporting requirements. As a result, there is no incentive for collecting standardized monitoring data and passing it upwards (unlike in the Uganda case above). Data collection for rural water supplies in Malawi was undertaken in some districts with encouragement and support from external agencies such as WaterAid and Engineers Without Borders Canada (initially working in partnership). However, there was no standard data collection across the country. From 2008, health surveillance assistants were encouraged to collect data on drinking water access. This information was collated and presented in district-level Excel-based systems.

While some districts made use of these systems, others failed to collect, update, or use the data. Meanwhile, in 2010, plans were made by the Ministry of Water Development and Irrigation to develop a comprehensive national monitoring system (funded by the African Water Facility). However, contracting the advisory support for this was delayed, and in the meantime other initiatives gained traction (Meek and Young, 2013). In mid-2011, the Ministry of Health started to develop a comprehensive monitoring and evaluation system for sanitation, which was linked to the ongoing initiatives of the Ministry of Water Development and Irrigation and Engineers Without Borders Canada/local government.

Within the framework, the Ministry of Health coordinates data collection on water and sanitation at village level by the health surveillance assistants. These assistants are employed by the Ministry of Health, are based in the field, and are responsible for health interventions and data collection in a catchment area of 1,000 to 1,500 people. The data should flow from health surveillance assistants to health centres to the district, where they are compiled in the district water office (Welle, 2007).

Alongside the work to improve national monitoring, efforts continue to strengthen definitions, provide easy-to-use templates for data analysis, and build the skills of those who collect, present, interpret, and use the data at district level (Meek and Young, 2013).

South Africa

Responsibility for water supply monitoring is set out in South Africa's constitution, and is detailed further in the country's *Strategic Framework for Water Services* (DWAF, 2003), the Water Services Act (Republic of South Africa, 1997), and the National Water Services Regulatory Strategy (DWAF, 2009). Numerous systems are used, some of which overlap (Table 3.2). National government monitors service provision through its National Treasury, the Department of Water Affairs (DWA), and the Department of Cooperative Governance and Traditional Affairs. The monitoring tries to reduce risks and incentivize improvements in the performance of water service authorities and water service providers. Some systems, such as the Blue Drop Certification Programme, seem to have taken off more than others. Water service providers have their own monitoring systems.

South Africa is an interesting case, as the country can be considered as both developed and developing. Arguably, the regulation of urban utilities is what has driven monitoring in South Africa. However, the information requirements may not be appropriate for rural settings, particularly in the case of small piped systems and point sources. De La Harpe et al. (2013) note that the district local governments that operate in predominantly rural areas have limited capacity and tend to be overwhelmed by the numerous reporting requirements.

Thailand

Thailand's history of concern for the supply of safe drinking water dates back to 1897, when King Rama V assigned Metropolitan (the government) to provide waterworks for Bangkok. Today, data on the water supply is available from the National Statistics Bureau, from which we see that rainwater has a significant role, providing almost 35 per cent of the Thai population with its drinking water. Water supply, sanitation, and hygiene in rural areas are considered to be fundamental for community health and Thailand has a history of community participation by volunteers (Wongpiyachon, 2013). The latter is particularly relevant when it comes to monitoring.

Table 3.2 Different water supply monitoring systems in South Africa

System	Purpose	Who monitors	Indicators	Intended result
Regulatory Performance Measurement System	To address regulatory compliance and performance of water service authorities (WSAs)	DWA	As per the regulations in the Water Services Act	Improve the performance of WSAs and water service providers (WSPs)
Water Services Audit	Compliance with the act	DWA – reports from WSAs	Quantity, quality, level of service, percentage of households, cost recovery	Reporting on compliance
Blue and Green Drop Certification Programme	National drinking water quality and effluent quality regulatory initiative	DWA – data provided by WSAs and WSPs	Water quality and related indicators	Improve drinking water quality and quality of discharged waste water and promote good operational practice
Auditor General	Ensure financial compliance	Auditor General based on WSA records	Financial data and procurement data	Financial accountability
Census	Determine service levels at household level	Statistics South Africa	Numbers of households serviced and interruptions to service	Independent information about water service coverage and functionality
Municipal Benchmarking Initiative	Develop performance benchmarks to inform the development of best practice, financial and support needs	South African Local Government Association and Water Research Commission	Wide range of metrics	Improve municipal performance in water and sanitation services
Rural Water Service Provider	Monitor provision of water services	WSPs	Water quality, quantity, and continuity	Improve service delivery and good operational and maintenance practices
National Integrated Water Information System (NIWIS)	Develop a strategic perspective on water services to inform macro-level planning	DWA	Wide range of metrics and key performance indicators (KPIs)	High-level strategic picture of water services performance nationally
Integrated Regulatory System (IRS)	Ensure integrated regulatory compliance nationally	DWA	Wide range of metrics and KPIs	High-level strategic picture of regulatory compliance of WSAs and WSPs

Source: De La Harpe et al., 2013.

Thailand does not have a comprehensive sector performance measurement system, unlike Uganda or Malawi, but the country is particularly innovative when it comes to the participation of water users in measuring water quality. In 2003, the Bureau of Food and Water Sanitation in Thailand's Department of Health took over responsibility for drinking water quality surveillance. It started a campaign to raise water quality standards that comprises a voluntary certification process for piped water supply systems. The process includes testing, and, if successful, leads to a ceremony at which the tap water is declared safe to drink (Wongpiyachon, 2013).

Timor-Leste

Timor-Leste used to have a water supply monitoring system, but indicators were not consistent, not everyone provided data, and information was missing for some parts of the country. The system therefore was not a very useful management tool. In recent years a new system has been introduced (with support from the Department of Foreign Affairs and Trade and Australian Aid) to monitor water services and sanitation coverage in rural areas at national, district, and sub-district level. It should provide an understanding of progress towards national targets for water and sanitation. It allows key aspects of sustainable service delivery to be analysed.

Data are collected by government-employed WASH facilitators across the country through their regular visits to villages to support community management. Updated information, in the form of community profiles, is

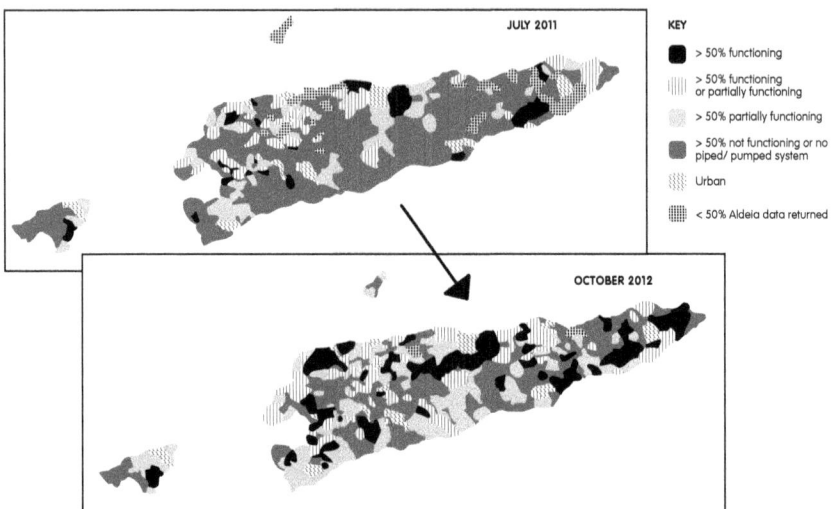

Figure 3.4 Comparison of water point functionality of water systems over time in Timor-Leste

Source: Willets, 2013.

sent from a mobile phone by SMS to a central database at national level. Mobile telephone services are available across approximately 85 per cent of Timor-Leste (Willets, 2013).

Every month, reports on the key indicators are produced and shared at district and national level. Excel spreadsheets and maps are used to report the data (Figure 3.4). Currently, district staff members are being trained to analyse data, which they are starting to use (for example, to inform budget debates). There is a desire by the government to share the data with the public, but first it wants to do more to ensure the data's validity (Willets, 2013).

Liberia

Having emerged from conflict, and with reliable information lacking, there was a drive to collect data on water points in Liberia. An exercise to map over 10,000 water points in the country in 2011 was led by the Ministry of Public Works, supported by UNICEF and the Water and Sanitation Program of the World Bank. Data was collected using android mobile phones; information included the GPS location, source type, and functionality. The data has subsequently been analysed and maps produced, and this has opened people's eyes to the reality on the ground. Liberia also held its first joint sector review in 2012, where the findings were discussed (Koroma, 2013). NGOs have been drawn into the process and are now also reporting using the Akvo FLOW technology for android phones. Putting information about NGO progress onto a website (http://wash-liberia.akvoapp.org/en/) has been an incentive for NGO reporting.

One of Liberia's current challenges is how to update the inventory. As enumerators were paid for the first round of data collection, there is an expectation that this should continue to be the case. Unfortunately, the country does not have the resources available for this, but work is ongoing to develop and use a framework for data updates (Koroma, 2013).

Ethiopia

Ethiopia's first national WASH inventory was completed in 2013, with the intention that it will provide the basis for a reliable, sector-wide monitoring and evaluation system. The scale of the operation in a country as large as Ethiopia was considerable. With the exception of the Somali region, data has been collected for the entire country, covering over 90,000 rural water supply schemes, 30,000 schools, and 20,000 health institutions, and 12 million households have been surveyed (Hailu Debela, 2013).

The inventory measured both water supply access (i.e. whether the rural population is within 1.5 km of a water supply point and can access 15 litres per person per day) and water use (i.e. whether the population is actually using water from the water point). This allows comparison between access and use (49 per cent and 62 per cent of the rural population respectively). The findings show considerable variation between regions.

The Ministry of Water, Irrigation and Energy has undertaken a preliminary analysis of the data. It is in the process of having the data officially verified by the Central Statistics Agency, which was also involved in the inventory design and data collection. In the future, the country will be able to use the findings for decision making and planning, among other things. Annual joint sector reviews already take place in Ethiopia, providing a platform for reflection. It is planned that training in data analysis will be provided to local (*woreda*) governments at a later date.

Emerging lessons

Inventories, more recently referred to as water point mapping, can provide a good baseline for a monitoring system. The findings often raise crucial questions. In Sierra Leone, the fact that 40 per cent of the 28,000 water points mapped are seasonal has triggered a discussion about why this is the case and what can be done (Danert and Adekile, 2013). However, an inventory is not the same as country-led monitoring. If data is not updated or reflected upon, it cannot reliably inform decision making or actions.

We draw this chapter to a close with some advice for establishing and developing a country-led performance measurement system:

1. *Monitoring is an incremental process not an event.* It should start simply but have the flexibility to expand and develop as local capacity develops and its usefulness is appreciated by all. A step-by-step approach should be followed to improve data collection, analysis, and reporting gradually to match the country's institutional framework and key concerns. Institutional and individual capacity needs to be developed gradually, depending on what is needed.
2. *Monitoring should be fit for purpose.* Systems should be designed with specific and defined objectives in mind, with a clear statement of how and why the data to be collected is to be used and for what purposes. Only the necessary data should be collected. Monitoring can be undertaken to inform national policies, strategies, and planning, and to support strategies, interventions, and regulation. These different purposes can be addressed in different ways (Norman and Franceys, 2013).
3. *Leadership.* National government should take the overall lead but involve a wide range of stakeholders. If there is resistance, or lack of interest, other champions can lead, innovate, and develop monitoring up to a certain point. There is plenty of scope for advisory support and mentoring of government provided that it does not undermine government leadership. Government capacity to lead can grow, provided that there are incentives for monitoring, other stakeholders remain supportive and constructively critical, and monitoring becomes an important political agenda.
4. *Try to build on what is already in place.* When piped systems are managed by public utilities or the private sector under regulation, contracts, or

licences, the accountability for service provision is clear. Normally, the service provider will be mandated to report to a regulator or the responsible asset holder, and there will be clear lines of accountability. Information from monitoring systems that are working well can be incorporated into wider sector monitoring.

5. *Roles, responsibilities, resources and incentives.* Institutional responsibilities need to be defined by those taking the lead for country-led monitoring. Responsibilities need to be mapped out, assigned, and agreed, and there should be a leader or group in place to undertake overall coordination. Individual responsibilities need to be assigned for who collects what data, who analyses and reports, by when, and to whom. The flow of data needs to be defined, as well as where and how data is stored and can be accessed. Trust needs to be built between different stakeholders and cooperation requirements need to be formalized. Reporting must be mandatory and incentives (and rewards) need to be in place for sharing information. These may be linked to resource allocation. These aspects need to be made operational from the start. Due attention also needs to be paid to the realities of human and financial resource availability, including issues such as the time needed for data entry, stationery and toner requirements, and transport. Ideally, monitoring activities should be integrated into the ongoing work of those responsible for water service delivery, in many cases local government.

6. *Indicators.* Effective monitoring is more than just a list of indicators. Keep indicators simple and do not have too many. It is better to monitor a few things well within an agreed sector framework than to cover too much. A monitoring culture can be developed from a starting point of one or two indicators with more added later. Agree on basic definitions for the indicators and note that different information is needed at different levels (e.g. by local government, by water providers, by the lead ministry, and by political leaders). Indicators may need to be modified, particularly if they are creating perverse incentives or if they are too complicated. Indicators provide a structure, but qualitative information and case studies can deepen understanding.

7. *Analysis and interpretation.* While systems should avoid duplication, it is useful to compare data sets from different sources. For example, user survey information from the national statistics office can be used to compare, triangulate, and validate information on outputs provided by the sector or line ministries and district local governments. Much can be learned from this process.

8. *Communicate widely for decision making and planning.* Various ways should be considered of providing feedback and communicating information from the monitoring process to government institutions, development partners, civil society, the public, and any other sector stakeholders, so that the findings can be taken into consideration in decision making and planning processes. Information that is useful locally should be disseminated and reflected upon locally.

Endnotes

1. The six monitoring stages are: Initiation and planning – where the purpose of the monitoring is developed, followed by agreement on what to monitor, how, by whom, and when; Data collection – collecting, collating, verifying, and storing data and information, employing a diversity of tools and systems and involving local governments, NGOs, and the private sector, which all help share the logistical burden and bring about data ownership; Analysis and interpretation – whereby data is transformed into useful information (although is it possible to establish automated analytical processes, drawing meaning from this information through interpretation requires skilled professionals); Communication – an aspect of the monitoring cycle that is often taken for granted, with the information put into a report or other useful format, and shared through appropriate channels (in order to enable public action, there is a need to carefully consider who to communicate with and how – feedback to the respective stakeholders is key); Reflection and decision making – a vital step that is often overlooked in the technocratic and political processes and that includes debate, discussion, and conflict resolution between different stakeholders as they consider findings and recommendations stemming from monitoring; Taking action – resulting in improved laws, rules, policies, practices, approaches, and methodologies leading to improved services, user satisfaction, and value for money.
2. The headline figure for rural water supplies in most countries tends to be the percentage access to a safe water supply. In most countries, this is measured through a proxy indicator such as 'the proportion of people that are using "improved" drinking water sources, defined as those that, by the nature of their construction, are protected from outside contamination, particularly faecal matter' (UNICEF and WHO, 2012). 'Improved' drinking water sources refer to protected springs, boreholes, dug wells, piped water, and rainwater harvesting facilities. Unprotected sources such as lakes, rivers, and streams are considered to be 'unimproved' (WHO and UNICEF, 2013).

References

Adank, M., Smits, S., Bey, V., Verhoeven, J. and Pezon, C. (2013) 'Development and use of service delivery indicators for monitoring rural water services in Ghana, Uganda, Burkina Faso, Colombia, Honduras, Paraguay, El Salvador', paper presented at the IRC Symposium 2013: Monitoring WASH Services Delivery, Addis Ababa, Ethiopia, 9–11 April.

Danert, K. and Adekile, D. (2013) *Tapping Treasure: Cost-effective Boreholes in Sierra Leone*, Consultancy Report, St Gallen, Switzerland: Skat Foundation.

De Albuquerque, C. (2012) *On the Right Track: Good Practices in Realising the Rights to Water and Sanitation*, Lisbon: Regulatory Authority for Water and Waste Services (ERSAR).

De La Harpe, J., Gibson, J. and Dungu, M. (2013) 'Monitoring for regulatory and contractual compliance: systems in South Africa', PowerPoint presentation by Jean De La Harpe at the IRC Symposium 2013: Monitoring WASH Services Delivery, Addis Ababa, Ethiopia, 9–11 April.

Désille, D., Rotbardt, A.and Faggianelli, D. (2013) 'Monitoring small piped water services in West Africa', paper presented at the IRC Symposium 2013: Monitoring WASH Services Delivery, Addis Ababa, Ethiopia, 9–11 April.

DWAF (2003) *Strategic Framework for Water Services: Water is Life, Sanitation is Dignity*, Pretoria: Republic of South Africa Department of Water Affairs (DWAF).

DWAF (2009) *Water Quality Regulation: A Strategy for Incentive-Based Regulation Blue and Green Drop Certification*, Pretoria: Republic of South Africa Department of Water Affairs (DWAF).

Flores Bacquero, O., Giné Garriga, R., Palencia, A.J.F. de and Pérez-Foguet, A. (2013) 'Piloting new indicators and methodologies to measure the human right to water in Nicaragua', paper presented at the IRC Symposium 2013: Monitoring WASH Services Delivery, Addis Ababa, Ethiopia, 9–11 April.

g7+ (2013) 'The Dili consensus', outcome document of the International Conference on the Post-2015 Development Agenda, Dili, Indonesia, 26–28 February.

Guzha, E. (2013) 'Personal communication' during panel debate and plenary discussion at the IRC Symposium 2013: Monitoring WASH Services Delivery, Addis Ababa, Ethiopia, 9–11 April.

Hailu Debela, T. (2013) 'Monitoring water supplies and sanitation in Ethiopia', PowerPoint presentation at the IRC Symposium 2013: Monitoring WASH Services Delivery, Addis Ababa, Ethiopia, 9–11 April.

IDPS (2011) 'A new deal for engagement in fragile states', statement during the 4th High Level Forum on Aid Effectiveness, International Dialogue on Peacebuilding and Statebuilding, Busan, Korea, 29 November–1 December.

Koroma, A. (2013) 'Monitoring wash services: the Liberia story', PowerPoint presentation at the IRC Symposium 2013: Monitoring WASH Services Delivery, Addis Ababa, Ethiopia, 9–11 April.

Lockwood, H. (2013) 'Project monitoring: a vicious cycle of donor accountability or a necessary stepping stone to better national WASH sector monitoring?', keynote paper presented at the IRC Symposium 2013: Monitoring WASH Services Delivery, Addis Ababa, Ethiopia, 9–11 April.

Meek, A. and Young, S. (2013) 'Development of a national monitoring and evaluation framework for WASH activities in Malawi', paper presented at the IRC Symposium 2013: Monitoring WASH Services Delivery, Addis Ababa, Ethiopia, 9–11 April.

MoWDI (2010) *The Current Status of Water Supply in Malawi*, Lilongwe: Ministry of Water Development and Irrigation (MoWDI).

MWLE (2004) *Performance Measurement Framework, Uganda Water and Sanitation Sector*, Kampala: Ministry of Water, Lands and Environment (MWLE).

Norman, R. and Franceys, R. (2013) 'Monitoring: fit for purpose?', PowerPoint presentation by Rachel Norman at the IRC Symposium 2013: Monitoring WASH Services Delivery, Addis Ababa, Ethiopia, 9–11 April.

O'Brien, F. (2013) 'The role of the UN in fostering national ownership and capacities in evaluation', unit 2 of the e-learning course on country-led M&E systems [online], My M&E <http://www.mymande.org/> [Accessed 13 January 2015].

OECD (2005) *The Paris Declaration on Aid Effectiveness*, Paris: Organisation for Economic Co-operation and Development (OECD).

OECD (2008) *Accra Agenda for Action*, Paris: Organisation for Economic Co-operation and Development (OECD).

OECD (2011) *The Busan Partnership for Effective Development Co-operation*, Paris: Organisation for Economic Co-operation and Development (OECD) <http://www.oecd.org/dac/effectiveness/busanpartnership.htm> [accessed 9 October 2014].

Republic of South Africa (1997) 'Water Services Act No 108, 1997', *Government Gazette*, 19 December.

Rasolofomanana, L. (unpublished) 'Data reconciliation process in Madagascar', WaterAid Madagascar.

Segone, M. (ed.) (2010) *From Policies to Results: Developing Capacities for Country Monitoring and Evaluation Systems*, New York NY: UNICEF <http://www.mymande.org/content/policies-results> [Accessed 13 January 2015].

Ssozi, D. (2013) 'Personal communication' during the session on national monitoring of water and sanitation in Uganda at the IRC Symposium 2013: Monitoring WASH Services Delivery, Addis Ababa, Ethiopia, 9–11 April.

Ssozi, D. and Danert, K. (2012) *National Monitoring of Rural Water Supplies: How the Government of Uganda Did it and Lessons for Other Countries*, RWSN-IFAD Series 4, St Gallen, Switzerland: Rural Water Supply Network.

Swann, P. (2012) 'Personal communication' during the GLAAS evaluation meeting, Bern, Switzerland, 2–3 October.

UNICEF and WHO (2012) *Progress on Drinking Water and Sanitation: 2012 Update*, New York NY: UNICEF and World Health Organization (WHO).

WASREB (2012) *Impact: A Performance Review of Kenya's Water Services Sector 2010/11*, Nairobi: Water Services Regulatory Board of Kenya (WASREB).

Welle, K. (2007) *Mapping for Better Accountability in Service Delivery: Assessing WaterAid's Work in Mapping Water Supply and Sanitation Delivery to the Poor*, Briefing Paper 29, London: Overseas Development Institute (ODI).

Welle, K. (2013) 'Monitoring performance or performing monitoring? Lessons on the politics of monitoring', PowerPoint presentation at the IRC Symposium 2013: Monitoring WASH Services Delivery, Addis Ababa, Ethiopia, 9–11 April.

WHO (2012) *UN-Water Global Annual Assessment of Sanitation and Drinking-Water (GLAAS) 2012 Report: The Challenge of Extending and Sustaining Services*, Geneva: World Health Organization (WHO).

WHO and UNICEF (2013) *Progress on Drinking Water and Sanitation: 2013 Update*. Geneva: World Health Organization (WHO).

Willets, J. (2013) 'Water and sanitation information system for Timor-Leste', PowerPoint presentation at the IRC Symposium 2013: Monitoring WASH Services Delivery, Addis Ababa, Ethiopia, 9–11 April.

Wongpiyachon, S. (2013) 'Monitoring rural and small towns water supply in Thailand: a focus on water quality', PowerPoint presentation at the IRC Symposium 2013: Monitoring WASH Services Delivery, Addis Ababa, Ethiopia, 9–11 April.

About the author

Kerstin Danert works for Skat Consulting in Switzerland and is Director of the Rural Water Supply Network Secretariat. An experienced rural water supply specialist, Kerstin Danert supported the Government of Uganda in the development of the country's water and environment sector performance measurement system, over a period of seven years from 2005, and the Government of Liberia to prepare its first *Sector Performance Report* in 2014.

CHAPTER 4

Transforming accountability and project monitoring for stronger national WASH sectors

Harold Lockwood

In spite of advances in alignment with country systems, many development partners still tend to focus monitoring efforts on their 'own' projects, driven by a strong burden of accountability to taxpayers and individual and institutional donors. Project-monitoring efforts are fragmented and often work around government-led systems. They tend to stop once the implementing agency withdraws. Conversely, project monitoring can offer flexibility and speed for testing innovative approaches and new technologies. The reality in many developing countries is that government-led water, sanitation, and hygiene (WASH) monitoring systems remain weak and are often underfunded. Despite these dilemmas, several recent trends indicate that project monitoring and government-led systems can be mutually beneficial. This can only be achieved if all actors communicate better and modify their organizational behaviours; much of this will be determined by changing the incentives for monitoring. When planned and communicated well, project efforts can contribute positively to permanent, comprehensive, national sector monitoring systems.

Keywords: project monitoring, accountability, development partner, national sector monitoring system, government leadership

Introduction

Over the last decade there has been a major shift in perspective in the water, sanitation, and hygiene (WASH) sector in line with broader efforts to reform the effectiveness of development aid and to promote greater country ownership. The Paris Declaration and subsequent agreements have set out clear principles pointing towards the need for greater alignment with government priorities and country systems, including monitoring frameworks. Support is increasing for common programming frameworks, including sector-wide approaches (SWAps), with the explicit acceptance of joint monitoring and reporting frameworks (WHO, 2012), and there is a growing number of examples of common nationwide monitoring systems.[1] The global monitoring architecture spearheaded by the Joint Monitoring Programme (JMP) calls for a process of alignment around more common standards and indicators. And yet the reality in many developing countries is that country-led WASH monitoring systems remain weak or fragmented, are often underfunded, and are de-linked from core public sector systems.[2]

Development partners of all shapes and sizes – from small charities to large international non-governmental organizations (NGOs), bilateral donors, and the major lending banks – support WASH interventions that often include a monitoring component. These externally financed programmes can provide valuable testing grounds for new, innovative approaches and technologies and are often flexible and responsive enough to allow for quick learning cycles. However, such agencies often focus monitoring efforts on their 'own' project interventions, driven by a strong burden of accountability to taxpayers and institutional donors. Despite public acknowledgement and commitments to promote the use of country systems, concerns remain over lack of capacity.[3] The result is that project-monitoring efforts may often work around, instead of working with, country-led systems. For many years this has resulted in a plethora of fragmented efforts to monitor WASH interventions that fall away once project funding has run out or the implementing agency withdraws.

One result of this tension over the long term is that development of truly comprehensive, well-functioning national systems has been undermined. But the reality is that such project monitoring, often linked to implementation on the ground, is not about to go away, particularly in many aid-dependent countries, and it is likely to be a continuing feature of the sector for the next 10 to 15 years. Accountability is the key driver in this equation and raises some fundamental questions: why do we monitor? For whom? And, by extension, what do we monitor? The challenge therefore is how to harness all of the positive elements and innovation that external aid projects can bring and find ways in which these experiences can be integrated, scaled up, and sustained within the predominantly low-resource realities of national and local government systems.

What is project monitoring?

Of course, the term 'project' in its purest sense has no value connotation, either positive or negative, and simply describes the action of planning or designing something to be done or carried out.[4] As such, all organizations across public, non-profit, and private sectors employ projects, typically following a common cycle. Well-planned, properly resourced projects are needed, as much in the WASH sector as anywhere else. Here we make a distinction between two types of monitoring: the first is typically geared towards reporting progress against the correct and timely inputs for construction of civil works and initial software interventions, against stated time frames or budgets. The second type also incorporates outputs and outcomes.

Externally funded projects tend to focus most closely on the former, but this is not universally the case; many 'projects' also seek to monitor outcomes and impacts (e.g. on health) – these have been labelled 'results-based monitoring systems'. There are also examples of development partner project monitoring aimed at sector reform processes. Equally, national systems track inputs of money and activities, as well as outputs and outcomes. The distinction or meaning we draw in the context of this discussion can perhaps be best captured by thinking of project monitoring as having some or all of the following characteristics:

- Monitoring is limited to the defined lifespan of a project or programme intervention and is generally short term (usually not more than five years maximum).
- There is monitoring of outcomes and even impacts that fall outside, or are de-coupled from, government-led or sanctioned data collection, performance management systems, and policy priorities. By definition, this includes all externally funded projects that are executed outside a SWAp or similar common framework.
- The pressure for accountability, and data flows, is typically upwards and outwards, and the primary – and in some cases sole – purpose is to inform external funders about progress and performance.
- Monitoring may be driven by a desire for (international) visibility and profiling.

There are, of course, examples of project monitoring that are a force for good, bringing new technologies or approaches to the table and testing these at scale to help trigger change and progress in national systems. Monitoring that is flexible and can test what works and what doesn't in short learning cycles is a great asset. This facet or benefit is illustrated by Kate Fogelberg of Water For People (WFP), when she explains the support WFP gives to the local government in the rural municipality of Cuchumuela, Bolivia. One of her claims is that WFP is small, and as such can '*fail fast*', but it can also inspire government to try new things. As part of the capacity support programme, WFP supports the authorities to monitor all projects in its jurisdiction, regardless of who constructed the systems, using smart phones to improve the data collection process and visualization of results. The work of WFP in this municipality has led to change, with new by-laws being established to improve the management of systems. In part this work at the local level is helping to bridge the gap between accountability to the donor (do our own projects continue to function over time?) and to local government (are we delivering services to all our citizens in the municipality?).

A related example is the fact that much of the recent exponential growth in the use of mobile phone technology for improving the speed, reliability, and effectiveness of data collection was initially driven by short-term project experiences.[5] But we also know of many cases where project monitoring is very extractive, with its main aim being to inform head office reporting requirements and enhance visibility, and does little to improve performance on the ground.

Why this debate matters for sustainable WASH services

In the end, comprehensive and robust monitoring is about improving performance and delivering better services. Measuring the right things at the right time and, most critically, ensuring a response (at both operational and policy level) to make things better are at the heart of why monitoring is done at all. And ultimately it matters because of the accountability of all stakeholders – operators, governments, and development partners – to the consumers and end users of WASH services. Government should be accountable to citizens for ensuring the provision of permanent WASH services, which is now enshrined as a human right (De Albuquerque, 2010). Good monitoring systems should translate this right into providing the poor with a 'voice', to demand and realize these (ever improving) services.

But the availability of reliable information has long been a major weakness in the WASH sector, especially for rural and peri-urban areas not served by formal utilities. Unlike in urban contexts where performance monitoring is much more commonplace,[6] many rural sectors lack comprehensive and regularly collected data. There is often disagreement over even simple information, such as access and functionality between government sector WASH institutions, the national statistical bureau, and external development partner stakeholders. Such data should provide the basic building blocks to inform good decision making about resource allocation and to support corrective actions at the local level. As well as supporting local-level performance, such monitoring also provides the evidence for improving sector policy and holding government and others to account. Conversely, lack of leadership and failure to support monitoring in the WASH sector may be a reflection of government not taking full responsibility and ownership, and instead relying on the easier – and short-term – fix of project financing.

Where monitoring does take place, approaches tend to focus on a limited set of indicators that measure coverage and (nominal) numbers served rather than quality aspects of the service, which can be proxy indicators for sustainability; these could include the level of downtime, the performance of operators, and the capacity to support local operators.[7] This is an area for improvement – for both country-led and project monitoring – that can be addressed through learning supported by project monitoring funded by development partners.

This debate matters because in low-income countries with highly aid-dependent WASH sectors, development partners often have a disproportionate influence on what is monitored and how data is shared and used. Ready use and ownership of data, especially by local government, is critical. And yet well-resourced development partner programmes are often much more powerful than their local counterparts and can drive the agenda simply due to their financial muscle, establishing monitoring frameworks that are simply too complex or costly for (local) government to take over and sustain. Indeed, it could be argued that monitoring systems led by development partners are a distraction that often aggravate, rather than contribute to, local capacity building. The end result is a patchwork of monitoring efforts that often co-exist in the same geographic area[8] but fall away as project funding winds down.

This situation has been further complicated by the growing pace of *decentralization and institutional reform*, both within the WASH sector and in public administration more broadly. The standard rallying cry now is for local government to be responsible for post-construction support and monitoring. The reality is that many (weak) local governments are left to manage a set of incompatible and parallel monitoring systems, including those of their own, which would be a challenge even for high-capacity organizations.

There are also differing needs for data at local government level. A district water officer will monitor to identify problems, which they would then act upon to improve or resolve. Data may be fed up to national level with the expectation that funding will be released to address these problematic communities. But if the national database is simply a repository, with no resulting action, this merely ends as a reporting exercise (Smits et al., 2013: 10). This debate then also throws into sharp relief the relationship between local government and central line ministries and the often weak and tenuous links between them when it comes to compatible data collection, storage, analysis, and action.

Main themes and challenges in project monitoring

The interface between project monitoring and country-led frameworks is complex and driven by a wide range of incentives that can go far beyond the confines of the WASH sector. One of the most important drivers of this relationship is accountability, which sits at the centre of this debate: why do we monitor? For whom? And, by extension, what do we monitor? But this interface will be influenced by other variables. On the one hand, it will be affected by the country and sector in question and, for example, the relative strength of public sector management systems, the national statistical bureau, and the vision and capacity of central government to set out programme-based approaches to sector support. On the other hand, individual development partner policies will have a major impact on how far monitoring efforts seek to align or diverge from country-led frameworks. For some agencies, there will always be an aversion to or mistrust of government; for others, there may be legal or institutional barriers to working more closely with public sector systems. Yet others may be providing sector or general budget support and will already be relying on common monitoring frameworks and joint sector reviews. Frequently, however, the partner countries themselves lack the will and/or capacity to manage donor support in this way; this is particularly acute among countries where capital and recurrent budgets are heavily dependent on external aid transfers.

Given this complexity and the fact that each country context is unique, how can we positively frame the discussion about the relationship between project-driven monitoring and country-led systems? One approach is to consider the main themes that appear to be important to this debate; Figure 4.1 below starts to group these issues, which are explored in brief in the following sections.

68 FROM INFRASTRUCTURE TO SERVICES

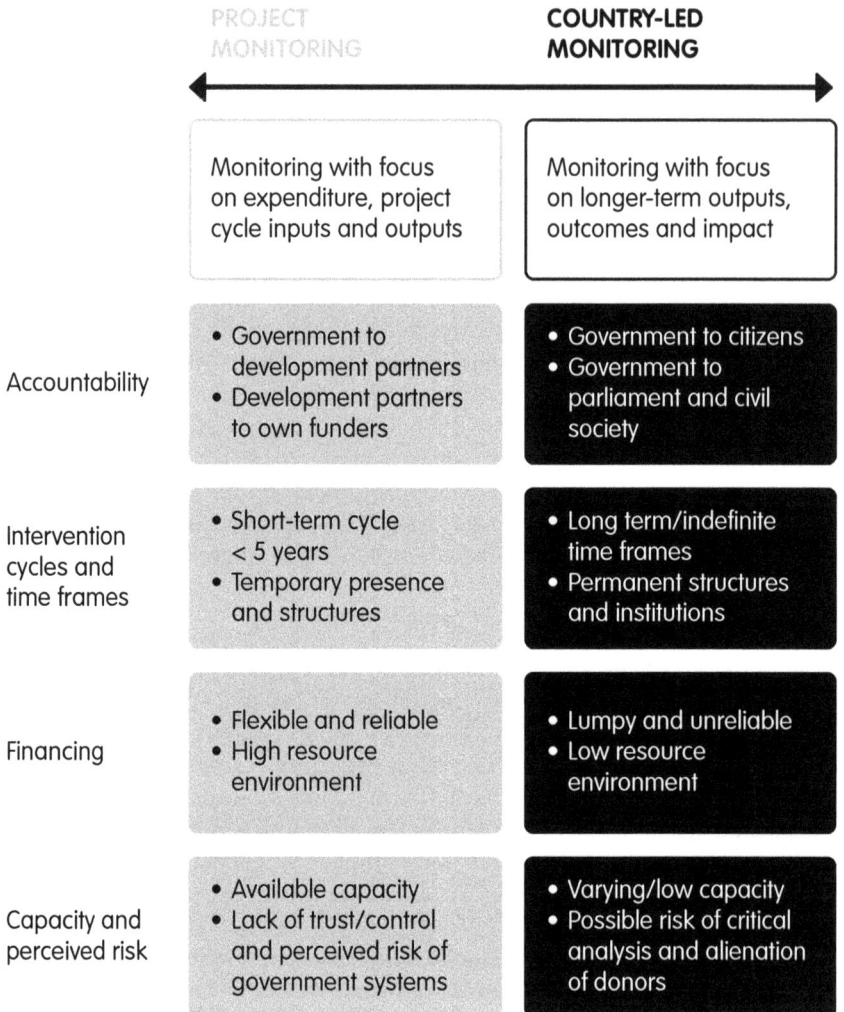

Figure 4.1 Central themes and challenges to integrating project monitoring with national frameworks

Accountability

Under the principles of the Paris Declaration, both development partners and governments share responsibility for achieving development goals – so-called mutual accountability. And yet, when it comes to monitoring and the use of the resulting outputs, each party comes under differing pressures and there is often a considerable gap between the theory and the reality:

- In theory, national government ministries are accountable to their citizens, either directly or through parliamentary oversight bodies, civil

society organizations, or umbrella groups. In reality, however, these indirect accountability mechanisms can be weak or there may be low capacity to place pressure on government by citizens in the first place.
- There may be perverse incentives to not make monitoring data more available if this exposes poor performance by national governments; in turn, low levels of accountability can lead to a cycle of low-quality data, or no data, and limited pressure to improve services.
- Where there is a heavy reliance by governments on external aid for sector investment, especially in situations where aid is project-based, then government accountability can often be skewed towards development partners.
- In the absence of strong, country-led frameworks, development partners tend to 'fill the vacuum' by establishing parallel systems.
- Development partner accountability is also two-way, with often strong pressure to report to their constituencies, for example donors to their taxpayers and NGOs and charities to their funders.
- This pressure can often lead organizations to show (superficial) results and to have visibility. This is particularly the case for NGOs, which may be fighting for a finite pot of funding, and it acts to undermine acceptance of common country-led, but perhaps more anonymous, monitoring systems.

In this situation, it is often very difficult for development partners to avoid the pressure to show results. This locks them into a type of 'vicious cycle' of accountability under which, even when there is intent to support country-led monitoring systems, the most pragmatic solution may be to establish their own parallel systems, as shown in Figure 4.2 below.

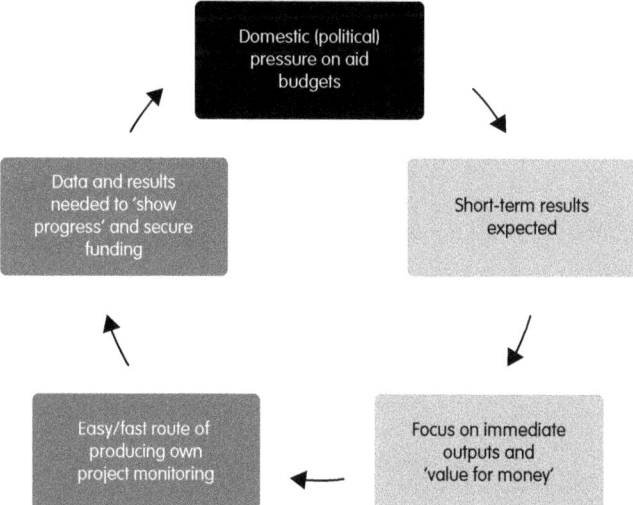

Figure 4.2 The development partner's dilemma – the vicious cycle of accountability

A pragmatic approach to bridging the accountability gap

The African Development Bank (AfDB) has designed and launched an innovative new strategy for monitoring that explicitly attempts to bridge this gap between organizational accountability (in this case to the shareholders of the AfDB regarding the exposure to risk for the loans that are extended to client countries) and accountability to national sector development.

Fabio Losa, monitoring and evaluation specialist at the bank, explains this dilemma and how a multilateral development organization such as the AfDB is simultaneously helping African countries strengthen their WASH sector monitoring and evaluation capacities, and pursuing the path towards a results-based organization, accountable to both development partners and beneficiaries, and retaining a focus on efficiency and effectiveness. Losa explains how the strategy of the Water and Sanitation Department (OWAS) of the AfDB is founded on a three-tier approach: to improve the bank's project monitoring and evaluation; to support country monitoring and evaluation capacities; and to link with global initiatives (see Figure 4.3).

At the country level, OWAS, in partnership with its regional member countries and other development partners, intends to help countries strengthen their capacities, collection processes, and monitoring systems and eventually improve information availability. At the level of WASH projects funded by the bank in its regional member countries, the goal is to improve OWAS capacities to monitor and evaluate interventions as a results-based organization that is accountable to donors and beneficiaries. The strategy is an ambitious one, spanning from 2012 to 2020, and it is starting with a first pilot phase in Malawi and the Central African Republic (Losa, 2013).

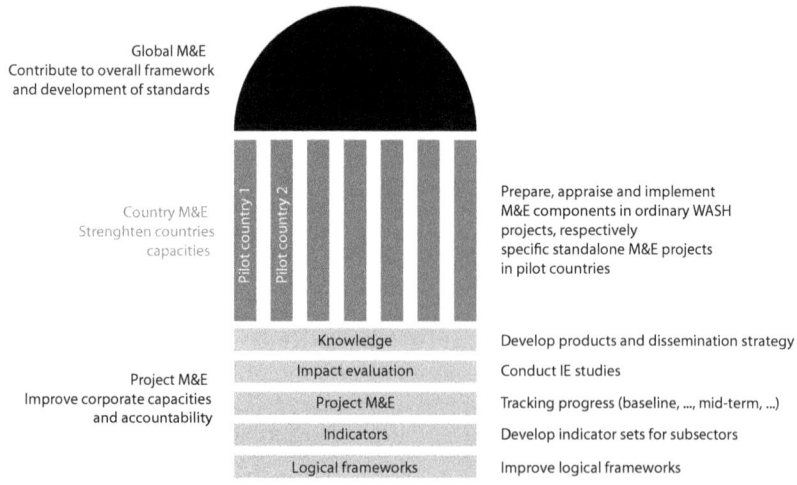

Figure 4.3 The three-tier approach of OWAS's monitoring and evaluation (M&E) strategy
Source: Losa, 2013.

Intervention cycles and time frames

Development partners have different cultures and visions in terms of their in-country presence. Some will seek to 'work themselves out of a job', while others make explicit commitments for years or even decades. Regardless of these commitments, most development partners are themselves subject to economic, political, and at times security factors that may cut short their programmes of support, or, conversely, they may extend funding periods due to domestic political pressures. All too often, these are not technical choices based on careful reasoning, but responses to the way in which aid is politically driven. Accepting that there is a range of different experiences, a number of general trends are apparent:

- Development partner project monitoring is almost always short term (two to four or five years) with less interest in going beyond the end of project-funding horizons. Further, donor interest and policies can be fickle and fluctuate markedly depending on the pressure exerted by domestic public opinion and sudden competing geopolitical demands.
- The responsibility and mandate to monitor, both for implementing NGOs and for lending banks, often terminate with the end of the life of the project. Adopting common monitoring frameworks as part of broader SWAps is the obvious solution. But, as noted above, even these frameworks are not respected by all stakeholders, and are not yet fully established in all countries.[9]
- Experience shows that the building of a truly comprehensive national monitoring system takes a prolonged period, sustained investment, and high levels of commitment – probably in the order of 10 years plus, which is often beyond the horizon of development partner funding cycles.
- Government time frames for monitoring are in theory infinite, but in reality they are also subject to administrative cycles or political upheaval and resistance to institutional or policy reform.
- Such political change can lead to the replacement of key individuals and the loss of institutional memory and capacity. The development of comprehensive national monitoring systems has stalled in a number of countries due to political and institutional paralysis, or simply because of a lack of political priority for monitoring, which may be seen as less important than direct service provision.

Interestingly, there have been a number of recent drives to extend development partner monitoring 'beyond the project'. One of these is based on the work of WFP, which guarantees a minimum time frame for monitoring of 10 years, regardless of funding cycles or presence in a particular country or district.[10] Although this has been a highly visible position, it can also be construed as counterproductive to the emergence of comprehensive country-led systems given that it commits to an ongoing (external) monitoring presence. However, the stated intention is for WFP to transition this monitoring commitment to country-led (or locally led) efforts. The second example is the decision of the Dutch government and its development agency,

DGIS, to require recipients of grants to commit to ensuring service delivery over an agreed time frame (also 10 years, with a concurrent commitment to monitoring), under what they refer to as a 'sustainability clause'.[11]

Another example of how development partners are starting to plan for 'beyond the project' is presented by Heather Skilling, Senior Water and Sanitation Advisor within the Water Office of the United States Agency for International Development (USAID). She explains that, as a cornerstone of the reform agenda, under the new 'USAID Forward' strategy, USAID has begun a critical shift in the way it administers assistance, placing a greater emphasis on public–private partnerships, channelling funding to local governments and organizations that have the in-country expertise to create sustainable change. This includes a concurrent shift in the focus of long-term monitoring that can support WASH service provision well beyond the actual implementation phase of any given USAID project. Skilling states that the USAID Water and Development Strategy will seek investments in longer-term monitoring in order to assess the sustainability and impact of project funds beyond the typical life of the project and to facilitate support to issues that arise after the completion of projects.

> **Box 4.1 USAID Water and Development Strategy**
>
> 'Will seek investments in longer-term monitoring and evaluation of its water activities in order to assess sustainability and impact of project funds beyond the typical life-of-project and to enable reasonable support to issues that arise subsequent to completion of projects.'
> *Source:* Heather Skilling, USAID, Addis Ababa, 2013.

Financing

Lack of sufficient investment, as well as lack of capacity to absorb financing, is a well-documented problem in many developing country WASH sectors. In contexts where there is still the need to provide first-time access, capital investment quite rightly takes precedence and 'softer' areas of support, including monitoring, may often have a much lower priority.

Development partners, particularly the bilateral donors and lending banks, are addressing investments in monitoring and capacity building, but, again, such sector-level support is often tied to particular grant or loan agreements, and financing for monitoring can fluctuate markedly without the benefit of a strong SWAp arrangement. However, there are success stories that illustrate the long-term benefits of sustained financing. Uganda is a case in point, with a relatively early adoption of a SWAp and very consistent long-term support from bilateral donors, along with strong government commitment, which has resulted in a robust sector performance measurement framework (Ssozi and Danert, 2012). The key lesson here is that there has been long-term donor commitment to Uganda with support for the monitoring system over almost

10 years.[12] But even in cases such as this, significant challenges remain with development partners, which continue to operate outside such common frameworks.[13]

Many of the smaller aid agencies, and even some large-scale grant programmes, invest in their own monitoring systems, relying on a proportion of grant funding to finance this work. Inevitably, once project funding ends, so too does the financing for monitoring. The sustainability checks introduced as part of DGIS funding to a range of partners are a case in point. Although these project-monitoring mechanisms bring a welcome focus to the issues relating to long-term sustainability, the costs can be prohibitive. In some cases the checks carried out by independent auditors cost in the order of US$100,000 plus per year for restricted sampling, which means that it would be difficult for ministries to scale up and replicate such checks across entire countries.[14]

Another critical challenge for the financial sustainability of monitoring systems is the capacity, especially of local government, to continue to pay for such systems. Development partners can often be hugely optimistic – or simply naive – about the financial capacity of local government to continue to bear the full costs of monitoring systems that are put in place as part of projects, as the example from Malawi shows (see Box 4.2).

Box 4.2 Bridging the financing gap for monitoring at district level in Malawi

In Malawi, GPS mapping work was done from 2002 to 2005 and provided useful data for national policy but was far beyond the financial capacity of the typical Malawian district to repeat on its own, despite the sector's stated aim of having districts lead ongoing data collection. This data typically cost US$10,000 to US$20,000 per district to collect once, while the average budget for all recurring activities in a Malawian district is only about US$4,900 per year, meaning that follow-up district-led data collection is almost impossible under this system. Engineers Without Borders (Canada) works with local government in Malawi, recognizing financial and resource constraints from the start, to design more affordable and replicable approaches to the monitoring of WASH services.

Source: Scott, 2012.

Capacity and perceived risk

The capacity of national institutions is often behind decisions of development partners to retain control over procurement, contracting, and monitoring processes. The same can be true in terms of the relationship between national and decentralized government, where 'lack of capacity' is frequently used by line ministries as a brake on devolution of real authority and budget allocations.

In a number of instances, the doubts of development partners about the capacity for effective monitoring are warranted. And it is also true that many decentralized authorities lack the technical capacity and recurrent budgets to support monitoring. Conversely, it should not be automatically assumed that all external projects can monitor effectively. Weak monitoring and an absence of effective measurement frameworks can also plague large-scale donor-driven programmes.[15] In fact, it is true that development partners will vary in their capacity to support national and sub-national monitoring systems; their levels of capacity are as heterogeneous as those of country partners' own national and sub-national systems.

There may be another factor at play that has more to do with the risk of losing control in cases where development partners cede the authority to monitor to national entities. This is a double-edged risk, however. The rhetoric of donors and demand for country-led processes are often strong, but may result in their own interventions being shown to perform poorly. At the same time, there may be a feeling on the part of national authorities that they should not be overly critical of development partner interventions in case this leads to less funding or a complete closing down of financial support (Segone, 2009).[16]

Of course, one way of breaking this capacity challenge is to make this an explicit aim of external projects that include monitoring. One such example from the AfDB was described earlier in the chapter and contrasts with a second example from the NGO sector as documented by Juliet Willetts, who presented lessons from monitoring the Civil Society Fund of the Australian Government Department of Foreign Affairs and Trade. These provided an insight into some of the challenges facing sector monitoring and how NGOs might support governments in improving such systems. The fund of US$25 million involved 11 NGOs implementing projects in 21 countries. The learning across this programme identified a wide range of possible strategies available to NGOs to support sector monitoring. This resulted in the development of a 'strategy map' or typology of roles that NGOs could play in strengthening country-led systems as part of their own project-monitoring efforts. This map resulted in three broad types of role:

- direct role in monitoring, by holding up a mirror to government about their own performance;
- building expertise in local government to improve their own monitoring;
- documenting and sharing new learning and innovation in monitoring and promoting their uptake by government.

According to this typology, strategies can be classified as *causal*, *persuasive*, or *supportive*, and either may be applied with a focus on particular individuals or groups, or may be applied to the broader enabling environment for service provision. Table 4.1 sets out this typology of the ways in which NGOs could support sector monitoring as identified by the team (Willetts et al., 2013).

Table 4.1 Typology of potential strategies for NGOs to support sector monitoring

Strategy	Causal	Persuasive	Supportive
	I-1	I-2	I-3
Focused on a particular individual or group (I)	Direct role in monitoring own direct implementation activities.	Providing awareness raising, education, or specific training to community members or other partners.	Providing frequent, sustained, ongoing mentoring and support or multipurpose capacity building; or developing support structures, committees, and networks.
	Potential NGO roles to support sector monitoring: Provide monitoring information to government concerning community, school, or public water and sanitation systems (either built by NGO or another agency).	*Potential NGO roles to support sector monitoring:* Build interest and motivation for local-level monitoring and support relevant skills development through training.	*Potential NGO roles to support sector monitoring:* Use systematic strategies to build monitoring skills and capacity of local government or service providers, private sector, or schools.
	E-1	E-2	E-3
Focused on the enabling environment (E)	Engaging in policy dialogue on specific issues, directly causing changes in incentives, rules, or guidelines; playing an advocacy or social accountability role.	Disseminating information widely to a broad audience; creating a persuasive environment for a specific behaviour or attitude; and conducting workshops and conferences.	Building partnerships, providing collective support, and promoting networking and coordination; also supporting higher levels of government in their role or supporting local research or action networks.
	Characteristic activities in this fund: Lead lobbying or mobilize community members or other partners and organizations to advocate for unified sector monitoring.	*Characteristic activities in this fund:* Document and share own learning and innovations with respect to WASH monitoring with broad set of other sector stakeholders and promote their uptake.	*Characteristic activities in this fund:* Initiate and participate in multi-stakeholder sector coordination groups that demand, develop, implement, or use sector monitoring systems; support central government in roll-out of sector monitoring.

Source: Willetts et al., 2013.

Convergence and examples of good integration

Communication and integration

There is no doubt that all development partners approach their monitoring work with the best of intentions. It is implausible that such organizations would explicitly set out to undermine the development of government-led systems. As such, a large part of the 'convergence' question is about communication and intent. Put simply, how well do development partners engage with government as part of their project monitoring from the outset? This is addressed by Elynn Walter of WASH Advocates in documenting the findings of a recent study into WASH in Schools monitoring (Walter, 2013). The findings are based on a set of qualitative surveys with 21 implementing and donor organizations, and identified obstacles to integration and current monitoring trends and challenges. The main barriers to integration of WASH in Schools monitoring between NGO and government systems identified in this study were:

- lack of government capacity and political will to monitor effectively;
- limited awareness of national government monitoring systems by NGOs;
- lack of willingness of NGOs to work within a system they feel 'isn't functioning';
- monitoring in silos within both NGOs and governments and not sharing results;
- education ministries focusing on measuring educational outcomes and not enabling environments including WASH.

As well as uncovering the challenges, the WASH Advocates study identified instances where some degree of integration has been achieved; these included cases of open communication and coordination between NGO and government monitoring for WASH in Schools in the Philippines, Uganda, and Zambia. The paper also recognizes that these efforts are all at different levels of the integration process; a typology of integration expressed as a 'ladder' was developed (see Figure 4.4).

Examples of good practice

Despite the strains and tensions noted above, the situation is improving and there is already greater awareness and intent to better support country-led monitoring systems. Initiatives such as the country-level Sector Information and Monitoring Systems (SIMS) for Africa promoted by the African Ministers' Council on Water (AMCOW), the Water and Sanitation Program (WSP) of the World Bank, and the African Water Facility point to this coalescence around establishing strong national systems (World Bank, 2007). Ultimately, the pathway to this outcome will lie with common frameworks, such as SWAps and common systems, allowing better and more effective alignment between national data collection and the global processes that are currently under review by the JMP for the post-2015 landscape.

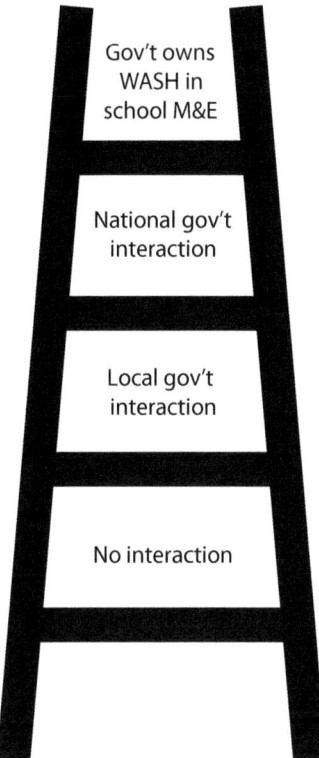

Gov't owns WASH in school M&E	Government-led WASH in Schools M&E. NGOs use national indicators and feed M&E data directly into national systems.
National gov't interaction	Some coordination with national systems but sporadic leadership from the national government. Civil society coordinators at national level on WASH in Schools M&E.
Local gov't interaction	NGO monitoring engages local level ministry representatives in data collection process but has not affected/strengthened national M&E for WASH in Schools.
No interaction	NGO data collection happens independently of any government system.

Figure 4.4 WASH in Schools monitoring and evaluation 'integration' ladder
Source: Walter, 2013.

But accepting that SWAps and other common frameworks may be some way off in all countries, in the interim there are lessons to be learned from some of the more positive examples of taking the best of project monitoring and using this to bolster country-led systems. The medium- to long-term implication is for development partners to wind down project monitoring and to do more to strengthen and pay for common government frameworks as these become better established and more refined. Some promising examples are presented in the following boxes.

Consensus and a way forward

Emerging consensus around project monitoring

A number of threads or themes in overcoming the negative consequences and tensions between 'project' monitoring and government-led monitoring emerged from the Monitoring Sustainable WASH Symposium held from 9 to 11 April 2013 in Addis Ababa, Ethiopia. The level of consensus points towards guarded

Box 4.3 Sustainability check tool – Mozambique

This instrument was developed under a joint UNICEF, government of Mozambique, and government of the Netherlands rural water supply and sanitation programme entitled the One Million Initiative. The aim of the tool is to provide an annual 'audit' or report on the sustainability of investments by looking at a number of core factors, including institutional, social, technical, and financial dimensions. The tool has been applied over a five-year period under this programme and has built up a cumulative picture of performance over this time.

More importantly, some of the elements of the sustainability check are now being taken up as a basis for the development of sustainability indicators for the National Rural Water Supply and Sanitation Programme (PRONASAR) by the government of Mozambique, with a scaling up of the tool within the framework of the National Directorate of Water's work plan (Godfrey et al., 2013).

Box 4.4 Scaled-up database for rural water and sanitation – Indonesia

The Australian government's Department of Foreign Affairs and Trade (DFAT) has been financing large-scale water and sanitation investments in Indonesia with the rural component supported through World Bank-led programmes, notably the Third Water Supply and Sanitation for Low Income Communities Project (PAMSIMAS) and the Water and Sanitation Policy Facility (WASPOLA). In the case of PAMSIMAS, the World Bank together with the Indonesian government's Ministry of Public Works have set up a management information system that collects project data from every district under implementation. The database is in the Bahassa Indonesian language and is available to the public. It includes project costs, community contributions, details of facilities built, number of beneficiaries, and sustainability data, entered by district facilitators. This information is then used at the central level to gauge project progress and performance; it is the only monitoring framework of this size in the country. However, it is still currently being maintained by staff from the PAMSIMAS programme, rather than by government, which calls into question the long-term viability of the system.
Source: Communications with DFAT Indonesia representative, 2013.

Box 4.5 Service delivery indicators – Ghana

In 2007, the Community Water and Sanitation Agency (CWSA) developed the District Monitoring and Evaluation System (DiMES), which was supposed to be used by local government, but it was never really populated or maintained. In 2011 the CWSA, together with the Triple-S (Sustainable Services at Scale) project, developed a set of indicators to assess and monitor the functionality of water facilities, the level of services provided, and the performance of the community-based operator. Akvo Field Level Operations Watch (FLOW) was piloted by local government staff as a technology in three districts to map water facilities and capture the level of services provided. The CWSA aims to build on past project results and feed the data collected with FLOW into the DiMES to make it readily available for decision making at local government level. The vision of the CWSA is to mainstream this monitoring system in all districts in Ghana, and it has found development partners willing to support this vision of a scaled-up DiMES. With this financial support, and building on the initial three pilot districts, 119 more districts will now be using FLOW to collect data and DiMES for improved analysis, planning, and decision making (Duti, 2012).

> **Box 4.6 SIASAR initiative – Honduras, Nicaragua, and Panama**
>
> The Rural Water and Sanitation Information System (Sistema de Información de Agua y Saneamiento Rural or SIASAR in its Spanish acronym) is a platform for monitoring, data collection, and analysis that has been developed as part of a Central American regional initiative supported by the Water Partnership Program (WPP) of the World Bank. The SIASAR tool has been developed in collaboration with government ministries and other national stakeholders to be a practical and interactive web platform that takes advantage of open source programming and mobile technology. It groups data into four key areas using commonly agreed upon indicators, and can produce different levels of data analysis depending on the needs of users. The long-term sustainability and scale-up of SIASAR is being addressed through strong institutional buy-in from regional governments; to date, under the pilot phase, over 1,200 communities have had data entered and there is strong interest from other Central American and South American countries (World Bank, 2013).

optimism, despite the very real challenges and constraints in this area. Firstly, there was a clear recognition that it is ultimately national governments that must deliver adequate monitoring and show leadership; conversely, where this does not take place, development partners will continue to fill the gap, with piecemeal and short-term solutions. Secondly, there was a general agreement that the efforts of development partners are valid and can bring valuable lessons and piloting solutions. For NGOs with a presence in the field, there is a vital role for innovation, as well as for 'holding up a mirror' to the sector, and especially to governments, in a more advocacy-type role. Thirdly, there is evidence that project monitoring has already influenced government-led systems in a positive way, particularly in relation to the debate around sustainability for service provision.

However, several serious challenges constitute a caveat to these positive messages. One of them is the difficulty of overcoming organizational behaviours and incentives that are driven by accountability to development partner funders. These are powerful forces that can work against better alignment with government systems; such patterns of behaviour are often difficult to 'unlearn'. And in many cases the desire to satisfy a demand for fast results and ever more detailed data is difficult to resist when visibility and fundraising – and therefore organizational self-preservation – are at stake.

One of the key barriers is the lack of communication and information sharing between project monitoring and national systems. Simple first steps to address when planning for project monitoring would include finding out about government systems, however limited or rudimentary they may be. Integration cannot happen without this basic first step and it is remarkable how often this step is not taken, whether through ignorance or simply through a lack of willingness to act.

A way forward towards better integration

First and perhaps foremost, it is clear that the tension between project- and country-led monitoring is both dynamic and complex, shaped by many variables; there is no 'one size fits all' approach to facilitating better integration and an ultimate transition to robust, comprehensive national systems. From this examination of key drivers and challenges that are shaping the way in which development partner project monitoring interfaces with country-led monitoring, we can draw a number of initial recommendations:

- When supporting project monitoring, development partners should have country ownership and country-led systems in mind *from the very beginning*; this should be associated with a diagnosis of these systems – in both the supply of and demand for information. Early and continuing communication with relevant sector authorities at national and local level is a key step in this process.
- Linked to the above, development partners should be realistic about the low-resource environment common in many countries, particularly at decentralized levels; project monitoring and innovation must fit with these financial and other capacity constraints, otherwise they are highly unlikely to be adopted or scaled up.
- The 'governance' and coordination of monitoring at country level are important to support effectively; how innovation and learning about monitoring are captured and fed back into country-led systems is critical. Understanding who is involved and how these processes happen are central to developing permanent capacity.
- Building comprehensive monitoring systems for a nation takes time. Long-term explicit development partner commitment – including funding – is important to engender and bolster government buy-in and leadership on monitoring, especially where there are competing demands for sector investments.
- Common programming frameworks, resulting in a SWAp or similar, are highly desirable if there is to be a critical mass around monitoring and to act as an incentive (both positive and negative) for development partners to support country-led systems.
- Development partners, particularly those working outside common programmatic approaches, should be challenged more vigorously and held to account in terms of adopting standard monitoring indicators and sharing of results.
- Efforts to strengthen country monitoring systems should be experimental and iterative, and should focus on the problem definition rather than pick from a (pre-set) menu of solutions: projects that support monitoring systems should ask first 'What is the problem?' rather than 'Which solution should we adopt?'
- Government leadership and political support matter. If national sector stakeholders do not show the desire for and commitment to building country-led monitoring systems, different development partner projects and programmes will simply move to fill the vacuum left behind.
- Development partners of all types must work harder to explain why national monitoring systems are needed and should be funded and work

to change the incentives for reporting back to their headquarters or to institutional or individual (taxpaying) funders.

Endnotes

1. Many countries in Latin America have common information frameworks and approaches to data collection. Although there are fewer comprehensive systems in place in sub-Saharan Africa, this is a growing trend; for example, in Uganda (see footnote 14) and Ethiopia, where the government has established a monitoring and evaluation system with common indicators and reporting as part of the One WASH National Programme (Ministry of Water and Energy, National WASH Coordination Office, September 2012).
2. For example, only 42 per cent of respondent countries to the 2011 GLAAS country survey reported WASH sectors that are informed by reliable monitoring systems.
3. For example, the 2011 evaluation of the Paris Declaration reports only 'moderate or mixed progress' on a greater use of country systems where such systems have been made more reliable (OECD, 2011).
4. See *Shorter Oxford English Dictionary*.
5. See the history of the development of FLOW (Field Level Operations Watch): <http://www.waterforpeople.org/what-we-do/?gclid=CInzo_bk-cECFarKtAodHxQA1g>.
6. The strength of performance monitoring in urban areas is reflected by the growth of the International Benchmarking Network for Water and Sanitation Utilities, which now collates data from over 2,000 utilities and 85 countries: <http://www.ib-net.org/>.
7. For example, a recent review of the rural sector in 13 countries found only two instances, Honduras and Uganda, with sector monitoring frameworks that included both composite indicators and targets relating to sustained service provision (Lockwood and Smits, 2011).
8. A recent study looking at one municipality in Honduras found four separate forms of monitoring being carried out in one relatively small geographic area, all using somewhat different approaches (IRC 2012).
9. In 2010, the AfDB commissioned a two-part study, entitled 'Water governance sector in Africa', in which it states that 'eleven African countries are using the sector-wide approaches (SWAps) in their water sectors and many more in health or education sectors', namely Benin, Burkina Faso, Ethiopia, Ghana, Kenya, Malawi, Mozambique, South Africa, Senegal, Tanzania, and Uganda: <http://www.afdb.org/en/news-and-events/article/afdb-to-launch-water-sector-governance-in-africa-report-7495/>. Nonetheless, the extent to which some of these constitute a full SWAp may be debatable.
10. See WFP's commitment to post-project monitoring: <http://www.waterforpeople.org/everyone/monitoring-evaluation.html>.
11. For a reflection on the value of the sustainability clause, see: <http://waterservicesthatlast.wordpress.com/2012/08/31/hitting-the-right-note-

the-dgis-sustainability-clause-is-complex-but-thats-no-excuse-for-being-timid/>.
12. The Danish aid agency DANIDA first started work in support of the sector in Uganda in 1991, moving from area-based programming to broader sector support. Since 2003, DANIDA, along with other development partners, notably the UK government's Department for International Development, has been one of the key donors supporting development of the national monitoring framework and the so-called 'golden' indicators (Ssozi and Danert, 2012).
13. Personal communications with senior staff of the Department for Water Development, Ministry of Water and Environment, Government of Uganda (2012).
14. Data for the cost and scope of the UNICEF sustainability checks is from an ongoing study being undertaken by IRC and Aguaconsult on behalf of DGIS, May to June 2013.
15. A recent, wide-ranging evaluation commissioned by the Policy and Operations Evaluations Department of the Netherland's Ministry of Foreign Affairs points to major weaknesses in large-scale programmes of the World Bank and UN Habitat (IOB Evaluation, 2012: 60).
16. For a more in-depth analysis of this so-called 'country-led evaluation paradox', see the presentation by Robert Picciotto, King's College London and former director general of evaluation at the World Bank: <http://mymande.org/content/country-led-evaluation-cle-paradox>.

References

De Albuquerque, C. (2010) *Report of the Independent Expert on the Issue of Human right Obligations Related to Access to Safe Drinking Water and Sanitation*, United Nations General Assembly 65th Session Item 69(b) of the provisional agenda 'Promotion and protection of human right', Geneva: Office of the United Nations High Commissioner for Human right (OHCHR).

Duti, V. (2012) 'Tracking functionality for sustainability', paper presented at the 2011 Community Water and Sanitation Agency Annual Review Conference, Ejisu, Ashanti region, Ghana, 23–27 April.

Godfrey, S., van der Velden, M., Muianga, A. and Xavier, A. (2013) 'Sustainability check: five year annual sustainability audits of the water supply and open defecation free status in the One Million Initiative, Mozambique', paper presented at the IRC Symposium 2013: Monitoring WASH Services Delivery, Addis Ababa, Ethiopia, 9–11 April.

IOB Evaluation (2012) *From Infrastructure to Sustainable Impact: Policy Review of the Dutch Contribution to Drinking Water and Sanitation (1990–2011)*, The Hague: IOB Evaluation, Ministry of Foreign Affairs.

IRC (2012) 'Everyone, forever? Scaling-up rural water and sanitation in Chinda, Honduras', *Water Services that Last: Case Studies for Change*, The Hague: IRC and Water For People.

Lockwood, H. and Smits, S. (2011) *Supporting Rural Water Supply: Moving Towards a Service Delivery Approach*, Rugby: Practical Action Publishing.

Losa, F. (2013) 'Bridging project and country WASH monitoring and evaluation: the new M&E strategy for the Water Supply and Sanitation Department of the African Development Bank', paper presented at the IRC Symposium 2013: Monitoring WASH Services Delivery, Addis Ababa, Ethiopia, 9–11 April.

OECD (2011) *Aid Effectiveness 2005–10: Progress in Implementing the Paris Declaration*, Paris: Organisation for Economic Co-operation and Development (OECD) <http://effectivecooperation.org/files/resources/2011%20Report%20on%20Monitoring%20the%20Paris%20Declaration%20ENGLISH.pdf> [Accessed 13 January 2015].

Scott, O. (2012) 'Supporting institutionalized monitoring systems for rural water supply and sanitation in Malawi', *Waterlines* 31 (4): 272–9.

Segone, M. (2009) 'Enhancing evidence-based policy-making through country led monitoring and evaluation systems', in M. Segone (ed.), *Country-led Monitoring and Evaluation Systems: Better Evidence, Better Policies, Better Development Results*, Evaluation Working Paper Series, Geneva: UNICEF Regional Office for Central and Eastern Europe and the Commonwealth of Independent States (CEE/CIS).

Smits, S., Schouten, T., Lockwood, H. and Foncesca, C. (2013) 'Background paper for Monitoring Sustainable WASH Service Delivery Symposium,' paper presented at the IRC Symposium 2013: Monitoring WASH Services Delivery, Addis Ababa, Ethiopia, 9–11 April.

Ssozi, D. and Danert, K. (2012) *National Monitoring of Rural Water Supplies: How the Government of Uganda Did it and Lessons for Other Countries*, RWSN-IFAD Series 4, St Gallen, Switzerland: Rural Water Supply Network.

Walter, E. (2013) 'Making the grade: a progress report on WASH in Schools monitoring and evaluation', paper presented at the IRC Symposium 2013: Monitoring WASH Services Delivery, Addis Ababa, Ethiopia, 9–11 April.

WHO (2012) *UN-Water Global Annual Assessment of Sanitation and Drinking-Water (GLAAS) 2012 Report: The Challenge of Extending and Sustaining Services*, Geneva: World Health Organization (WHO).

Willetts, J., Bailey, B. and Crawford, P. (2013) 'Reflections on monitoring a large-scale civil society WASH initiative: lessons for sector monitoring and potential contributions from NGOs', paper presented at the IRC Symposium 2013: Monitoring WASH Services Delivery, Addis Ababa, Ethiopia, 9–11 April.

World Bank (2007) *Country-level Sector Information and Monitoring Systems (SIMS) for Water and Sanitation in Africa*, Water and Sanitation Program Field Note, Washington DC: World Bank.

— (2013) *The SIASAR Initiative: An Information System for More Sustainable Rural Water and Sanitation Services*, Briefing Note, Washington DC: Water Partnership Program of the World Bank.

About the authors

Harold Lockwood is director of the UK consulting agency Aguaconsult. He has extensive international experience of sector policy development, decentralization of service provision, and monitoring and evaluation. His focus in recent years has been on sustainability of WASH programmes, collaborating with a range of organizations, including national governments, donors, NGOs, foundations, and research centres. In 2013, Harold Lockwood supported IRC in an evaluation of the sustainability-contracting instrument applied by the Dutch Ministry of Foreign Affairs. He has also carried out similar monitoring work for a range of other donors, including USAID and DFID.

CHAPTER 5

Technology, data, and people: opportunities and pitfalls of using ICT to monitor sustainable WASH service delivery

Joseph Pearce, Nicolas Dickinson, and Katharina Welle

Innovations in information and communication technology (ICT) provide new opportunities to open up monitoring practices to more stakeholders. Accurate data on the level of service received by users and the performance of service providers makes it possible to improve water, sanitation, and hygiene (WASH) services. However, WASH data alone is not enough to encourage action. There remain technological and governance challenges to lasting WASH improvements. Data collection remains infrequent in many countries and many ICT-related innovations are limited to 'islands of success'. Technological glitches are still prevalent and often unaddressed. ICT builds on processes that are already in place and by itself cannot strengthen the processes required in order to act on monitoring data; for improved services, ICT design and application need to go hand in hand with changes in people, processes, and institutions.

Keywords: information and communication technology, transparency, national inventories, mobile phones, automated data collection

Introduction

Information and communication technology (ICT) 'consists of the hardware, software, networks, and media for the collection, storage, processing, transmission and presentation of information (voice, data, text, images), as well as related services' according to the World Bank's ICT glossary. Established ICTs include radio, television, video, and compact disc, while new ICTs relate specifically to cell phones and the internet (World Bank, n.d.; Juma and Yee-Cheong, 2005).

Within the context of water, sanitation, and hygiene (WASH) monitoring, ICT commonly includes internet services, mobile telecommunication networks, smartphones, and feature phones. Throughout this chapter the term

'ICT innovation' is used to describe any innovation in ICT hardware, software, networks, and services. ICT tools refer to both hardware and software. ICT e-services include software updates, websites, databases, and other cloud or networked services that are provided on a regular or continuous basis to ICT users.

ICT is a key driver for long-term economic transformation, serving as an 'enabler of development of key sectors of the economy' (Juma and Yee-Cheong, 2005; Dzidonu, 2010). Rapid reductions in the costs of ICT services alongside increasing efficiency and quality have encouraged wide investment in ICT over the past two decades (Okogun et al., 2012). In the context of global development, ICTs make important contributions to achieving the millennium development goals (MDGs) as they stimulate economic growth by increasing productivity as they become embedded within public and private practice (Dzidonu, 2010).

Through better information flows and communication, the use of ICTs can improve service delivery in the public sector. Furthermore, ICTs can facilitate new communication channels between government, the private sector, and citizens. In so doing, ICT-supported public service delivery has the potential to increase the transparency of government services and to make them more responsive to citizens' concerns (Deloitte, 2012). The use of mobile phones has the potential to make government available anytime, anywhere, to anyone (World Bank, 2012).

Increases in mobile phone penetration and in access to mobile internet in rural areas in developing countries are encouraging the use of ICT to monitor rural water supplies, but there are still important gaps, as illustrated in Box 5.1.

However, ICTs are not, in themselves, sufficient to improve the effectiveness of service delivery. While they can facilitate new ways of engagement through information and feedback flows, the enabling role of ICT is subject to other governance factors such as public administration reforms, basic infrastructure, the availability of human resources, and skill sets at decentralized levels. Gaps between government policies, ICTs, the economy, and service providers need

---

Box 5.1 Mobile and internet penetration worldwide and in developing countries

Worldwide, mobile broadband grew by 45 per cent annually between 2007 and 2011, and between 2008 and 2010 there was a 22 per cent drop in the price of mobile broadband in developing countries (ITU, 2012). Even with these great improvements, per 100 people, there were only 5.3 mobile broadband subscriptions in developing countries compared with 46.2 in developed countries in 2010. In developing countries, subscribers paid almost 75 times more for wired broadband and almost six times more for mobile broadband than in developed countries. In most developing countries, households, schools, hospitals, and other public institutions located outside major urban areas were not yet connected to high-speed internet (ITU, 2012). In order to deal with these challenges, it is still critical to ensure that implemented services can operate in low bandwidth settings and do not require constant mobile network connections for use in rural areas (Dickinson and Bostoen, 2013).

to be bridged in order to harness the expanding potential of ICTs within the field of development (Okogun et al., 2012).

Harnessing ICT innovations for monitoring WASH services

Between 1990 and 2010, more than 2 billion people gained access to improved drinking water sources, and the MDG for water supply has been met five years ahead of time. However, 780 million people lack access to safe water (UNICEF and WHO, 2012). As coverage increases, the need to monitor and ensure sustainability of water services grows.

A particular challenge in rural water supply is the high non-functionality rate of water supply schemes of over 30 per cent (RWSN, 2009). The low sustainability of water services makes reaching everyone more difficult than expected, and obtaining up-to-date information on scheme sustainability is particularly urgent in the rural water supply sub-sector. In many of the countries that are facing major WASH challenges, national water supply scheme inventories are not updated regularly and routine monitoring data for the sector is not considered reliable. Both ICT- and WASH-related challenges will need to be addressed in these contexts in order to improve both the speed of information updates and the actions that are required until everyone has access to water and sanitation services.

High-income countries and countries with relatively stable institutions and high population densities are often better positioned to establish innovative ICT than lower-income and lower-density countries – a situation that often parallels WASH sector progress. Governments, donors, non-governmental organizations (NGOs), and other stakeholders need to tackle the dual challenges of ICT and WASH together to ensure sustainable rural water services for everyone.

Overview of ICT applications used for WASH monitoring

WASH-related ICT-based monitoring innovations have grown steadily since the early 2000s. The many early attempts to use ICT for monitoring included the use of Microsoft Access and other local computer databases and management information systems to organize and distribute monitoring data collected on paper. However, in recent years, the ubiquity and low cost of mobile telecommunications and internet access in the South have prompted innovations in the use of mobile technologies to collect and distribute information; for instance, a recent study of mWASH monitoring identified 40 mobile initiatives in the sector (Hutchings et al., 2012). The use of mobile telecommunications, internet-based cloud services, and smartphones is revolutionizing monitoring in the WASH sector. Table 5.1 includes examples of ICT use within the various steps of sector-wide WASH monitoring. Individual WASH ICT methodologies are described in more detail in Table 5.2.

Table 5.1 ICT within the flow of monitoring information

Steps in the sector-wide monitoring information flow		WASH example
Collection	Capturing data in a format that can be recorded. ICT technologies support different methods of data collection, such as crowd sourcing, administered surveys, and automated data collection. The technologies used include digital sensors and loggers, smartphones, and web, mobile, and computer software to support data entry.	Mapping facilities using Android phones with Akvo FLOW[1]
Transfer and communication	Transporting data from the field and storing the information temporarily. The most common forms of transport include physical transport of digital media, wireless data transfer through GSM networks or WIFI, and wired data transfer.	Using FrontlineSMS to send monitoring surveys via SMS[2]
Data management	Storing and organizing data and enabling access after the information has been stored for data cleaning, reconciliation, and other purposes. Data storage technologies include storage media or hardware, storage architecture, and the way in which data is organized, and the software used to manage the data. In general, storage is increasingly decentralized, with the use of cloud services and websites to store and manage data.	Using Manobi to manage asset inventories of piped systems in small towns[3]
Analysis and reporting	Manipulating the data and related information to understand patterns and answer questions about rural water supplies and their sustainability. There is a broad range of tools and innovations possible, including reports and visualization, analysis and statistics, knowledge management, decision support systems, and surveillance and alert systems.	Using Water Point Mapper to generate maps of water quality or water point functionality[4]
Use	Applying the information to guide decisions at district, regional, and national levels. This includes enforcing sector guidelines, repairing facilities, supporting service providers, monitoring standards, and planning the equitable extension of services.	The M4W project sending an SMS to a handpump mechanic to request the repair of a pump after a problem is reported[5]

Table 5.2 Methodologies for ICT-based data collection in WASH

Methodology	Technologies	Description
	Open Data Kit (ODK)	ODK is an open-source set of tools that assists in creating and managing data collection processes. ODK functions include building data collection forms, collecting data on mobile devices, aggregating data on a server, and exporting the data for analysis. It is used by governments, NGOs, academic institutions, and the private sector for monitoring in water and sanitation. The ODK software can be downloaded free from the ODK website. A vibrant user community shares experiences and developments.
Smartphone data collection	Akvo Field Level Operations Watch (FLOW)	Akvo FLOW, started by Water for People, enables survey-based data collection and is offered as a supported software service by Akvo. A contract is required for its use but the software may also be downloaded and run separately, although there is limited community support for running a separate version of the application. This service has been used by the governments of Liberia and Ghana, IRC, and others.
	mWater.co	mWater.co was developed to identify water sources and record water quality data as open data available online. It can be used for water point mapping surveys. The mWater app is free to download from the Google app store. UN Habitat has used mWater in Kenya and Tanzania.
Feature phone data collection	FrontlineSMS	This enables users to design, build, send, and receive forms via SMS. It is simple, fast, and easy to set up, and there are working examples from all continents.
	M4Water	This enables survey-based data to be collected using simple, low-cost feature phones that support Java applications. In addition, it allows reporting by communities of handpump breakdowns using SMS. M4Water was developed by Makerere University and is supported by a private company in Uganda.
Automated data collection	Oxford smart handpumps	Motion sensor technology coupled with a communications device has been fitted to handpump handles and can record and send data about frequency of use. Information is sent via SMS and is received by handpump mechanics. WaterAid's Water Point Mapper software has been used to analyse the data.
	MoMo	This is a flow rate sensor that can be embedded into handpumps or piped systems. Initial tests are still ongoing.

Typically, a single technology will not cut across all these steps. Instead, sector monitoring information systems will include a number of different technologies, requiring different skills and resources. These information systems are usually customized and/or configured for a specific country, organization, or project.

Technologies for data collection

Common ICTs for data collection can be divided into three categories based on the type of device used: smartphones, feature phones,[6] and smart devices embedded in water facilities. Table 5.2 provides some examples of these; however, it should be noted that the features and support provided for each tool change very quickly and this table provides only a snapshot at the time of writing. It should be noted that the FrontlineSMS and the smartphone data collection tools are the most mature tools in terms of reliability and usability at the time of publication. Smart handpumps and other affordable embedded devices have not yet undergone mass production, are still being piloted, and usually require specialized skills for implementation.

The increasing availability and affordability of smartphones makes it likely that applications will continue to improve and they will become increasingly accessible and prominent, especially in urban areas. The use of visual interfaces can overcome some language issues. However, challenges to smartphone data collection include battery life, different operating systems, and uneven implementation of GPS.

The use of feature phones for data collection is significant among field workers in both rural and urban areas. As a result, there is still substantial demand for applications that use SMS, voice, and shortcodes (for example, the user enters a code, such as *334#, and is provided with a text-based menu) that can work on all low-cost feature phones. SeeSaw, based in South Africa, has piloted an innovative technology that allows entrepreneurs to report maintenance issues using a simple list of phone numbers that no one answers (a 'missed' call). Calling the number costs nothing.

In the near future, we are likely to see an increasing use of mobile applications using a combination of both basic mobile services and smartphones, depending on the differing needs of organizations collecting the data, access to smartphones, and the requirement to work without having to install software on phones.

In order to integrate the data collection tools with sector monitoring, there is also a need to ensure that the data collected feeds into monitoring and decision making. This may require linking the data collection systems to the national- and district-level databases as well as to tools for analysis. While some of these tools support some data management and visualization, it is not likely that any of them can provide a complete system for sector monitoring. Repeat data collection functions are critical – these allow existing entities such as water points to be updated while seeing the results of previous surveys on the data collection tool – and will need to be tested further in future applications of any of these tools in order to support monitoring data collection effectively. Enabling enumerators to search for data based on their location in the field or keywords can help them easily update information on water points nearby and ensure that data is kept up to date. Finally, one way to reduce the data collection burden but gain access to useful monitoring information is to automate data collection. This is treated in more detail later in this chapter.

Technologies for management and analysis

In the last decade, many new tools have become available to facilitate the management of data and to analyse geospatial data. However, local governments and community-based service providers often lack the technical capacity or training to use the software. In response, WaterAid developed a spreadsheet-based tool called the Water Point Mapper (WPM). The WPM, operated via Microsoft Excel, is capable of generating maps that can be viewed in Google Earth or Google Maps. Spreadsheet-enabled mapping has become a popular solution for government-led monitoring initiatives that lack the resources, finance, and skills required to implement smartphone data collection, cloud-based data storage, or online dashboards for spatial representation and graphical analysis. The Excel-based option remains locally accessible, has a minimal cost, can be managed offline, and is simple to operate and customize while generating effective spatial analysis.

At a national level, Microsoft Access database systems and Excel spreadsheets, as well as a variety of other relational databases, have commonly been used for national monitoring and for storing data by both WASH projects and governments. Not all of these relational systems, such as Microsoft Access, are easily available from computer browsers or on mobile devices and so the scalability of these systems to district level using mobile networks is limited. In addition, many of the Access databases and relational systems were expensive to develop and are difficult to update. Offline relational databases encouraged a centralization of data while responsibilities for monitoring water supply have typically been decentralized to districts. In the future, it is likely that web-based and mobile-friendly portals to WASH data and analysis will become increasingly common and user friendly. This is essential to ensure that, as mobile network coverage increases, so does access to data management and analysis for monitoring.

There is a new category of applications that have both data collection functions and data management and analysis tools (see Table 5.3 for a snapshot of some of these functions). The strongest tools will provide options for both online and offline access, relational data types, an application programming interface (API) that allows the third party tool to communicate with national databases, and visualization such as maps, charts, and time series. The most sophisticated tools will also include some statistical analysis and the computation of indicators, such as coverage based on several input questions. For the moment, complete monitoring systems will probably still

Table 5.3 Some applications that support data management or visualization 'out of the box'

Tool	Data			Analysis				
	Online access	Offline access	Tables	Relational database	API	Maps	Charts	Time series
WPM	✗	✓	✓	✗	✗	✓	✓	✗
Akvo FLOW	✓	→	✓	✗	→	✓	✓	→
FulcrumApp[7]	✓	✓	✓	✗	✓	✓	✓	✓
WASHCost Calculator[8]	✓	✗	✗	✓	✓	✗	✓	→
SIASAR[9]	✓	✗	✓	✓	→	✓	✓	→

Key: ✓ = yes; ✗ = no; → = planned.

include a combination of the software below with custom-built databases. However, as third party tools and e-government policies on data storage and open data mature, it is likely that more and more functions will be available to governments at national and local level 'out of the box'.

Automated monitoring and operational data

Automated ICT can be used in the WASH sector to remotely monitor services and address systematic and predictable tasks or challenges. These systems can be used across the monitoring information flow, from the use of remote sensors to collect and transfer data to the automation of data management, analysis, and report generation. In addition, some actions can be triggered through alerts and information targeted to specific individuals. Some examples are automated reports about breakdowns sent to area mechanics, the ordering and delivery of spare parts, and letting water committees know that their mobile money account is getting low. Some such technologies are identified in Table 5.4.

The most common forms of automation are software applications that generate automatic reports in standard formats or web-based maps from data collected (such as SweetData and mWater.co). Much automation occurs without the knowledge of the users, such as recording the date when the functionality of a water point is reported.

Advanced ICT that is available for monitoring rural water supply services incorporates the relatively low-cost functionality monitoring of SMS and mobile data technology embedded in the water supply infrastructure, whether a piped system or a handpump. Small devices, such as digital sensors and loggers, are installed to measure the flow of water in piped networks or the movement of the handpump mechanism, and they transmit the data to a server where it can be disseminated to field staff or mobile mechanics. This development promises to generate information at scale that can be used by institutions for improving management and service delivery. It has the benefit of providing fine-grained operational-level data that can inform improvements

Table 5.4 Some automatic technologies for data collection

	Digital sensors and loggers	Computers and integrated devices	Software applications	Implications for data
Automated data collection	Flow and pressure sensors to monitor water use, satellite imagery to track changes in water bodies	Smart handpumps and other devices with integrated sensors	Platforms and customized software for automated data management and visualization and for triggering actions with messages to users	Quantity and quality can be configured but quantity can also be overwhelming; the frequency of collection depends on a connection to the network; malfunctions in devices or connectivity can corrupt data

in service delivery. Some 'all-in-one' automated systems even incorporate payment and billing as well as monitoring the usage (by households) of rural water supplies. An example of such a system is the Grundfos Lifelink,[10] which is currently used by both Grundfos and Water Missions International to provide a solar-powered water source with a standpipe and allows payment with credit purchased in advance. So far, these systems have not been used on a significant scale. High capital costs and slow cost recovery from user payments may be reasons for this, but such systems may play a greater role in the future as capital costs are expected to decrease dramatically. These technologies also often create dependency on a virtual financial system of credits, and it may be that the prepaid financial models in place are not yet working for the poor and ultra-poor who have variable access to cash.

Oxford University has been piloting smart handpumps. The device is capable of measuring water point handle movements and sending data over SMS messages, as demonstrated in Figure 5.1. The device consists of three essential elements: 1) an ICT-based accelerometer; 2) a microprocessor; and 3) a GSM modem (Thompson et al., 2012). Tested first in Zambia, by Oxford University and a local private service provider, these devices have now been fitted to water points in 70 village handpumps in the Kyuso district of Kenya (University of Oxford, 2012). Areas with these smart handpumps have reported a reduction in non-functional days from 40 per year to four per year. This provides a positive indication of how smart handpumps could facilitate successful business models for rural service delivery.

It still remains to be seen whether these devices will continue to operate reliably outside research settings. The MoMo device, developed by the organization WellDone, found a clear example of the challenges involved in the application of innovations in ICT. The devices, which work by transmitting data received through sensors via SMS messages from the water point to a server, failed to transmit data during one early pilot because they were installed in an environment lacking mobile phone reception. The Oxford pilots found

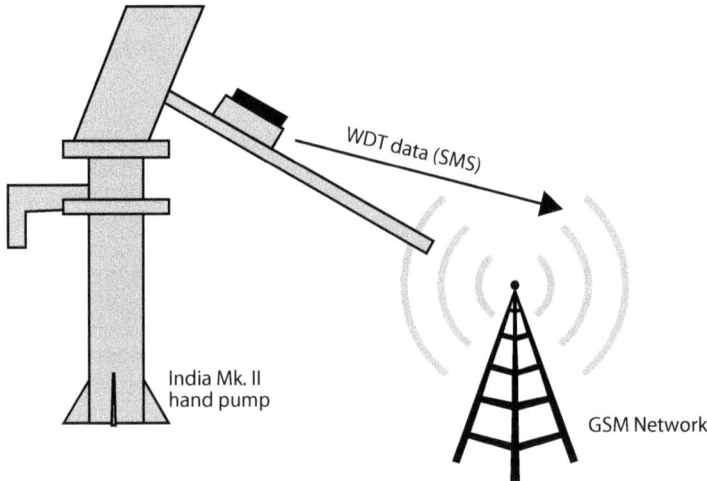

Figure 5.1 Water point data transmitter, sending data periodically by SMS, attached to an India Mark II handpump

Source: Adapted from Thompson et al., 2012.

that a high proportion of SMS messages were lost due to irregular network connectivity. Even with these challenges, remote monitoring of rural water supplies is likely to increase and could revolutionize both service delivery models and the ways in which these services are monitored.

In evaluating these devices, key considerations will be whether the remote monitoring devices will be serviced and repaired when they break down and whether they are reliable enough in real-world applications to reduce the overall costs relating to travelling to water points to check, maintain, and repair them consistently. Other factors include the unit costs for installation, the cost of maintaining and running the systems that collect the data, the costs of mobile data and/or SMS and power for the devices, security, spare parts, the lifespan of the technology, and the availability of a constant mobile network connection.

Case studies: using ICT for sector monitoring

This section explores country studies from Liberia and Timor-Leste to examine sector-wide uses of ICT for WASH monitoring. The experiences of these countries underline the potential for ICT to provide improved data for investment decisions and planning. They also help highlight some common challenges that may be faced when ICT is rolled out at a national scale, especially in relation to ensuring that improved information is kept up to date.

Liberia

In 2003 Liberia emerged from a 14-year civil war that decimated infrastructure and led to a dramatic deterioration of WASH services, including safe water points, and to the looting and damage of all data on facilities. The signing of the Comprehensive Peace Accord in August 2003 initiated emergency WASH interventions, providing critical relief after the war. However, these were ad hoc and often uncoordinated and limited; still only 51 per cent of the population has access to safe drinking water (UNICEF and WHO, 2012).

Planning and data collection became of critical importance and the Ministry of Public Works (MoPW) took the lead to address this shortcoming. With targeted investment following 2010's HIPC (heavily indebted poor countries) debt relief and additional support from the Water and Sanitation Program of the World Bank (WSP) and UNICEF, MoPW mapped 10,000 rural and urban water points across all 15 counties between December 2010 and May 2011. To gain greater insight into the planning and allocation of resources, MoPW created the nation's first comprehensive inventory of water point assets. The inventory has improved analysis with regards to water infrastructure and improved the accuracy of data used for fund mobilization.

The ICT used for the exercise enabled rapid data collection and represented a national-scale pilot for using mobile technology for data collection. Surveys were assigned to Android smartphones with Akvo FLOW enabling enumerators to complete the surveys via their touchscreens. In addition, they could use the phone camera and GPS to capture images and geographical coordinates of the water points. Data was then automatically submitted to the web-based dashboard for data management, cleaning, and analysis.

Attributes of water points were identified and verified, including the source type, functionality, construction details, and the prevalence of water committees. Water quality testing, which analysed biological and chemical composition, was carried out on sample wells in the capital, Monrovia.

Since the baseline collection in 2011, the main challenge has been updating the database with newly developed infrastructure and keeping the status of existing water points up to date. This is both a technical and a logistical challenge. To overcome this, a framework was developed involving the Ministry of Health and community health volunteers to collect data continuously. They utilized existing networks as well as engaging focal points at community, district, county, and national levels (see Figure 5.2). At the time of writing, Akvo is planning a repeat data collection tool to support the updating of existing data points when there is no internet connection in the field. The repeat data collection tool will help FLOW graduate from a baseline data collection tool to a continuous monitoring tool.

Many NGOs delivering water services in Liberia now have FLOW applications on phones with digitized standard questionnaires. Additionally, a website has been developed featuring Akvo RSR (Really Simple Reporting) tools to facilitate the piloting of continuous monitoring of projects in Liberia (not only water points). Nevertheless, prevailing challenges involve slow adaptation to new technologies or systems, and the capacity and motivation to collect data remain issues at sub-national level.

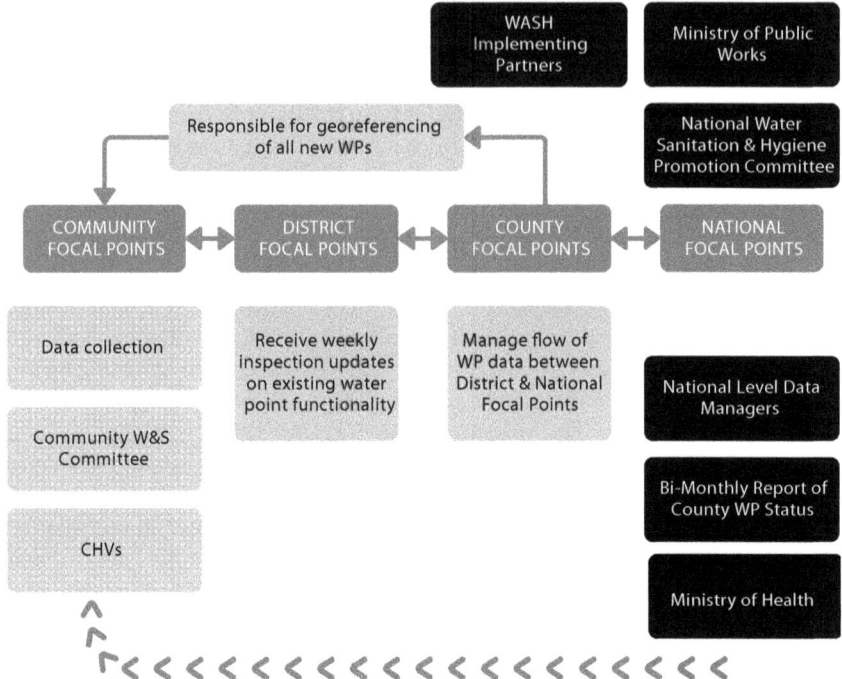

Figure 5.2 A framework for updating water point data in Liberia
Source: Koroma, 2013.

One definite success of this process was the production of a quarterly report on access and coverage. This has been partially updated using a template completed by NGOs and government partners to capture new construction and rehabilitation work. However, this fails to capture the functional status of existing water points.

While there are significant difficulties, the Liberia case provides an example of how incorporating NGOs into monitoring ICT systems can help address challenges to sustainable monitoring at scale. However, there is still a need to continue to incentivize at sub-national levels due to failures of existing water points, and local capacity building is required in the use of new tools in order for this to become a driver for sustainability. The addition of repeated data collection tools that provide access to previous data on phones and that encourage the use of data in planning can help create the right environment to stimulate repeated data collection.

Timor-Leste

Until recently, Timor-Leste has been marked by civil war and violence resulting in poverty, insecurity, and challenges for the WASH sector, including shortfalls in administrative and human resource capacity to implement policies and programmes (ISF-UTS, 2011). However, since independence in 2002, the government has significantly built the profile and priority of the WASH sector, moving away from donor finance dominance and towards improving WASH services and sector management through the Ministries of Finance, Infrastructure and Health, with continued support from the Australian government's Department of Foreign Affairs and Trade (DFAT).

Prior to 2010, Timor-Leste had a water supply monitoring system, but much data was collected on paper, there were different indicators collected, partners were not engaged, many geographical areas were neglected, and there was a lack of system functionality and service-level data. In addition, there was no scaled-up updating mechanism and no sanitation information. As a result, data analysis for decision making was limited and it was not easy to use the monitoring system as a management tool. Improving the sustainability of rural water service provision in Timor-Leste thus required a reorientation of the sector – from an infrastructure focus with poor monitoring to a service delivery approach, where progress is measured.

Between 2010 and 2012, the Water and Sanitation Information System (SIBS) was developed as a national monitoring tool, funded by DFAT through the BESIK Rural Water Supply and Sanitation Programme. In order to provide data for use at sub-district, district, and national level, government staff, as part of their day-to-day work, collected water and sanitation data in all rural villages in Timor-Leste. As a government system, the monitoring indicators were aligned with national standards and policies. This tool was designed to manage and monitor rural water and sanitation services at national, district, and sub-district level, as well as to measure functionality down to village level.

To overcome the challenges of data entry from paper-based forms, SIBS used feature phone SMS mobile technology for data transfer and Timor-Leste's limited internet and mobile data access. Mobile network services are available across approximately 85 per cent of Timor-Leste, enabling 88 government-employed WASH facilitators to collect data by downloading and inputting forms, storing the information, and then transmitting the data by SMS when mobile network coverage is available. In principle, updated information is sent every three months by SMS to a central database held at national level.

The data collection process involved creating baseline community profiles (56 questions) and collecting water system asset information and social information. It includes quarterly updating of information through regular visits by sub-district facilitators as part of their role to support WASH community management. The collected information is analysed using Microsoft Excel. Presented data is shared at district and national level, where staff have been trained in data analysis and use, but also at sub-district level; at this level, printed copies are used due to the lack of computer availability. Next steps involve making information openly available to all in order to hold service providers to account.

Some of the elements required by SIBS, and that relate to the costs of the system, are:

- FrontlineSMS open-source software;
- an ICT technician for 1.5 years to establish the system;
- simple feature phones for 88 WASH facilitators, with a small Java app for data collection;
- SMS for water and sanitation forms – two SMS messages were needed for each village, at a cost of US$0.08 per SMS, so covering 2,225 villages cost approximately US$35.60 for data transfer;
- community visits as part of the ongoing role of WASH facilitators;
- information management system support – establishing the database and SMS system and for ongoing systems support;
- equipment for users to access maps or data;
- bringing key people together to analyse and respond to data;
- investments in data checks (of 5 per cent of the data) to ensure accuracy.

By early 2013, there had been limited improvement to the scheme's functionality. This highlights the importance of being able to act on the data provided by ICT-driven monitoring systems and the need for planning on the basis of the data and corrective action to take place. It may also take more time than initially anticipated to make use of the information coming from new ICT systems. There are still lessons to be learned on how to effectively use ICT systems to improve services.

Overall, however, a national monitoring tool has been established in Timor-Leste, utilizing mobile technologies to monitor water and sanitation information at national, district, sub-district, and village levels. Staff training and external technical support are likely to continue for some time. Yet by updating data every three months, the government staff of Timor-Leste demonstrate the great potential of using ICT for monitoring WASH services in fragile states.

Discussion of country cases

The two case studies highlight the use of ICT to manage and monitor rural water and sanitation services at national, district, and sub-district level. They illustrate different ways in which ICTs can capture functionality at the level of facilities and villages, support the implementation and analysis of service delivery indicators, and measure national performance. Being government-led, the data collected was aligned with national standards and policies. It is important to examine these country cases to counterbalance the many small-scale pilots of ICT innovations in the WASH sector, which do not provide sufficient lessons on the scaling of sustainable monitoring ICTs.

The leadership in both countries also helped to clarify the respective roles and responsibilities of those who were collecting the data, validating data, and planning. It is clear that introducing new technologies must go hand in hand with changes in sector governance, and this requires a clear vision and leadership. The same level of leadership needs to go into the use of the data and enforcing sector standards in order to ensure that monitoring makes a difference when applied at scale.

At the same time, in both countries, staff turnover and a need for ongoing training also constrained the use of new technologies and monitoring processes, especially at district level. This required constant investment from outside sources of funding. Both countries face challenges, albeit different ones, in keeping their data inventories 'live', but Timor-Leste seems to be able to keep its data relatively up to date in some areas.

The case of Liberia also offers an example of how non-government actors can be used to provide updated information for national inventories. In many countries, NGOs are required to report their plans and the installation of new facilities. Providing these actors with national or district monitoring tools could strengthen national monitoring systems. However, even these actors require training, and the use of these systems will need to be enforced in order for them to be cost-effective. Additionally, it is still critical that government does at least some sampled repeat data collection to cross-check and verify data, even if that data is provided by service providers or NGOs.

By contextualizing processes, acknowledging stakeholder responsibilities, and encouraging high-frequency reporting by government staff and existing health networks, ICT tools are being enhanced. Forthcoming challenges, however, involve strengthening administrative systems, enhancing absorptive capacity, clarifying institutional arrangements for ongoing monitoring, and dedicating investment in sustainable service provision.

Finally, the cases highlight the capacity and time required to analyse data locally. District governments are further limited by a lack of internet connectivity and by electricity breakdowns. It is crucial that data is analysed and understood by the local stakeholders who will use it.

Successful design of ICT for improving services

This section presents and discusses lessons from the country cases above, from presentations under the ICT theme at the 2013 IRC Monitoring Sustainable WASH Service Delivery symposium, and from the wider sector literature for successfully using ICTs to support WASH monitoring. The lessons are organized along questions of social, operational, and programme design.

Social design

The social design of an application is the way in which the ICT is matched to a given social context or dynamic. The use of ICT is ultimately driven by a combination of people, institutions, and technology and how they interact. While some ICT functions are seemingly generic, such as using a mobile phone to make a normal voice call, the ways in which they are used are still largely shaped by the needs and the social and cultural norms of users and whether or not they are familiar with the particular use of that technology.

Monitoring is usually driven by the needs of a particular institution or set of stakeholders: for example, national governments might need to track access to water and sanitation services by their constituents, or an NGO might need to show donors how their money has been spent to achieve the new water and sanitation services. Because of this, it requires extra effort to ensure that those intended to *use* the system are also included during the design phase. For example, if national monitoring is being designed for use by local governments but has been initiated by national government or international donor agencies, then it is essential that local governments are involved in the design and testing phases of the ICT and that they help set the objectives of the monitoring system.

User perceptions and acceptance. User perceptions are critical to the use of ICTs. The emotional response of a user to a new technology – whether fear, interest, or excitement – can have an impact on adoption. For example, young users may find it easier to adopt new smartphones for data collection. Older users may benefit from their additional care. Hutchings et al. (2012) underline the importance of developing ICT tools that are customized to fit the local context, even going beyond the use of local language or terminology. Interactions can be localized based on social hierarchy, which has an impact on who has access to technologies or who is allowed to express dissent. Economic, socio-cultural, and environmental factors should be considered.

At a more fundamental level, the perceived ownership and objectives of monitoring systems shape the ways in which people use an ICT in the long term. A project-monitoring system may be designed to support project objectives and the collection and analysis of monitoring data may be supported financially by the project. However, if the perceived benefit to local users and institutions does not outweigh the costs of the system, data collection and analysis are unlikely to continue after the project period. National monitoring systems may face the same challenge with regard to ensuring that local governments and other stakeholders use the mobile data collection tools, databases, and web portals that have been developed.

The Community Water and Sanitation Agency and IRC piloted the monitoring of water services and the performance of community-based water service providers in three districts in Ghana. The data revealed that some systems were not performing well enough and that communities had not received enough support from the district. The focus on analysing and using the data with district water department staff and presenting it to assembly members encouraged repeat data collection without pilot funding and suggests the strength of local ownership of data and analysis (Atengdem, J. and Gyamfi, P., 2013). WaterAid's WPM focuses on the use of a locally stored Excel spreadsheet to ensure that data is owned and analysed locally. Even when scaling up these types of monitoring systems to national level, sufficient attention and support must be provided so that ICT meets the needs of local stakeholders and so that they are aware of the role of ICT.

User perception is also greatly shaped by how the data is used and by the actions that are taken after monitoring and reporting have taken place. If users repeatedly see that reported problems persist, then they may stop reporting without external motivation (Taylor, 2012). In fact, reporting may never start if people do not believe that action will take place. Another problem may be that people have alternative ways of reporting and resolving issues. Both the costs and benefits of using the ICT systems, in comparison with either not using those systems or using alternatives, should be taken into account. The actual choice of technology is almost irrelevant if the people meant to collect the data do not see any benefit in reporting.

Finally, the legitimacy and credibility of the data are another key issue. In both small-scale and large-scale monitoring systems, verification of data through triangulation and spot checks can be an important way to ensure that data is both accurate and taken seriously by all users. It is worth noting that ICT can play an important role in improving the reliability of data by, for example, cutting out data entry and reducing the time taken between data collection and verification. Tools such as Akvo FLOW have allowed remote monitoring experts to check for errors and inconsistencies on an online dashboard and to call the data collector directly to correct any potential mistakes before the data collection is finished. In the Water Missions Trade Water project (Armstrong et al., 2013), the financial accountability of agents was verified by checking the volume of water dispensed against the money deposited into the bank. However, for high-quality data, sampled spot checks by independent enumerators may be the best way to ensure that data is not manipulated.

Participation. Each ICT tool supporting a monitoring process almost inevitably creates barriers and opportunities for participation in monitoring. A new web-based portal may provide access to data for new stakeholders, while simultaneously reducing the perceived need for paper-based reports and therefore excluding those without internet access.

Participation can be affected along the whole monitoring cycle, from those who are involved in data collection, to the people who have access to and use the data for corrective action. Familiar technologies (such as voice calls and SMS) may encourage participation (for example, SeeSaw's use of 'missed' calls; Schaub-Jones, 2013). Software installation requirements or training can equally provide barriers to participation and have an impact on the cost of scaling the use of monitoring systems. Engaging users in system design can eliminate barriers to using technology, and working with users provides information and insight often beyond what is expected. There is value in involving primary users throughout the design and development stages; this can develop appropriate expectations of the tool's purpose and capabilities, as well as preparing users to begin utilizing the technology once implemented.

Improvements in sustained system uptake and relevancy can be made if user needs and preferences are addressed throughout the design and development of an ICT system. Greater involvement of communities and WASH stakeholders is required to build systems that meet the true needs of end users. A participatory process can be used in order to identify user requirements, which then inform the design of contextually appropriate technology.

Privacy and security. Monitoring data has the potential to reveal personal details about water users, community-based water providers, and other WASH sector stakeholders. These details can include names, phone numbers, place of residence, and income. Monitoring data needs to be accessible to those who should use it. However, this access to personal information could be abused due to negligence (unwittingly publishing it on an online map) during the standard use of ICT products, or from a motivation to use the information for personal gain.

Some governments have policies on the security of data and who should have access rights to different ICT system features and relevant databases. The privacy and security of data are key issues that need to be taken into account in the social design of a product. If a product is geared only to open data, it will not be the right tool for a government that requires access to information to be limited to specific WASH sector staff.

Technical design

The choice of technology, and how it is implemented, can have a strong impact on the scalability of systems. Technical considerations for the use of particular ICTs may include the geographical coverage of mobile phone networks, the battery life of devices (and backup chargers) in places with limited electricity, the cost of devices and services, and the ability of the technology to operate with intermittent internet connections in local offices.

In Ghana, the version of the district monitoring and evaluation system (DiMES) based on Microsoft Access, which was developed in 2007, requires a working computer, electricity, and training for each district: conditions that are difficult to maintain across all districts. A new version is being developed in order to overcome these challenges and will be partly web-based. In Timor-Leste, simple feature phones and FrontlineSMS software were used to implement a simple survey-based monitoring system. Saiful Islam Raju, from BRAC in Bangladesh, shares lessons for improving the sustainability of ICT systems, including developing lighter versions of the tools with a few key indicators, designing systems that fit within capabilities and existing organizational capacity, and designing for the existing capacities of staff responsible for implementing the system (Raju, 2013).

Data collection. Increasingly, evidence shows that mobile and automated data collection can have a significant impact on the ability to monitor at low cost and speed up data collection and verification. Ranijiv Khush from

Aquaya presents lessons on the use of mobile data collection in Mozambique and emphasizes that manual data management is a problem that leads to uninformed resource use and an uninformed public. As a result of this data was available at upper administrative levels in Mozambique (Ball et al., 2013).

The choice of type of technology, whether smartphone, feature phone-based or paper, will ultimately depend on the context. Surveys have been administered in national monitoring exercises using smartphones and feature phones. Access to the device is critical and may determine the choice of data collection application. When communities in developing countries have to monitor or report information, systems that require the use of simple phones to either make a call or dial a shortcode (USSD) are likely to remain common where internet access and mobile coverage are limited. Paper-based data collection will still play an important role in some cases, especially when the data is being collected on a regular basis and logged locally, such as in local service provider offices.

Data management. The technical design also takes into account the technologies used for data management. Some key aspects of technical design include the location of data, the application used to manage the data, and functions such as the ability to run custom queries and analysis and to communicate with third party applications.

The location of the data storage, whether in country or distributed in the cloud, may be determined by e-government policies on preferred suppliers, the reliability of the service required, and the cost. International services can often provide cost-effective solutions for smaller WASH sector organizations and agencies. Some organizations or governments may choose their own solutions for security reasons and because they have the scale required to lower costs. Another consideration will be the expected quantity of data. In sector information systems that require the storage of images, or near real-time data, it is likely that data storage requirements will increase over time as devices produce high-quality images and send more data. This can render ICT systems obsolete if growth in data storage and bandwidth is not taken into account. The same can be true for web-based and mobile-based portals that disseminate the information collected. As the use of these systems increases along with mobile data coverage and access to browser-based devices, these portals must have the capacity to absorb new users.

The interoperability of an ICT – how easily it can operate with other systems to share data and functionalities – is another technical design element that is sometimes forgotten. It can be valuable to share data management services and responsibilities across different organizations, which may use different information systems. BRAC's Integrated Collaboration and Rapid Emergency Support Services (iCRESS) system (Raju, 2013) is designed to integrate data across different sectors that traditionally have used a variety of data storage systems for their monitoring data, including simple Excel spreadsheets. Communication between these Excel spreadsheets and iCRESS had to be programmed manually, which represents a relatively high investment cost. Newer web-enabled technologies, and some mobile data collection tools, include API or data import and export functions, which can greatly simplify data exchange between systems. Through the use of APIs, BRAC has the capability to align with government and Red Cross information systems within the WASH sector. An interesting lesson from BRAC was that the system is more resilient because it uses many different sources of information: if one information input fails, another one can be used.

Programme design

Programme design refers to the management of the system and its institutional location to ensure the sustainability of the ICT and its related monitoring system. Hutchings et al. (2012) outline three key components: financing, technical partnerships, and metrics for effectiveness. In terms of sources of financing, the monitoring ICT can be funded through external donors, project partners, local or national agencies, internal funds (e.g. districts funding their own data collection), or even profits where the private sector is involved. More simply, options exist in terms of taxes, tariffs, and transfers.

While the cost of running baseline data collection is crucial, financing models must also be able to match the recurring costs of ICT services for technical support and for updating and debugging software over time. Even with the cost savings associated with the implementation of some ICTs, the cost of system maintenance can be difficult to budget when there is no precedent and new activities need to be factored (such as regular retraining for mobile data collection). This is particularly the case when funding is channelled through one- to three-year projects funded by external donors.

New ICT business models, such as Software as a Service (SaaS), require periodic fees to be paid for access to the ICT, which is kept up to date and improved over time. This contrasts with software that is bought once and installed and then never changes. The goal of SaaS is to spread the costs for software improvements over a larger number of users. Building monitoring systems with SaaS models can be cost-effective but requires long-term budget commitments and technical partnerships to ensure that these monitoring systems are not undermined by cash flow problems or changing suppliers. Sometimes, strategic technical partners may help provide long-term support for aspects of the system. Local telecoms, for example, may receive benefits from using a monitoring system on their network, for example more users on their network.

There are numerous examples of custom-built ICT systems that have been started but not yet finished due to contractual problems with the service provider. In these conflicts, licensing and ownership of the software code can become critical issues if they are not well defined in advance. Choices can include ownership being retained by the client or the establishment of a common open-source licence. Some intellectual property rights associated with the code can become a source of contention and lock a client into a particular software development firm. Some alternative choices include purchasing software that can be configured 'out of the box' or purchasing subscriptions paid over time. Typically, a custom-built system will need to be developed over time and tested with stakeholders in an iterative manner.

Measuring the effectiveness of a monitoring system should ideally be built into the system itself, for example by tracking the users of mobile systems, the volume and comprehensiveness of data collected, and the costs of maintaining the services. This is helpful when developing a monitoring system incrementally and in guiding how investment over time and recurrent costs can lead to improved ICT for monitoring. In addition, annual reviews of progress by users and key sector stakeholders can help to renew objectives and ensure that the system design goals are adjusted where necessary.

Conclusions: participation in producing, access to, and use of ICT-related data for improving water and sanitation

This chapter has explored and presented current examples of ICT innovations and their application within water and sanitation monitoring, with much of the information emanating from a wealth of papers and presentations authored for the IRC 2013 symposium on Monitoring Sustainable WASH Service Delivery. We show how ICTs can improve communication flows and service delivery and provide new opportunities for governments, institutions, and citizens. ICT can increase the transparency of government-regulated services and ensure that governments are more responsive to citizens.

As the availability of ICT increases, so does the potential for integrating technical solutions to fix existing problems. With the rise in ICT, we have the opportunity to collect and access greater knowledge about the sustainability of service delivery. New tools can identify trends and inform improvements in planning in ways that could address factors such as equity and ensure sustainable service provision.

In order to be successful, monitoring with ICT needs to take account of all three aspects of system design – social design (user perceptions, participation, privacy), technical design (the choice of technologies), and programme design (recurrent funding and resources). Successful monitoring systems match their users very well, as there are likely to be significant investments and recurrent costs if, for example, the tools require complicated training and support. Few if any ICT systems for national WASH monitoring are capable of including participation from all sector stakeholders (communities, district government, national government, NGOs, and the private sector), which suggests that ICT system designers should be careful not to be overambitious; rather, they should define exactly who their target users are and why. At the same time, broad access to the information generated and its wide dissemination are likely to increase the value of ICT systems.

The country cases have shown how difficult it is to pilot new technologies at a national level. For this reason, we argue that adaptive design and frequent user testing in regular and small iterative steps are required for large-scale ICT systems to be implemented successfully. Using ICT to potentially reduce the costs per unit of data still requires regular investments over time to ensure that the relevant ICT systems and monitoring processes are in place. Regular investments in interoperability between the systems of different agencies, training, product support, user testing, recurrent software costs, and data verification are just some of these budget items.

The focus on current tools is undergoing a much needed shift from data collection or database management only to using ICT to build sector monitoring systems for long-term use, with many stakeholders able to access and use the data. This means covering the entire monitoring process as outlined in this chapter. Future systems should encourage the use of information to improve sustainable services, enhance learning, and aid coordination between different actors. This will also require buy-in from sector leadership. Ultimately, monitoring systems will need to be enjoyable to use, provide trusted information, and add value to the different actors involved in improving WASH services.

From early attempts to integrate ICT for monitoring water and sanitation programmes, we have gained knowledge that we have used to build a basis for establishing shared understandings and defining best practice. Platforms such as the Rural Water Supply Network's mapping topic have provided a space for sharing and debate, much of which continues to inform ideas and influence actions. The plethora of mobile data collection tools available are an indication of the interest and investment in accessing better-quality information. However, there is still a limited number of accounts that detail cases where the availability of data has improved access to WASH services. This chapter shows that we are now struggling with issues that ICT solutions may solve only partly. Part of the challenge is the result of government-led monitoring supported by external agencies on a project basis with a short time frame. In this environment, only a few national water and sanitation inventories have been updated and it will take more time to establish the processes required to complement these ICT systems. But lessons are being learned and there is increasing opportunity for greater coordination of ICT interventions across organizations and governments. There is a growing need to share and document honest experiences of ICT, both the successes and the failures, as we move away from small-scale and short-term pilots. As the monitoring tools continue to improve – with more repeat data collection functions, automated monitoring, and improved dashboards for analysis and dissemination – we will still need to get right the social, technical, and programmatic aspects of updating monitoring data and improving WASH services.

Endnotes

1. <http://akvo.org/products/akvoflow/>.
2. <http://www.frontlinesms.com/>.
3. <http://www.manobi.net/?IDPage=3&M=3>.
4. <http://www.waterpointmapper.org/>.
5. <http://m4water.org/>.

6. <http://en.wikipedia.org/wiki/Feature_phone>.
7. <http://fulcrumapp.com/>.
8. <http://www.washcost.org/>.
9. <https://dgroups.org/?nmr9472s>.
10. <http://www.grundfoslifelink.com/>.

References

Armstrong, A., Melchers, C. and Bazira, M. (2013) 'Remote monitoring of privately-managed rural water supplies using Grundfos Lifelink', paper presented at the IRC Symposium 2013: Monitoring WASH Services Delivery, Addis Ababa, Ethiopia, 9–11 April.

Atengdem, J. and Gyamfi, P. (2013) 'Acting on water service monitoring and performance management data in Ghana', PowerPoint presentation at the IRC Symposium 2013: Monitoring WASH Services Delivery, Addis Ababa, Ethiopia, 9–11 April.

Ball, M., Rahman, Z., Champanis, M., Rivett, U. and Khush, R. (2013) 'Mobile data tools for improving information flow in WASH: lessons from three field pilots', paper presented at the IRC Symposium 2013: Monitoring WASH Services Delivery, Addis Ababa, Ethiopia, 9–11 April.

Deloitte (2012) *eTransform Africa: Modernising Government through ICTs, Transformation Ready: The Strategic Application of ICTs in Africa*, Place of publication unknown: Deloitte.

Dickinson, N. and Bostoen, K. (2013) *ICT for Monitoring Rural Water Services: From Smartphones to Cloud Computing*, Triple-S Working Paper, The Hague: IRC.

Dzidonu, C. (2010) *An Analysis of the Role of ICTs to Achieving the MDGs: A Background Paper*, New York NY: Division for Public Administration and Development Management, United Nations Department of Economic and Social Affairs (UNDESA).

Hutchings, M., Dev, A., Palaniappan, M., Srinivasan, V., Ramanathan, N. and Taylor, J. (2012) *mWASH: Mobile Phone Applications for the Water Supply, Sanitation and Hygiene Sector,* Oakland CA: Pacific Institute.

ISF-UTS (2011) 'Timor-Leste water, sanitation and hygiene sector brief', prepared for AusAID by the Institute for Sustainable Futures, University of Technology, Sydney, October.

ITU (2012) *Measuring the Information Society 2012*, Geneva: International Telecommunications Union (ITU).

Juma, C. and Yee-Cheong, L. (2005) *Innovation: Applying Knowledge in Development*, London: Earthscan.

Koroma, A. (2013) 'Monitoring WASH services: the Liberia story', PowerPoint presentation at the IRC Symposium 2013: Monitoring WASH Services Delivery, Addis Ababa, Ethiopia, 9–11 April.

Okogun, O.A., Awoyele, O.M. and Siyanbola, W.O. (2012) 'Economic value of ICT investment in Nigeria: is it commensurate?', *International Journal of Economics and Management Sciences* 1 (10): 22–30.

Raju, S. (2013) 'Monitoring service delivery: BRAC's experience with iCRESS', paper presented at the IRC Symposium 2013: Monitoring WASH Services Delivery, Addis Ababa, Ethiopia, 9–11 April.

RWSN (2009) *Handpump Data 2009: Selected Countries in Sub-Saharan Africa*, St Gallen, Switzerland: Rural Water Supply Network (RWSN).

Schaub-Jones, D. (2013) 'Considerations for the successful design and implementation of ICT systems in the WASH sector', paper presented at the IRC Symposium 2013: Monitoring WASH Services Delivery, Addis Ababa, Ethiopia, 9–11 April.

Taylor, D. (2012) 'The failure of Maji Matone phase 1', in Daraja, Bora Kujenga Daraja/Better to Build a Bridge [blog] <http://blog.daraja.org/p/failure.html> [accessed 7 October 2014].

Thompson, P., Hope, R. and Foster, T. (2012) 'GSM-enabled remote monitoring of rural handpumps: a proof-of-concept study', *Journal of Hydroinformatics* 14 (4): 829–39.

UNICEF and WHO (2012) *Progress on Drinking Water and Sanitation: 2012 Update*, New York NY: UNICEF and World Health Organization (WHO).

University of Oxford (2012) 'Mobile technology to fix handpumps in Africa' [blog]. Oxford: University of Oxford <http://www.ox.ac.uk/media/news_stories/2012/120608.html> [accessed 8 October 2014].

World Bank (2012) *Information and Communications for Development: Maximising Mobile*, Washington DC: World Bank.

— (n.d.) 'ICT glossary guide: 100 ICT concepts' [website]. Washington DC: World Bank <http://web.worldbank.org/WBSITE/EXTERNAL/TOPICS/EXTINFORMATIONANDCOMMUNICATIONANDTECHNOLOGIES/0,,contentMDK:21035032~menuPK:282850~pagePK:210058~piPK:210062~theSitePK:282823,00.html> [accessed 8 October 2014].

About the authors

Joseph Pearce is a Programme Officer at IRC with 10 years of experience developing and supporting WASH programmes through ICTs. Formerly Technical Adviser to WaterAid, Joseph Pearce led the design and development of the Water Point Mapper launched in 2010 – open-source software that generates maps showing the status of water supply services.

Nicolas Dickinson is Senior Programme Officer at IRC and its ICT and monitoring specialist. Nicolas Dickinson led in the design and development of WASHCost Share, an open-source tool that supports basic and advanced analyses of the lifecycle costs of water and sanitation services.

Dr Katharina Welle is a Senior Consultant with ITAD. Dr Katharina Welle specializes in the interface between research, policy, and practice of development. Since 2003, she has been carrying out applied research, reviews, and evaluations in the water sector relating to politics and governance, aid relationships in the sector, and sector-based monitoring and evaluation.

CHAPTER 6

Behaviour, sustainability, and inclusion: trends, themes, and lessons in monitoring sanitation and hygiene

Carolien van der Voorden and Ingeborg Krukkert[1]

In sanitation and hygiene, the programmatic focus is shifting from the construction of toilets to changing the behaviour of people and strengthening the public and private sectors to deliver the policies and products people and communities need to live hygienic and healthy lives. So, rather than counting toilets, monitoring systems need to measure whether people, in particular the poorest, are using toilets; whether there is a thriving market to respond to the demand for sanitary products; and whether waste is being collected and disposed of in a safe and environmentally friendly way. This involves measurement at different levels and among different stakeholders – households, communities and neighbourhoods, entrepreneurs, and the public sector – and this involves more complex monitoring processes. This chapter looks into incentives, methods, tools, and systems for the complexity of monitoring sanitation and hygiene.

Keywords: behavioural outcomes, open defecation-free (ODF) status, total sanitation, hygiene effectiveness, sanitation as a business

Introduction

Despite huge efforts, it is now increasingly obvious that the sanitation-related target of the millennium development goals (MDGs) will not be met by 2015. There are many causes to explain this shortfall, mostly based on the understanding that sanitation, and hygiene, are 'messy, complex and complicated' fields (Sparkman, 2012), where multitudes of actors operate in scattered sector environments without clear institutional leadership and with weak policy frameworks and capacity. Where water supply is largely a communal service, sanitation and hygiene are highly personal, and mostly dealt with at a household or individual level – but they have an impact on the whole community.

http://dx.doi.org/10.3362/9781780448138.006

These complexities justify the need for thorough and specific sanitation and hygiene monitoring, to increase our understanding of *why* and *how* sanitation and hygiene services and practices increase or improve, and how to ensure *sustainable* change.

So why monitor? As in any field, monitoring in sanitation and hygiene aims mainly to measure inputs and activities and ensure that they lead to their intended results and outcomes; to adjust programmes and planning where necessary; and to establish whether progress is being made towards given targets. Taking a broad definition, the goal of sanitation- and hygiene-related programmes and interventions could be described as achieving a situation where sustainable and equitable hygiene practices and sanitation service chains are accessed and used by all. Monitoring this goal requires going beyond monitoring numbers and access to include assessments of sustainability, service delivery and the sanitation chain, equity, behaviour, and more. It also implies taking into account a broad spectrum of players, both as subjects of monitoring and as contributors to the process.

The following sections will lay out some major shifts and trends in the sanitation and hygiene sectors with implications for monitoring, analyse some of the complexities involved, and discuss some key methodologies and findings.

A shifting field for sanitation and hygiene monitoring

In recent decades, sanitation and hygiene programming has seen some major paradigm shifts, with implications for sanitation and hygiene monitoring.

Basically, sanitation and hygiene programming has moved from using supply-driven, infrastructure-focused approaches, where government and support agents were the main 'drivers' of change, to a demand-driven, behaviour-focused approach where government and support agents facilitate communities' own change processes and where there is increasing scope for the private sector to respond to household demands. It has become accepted that a sense of ownership, be it communal or individual, emotional or physical, is key to sustainability. This has presented a real paradigm shift, as it includes changes in everything from approaches (from education to promotion; from supply to facilitation; 'hardware' to 'software'; enforcement to encouragement, etc.) to planning processes, to roles and responsibilities of all those involved, and to more wide-ranging roles for actors such as the small-scale private sector.

A second, related shift currently under way is that from a project implementation to a service delivery perspective. Rather than sanitation and hygiene interventions being approached as one-off projects, they need to be placed in a wider framework and a longer time horizon for service delivery. The sanitation service framework as interpreted by IRC is divided into two phases, as depicted in Figure 6.1. The first phase is the establishment phase and is about stepping onto the sanitation ladder. It focuses on providing easy

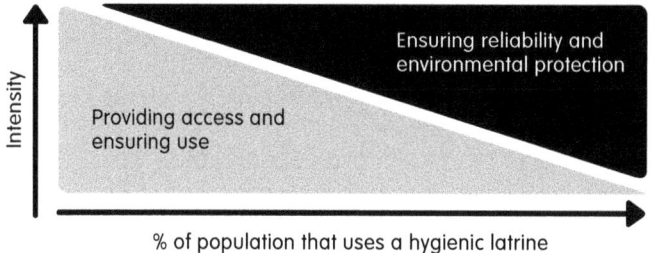

Figure 6.1 The shift in the focus of sanitation services as sanitation coverage increases

Source: Verhagen and Carrasco, 2013.

access to sanitary household latrines and ensuring use by all. It includes a process of establishing relationships between stakeholders, of constructing infrastructure, and of advocating and affirming hygiene behaviour patterns. The second phase is the consolidation phase and is about staying on the ladder and climbing the ladder. While still predominantly focused on non-sewered sanitation, this phase seeks to ensure that services are reliable, and that faecal sludge is disposed of safely to protect the environment from future degradation. In this phase, systems are put in place and households affirm their adherence to safe and acceptable sanitation practices. During this phase, specific attention is paid to operation and maintenance, replacement and improvement, and the safe and final disposal of faecal sludge or its productive use.

Lastly, there is a growing recognition that, no matter how inherently individual sanitation and hygiene behaviours are, they impact on the whole community. Whether or not someone uses a toilet has huge implications for the wider community environment, health, and well-being. Specifically in the field of sanitation promotion, this realization has led to a major shift away from individual- and household-based approaches towards community-led approaches such as community-led total sanitation (CLTS) or, more generally, community approaches to total sanitation (CATS). These approaches have seen remarkable successes by building on the fact that individual behaviours have communal consequences and that therefore it is in the community's best interest to change the sanitation behaviours of all individuals within the community. A further key element in the success has been that these approaches place responsibility and decision-making power squarely in the hands of the community and its people, and so can be very empowering.

Trends in monitoring

Alongside these paradigm shifts in approaches to improve sanitation and hygiene, monitoring methodologies and focus have to change as well. Broadly speaking, four distinct and current trends can be identified with regards to monitoring sanitation and hygiene:

1. a shift from monitoring (infrastructure) outputs to monitoring (behavioural/quality) outcomes;
2. a diversification of monitoring aspects and actors, whereby the actors are approached both as subjects and implementers of the monitoring;
3. a growing focus on monitoring the sustainability and equity of outcomes and services;
4. a move towards systematization and harmonization, linking local-level monitoring to national-level systems.

A shift from monitoring (infrastructure) outputs to monitoring (behavioural/quality) outcomes. In keeping with the paradigm shifts and a growing appreciation of the importance of behaviour change, the focus of monitoring is shifting more and more away from counting numbers and focusing on infrastructure; instead, it is beginning to concentrate on monitoring the outcomes of interventions in terms of access and use, and lasting behaviour change. The growing focus on outcomes is also linked to growing interest in assessing the actual impact of services (health, environmental, economic, etc.), although this still remains, and possibly ought to remain, mainly in the remit of evaluation. Overall, as will be highlighted later in this chapter, the key challenge remains finding feasible, affordable, and reliable methodologies and systems to monitor qualitative and quantitative aspects of behavioural outcomes at scale.

A diversification of monitoring aspects and actors, both as subjects and implementers of the monitoring. Both the desire to monitor the entire service delivery chain as well as the strong sector focus on total sanitation have influenced the content of what gets monitored, the actors being monitored, and the way in which different actors engage in the monitoring itself. As will be illustrated in the section on CATS, in CLTS and CATS, as in many other sanitation and hygiene development strategies, participatory monitoring is key in catalysing and sustaining change. And in order to understand and strengthen the various elements of the sanitation and hygiene service chain, many different actors need to be monitored in terms of their roles and functions, the value they add, the problems they face, the support they need, the costs they incur, and so on. There have been many attempts to do this, each of them focused on a subset of factors, as illustrated later in this chapter.

Challenges remain around further development and adoption of methodologies to monitor the different aspects and actors; around building widespread capacity to perform quality monitoring; and around developing systems to both display and ensure links between the various actors and elements of the service chain.

A growing focus on monitoring the sustainability and equity of outcomes and services. Sustainability and equity are key considerations of any development practice. In terms of monitoring sanitation and hygiene, this covers efforts to measure cost-effectiveness; the social, environmental, and financial sustainability and the self-sustaining capacity of the sanitation service chain (see, for example, the sections on cost-effectiveness and monitoring for inclusion); efforts to monitor sustainability of 'open defecation-free' (ODF) status and other hygiene behaviours (see the section on CATS); and efforts to measure acceptability, accessibility, affordability, appropriateness, and safety of services for different people at different stages of life (see the section on equity and the right to water and sanitation).

Many programmes and governments struggle to identify and put in place monitoring targets, indicators, and methodologies that can be feasibly, affordably, and reliably implemented over time and at scale and that will provide accurate, disaggregated data on the level and quality of (access to) services and hygienic behaviours of any given community, household, or individual.

A move towards systematization and harmonization, linking local-level monitoring to national-level systems. There is a growing recognition of the need for more harmonized monitoring and evaluation systems, globally and nationally. Global approaches such as the Joint Monitoring Programme (JMP)-led process towards development of water, sanitation, and hygiene (WASH)-specific indicators to feed into post-2015 target setting can be very helpful in this respect. As illustrated below, many programmes have also started to collaborate with (local) government institutions to ensure harmonized data gathering and the development of central database systems for collection, analysis, and planning.

But national government agencies, United Nations (UN) agencies, donors, non-governmental organizations (NGOs), and service providers still too often use different methodologies and approaches for data collection and analysis, different definitions and indicators, or different data sources to monitor progress in sanitation and hygiene, even within the same countries. The need to consolidate and harmonize is not yet recognized strongly enough.

Challenges and responses

The next sections go into detail on some of the challenges mentioned above, and consider the concrete monitoring responses, findings, and methodologies linked to some of the key approaches and priorities in sanitation and hygiene, by discussing recent experiences to:

- assess **the enabling environment** for sustainable sanitation and hygiene services, from public sector and market points of view;
- focus on **behavioural outcomes**, particularly by examining hand-washing behaviour change and consistency;

- monitor **total sanitation** and improve and standardize national protocols and approaches to plan, monitor, verify, and certify ODF areas and the impact on sustainability;
- measure **the cost-effectiveness of hygiene interventions**;
- adopt an **equity lens** for sanitation and hygiene monitoring;
- monitor **inclusion**, **quality**, and **sustainability**.

Current monitoring responses

The enabling environment

Starting at a national level, there is growing understanding of the various policy, institutional, financial, social, and programmatic elements and arrangements that impact on successful and sustainable service delivery. A number of initiatives are under way to assess the various elements of the enabling environment. Some of these assessments, for example the country status overviews in Africa developed by the Water and Sanitation Program (WSP) of the World Bank and commissioned by AMCOW (African Ministers' Council on Water), are politically motivated and aim to show progress against commitments. Others are intended to assist governments in assessing the strength of their programmes and identifying where improvements may be needed.

In this latter category, WSP, through its 2007–10 three-country Total Sanitation and Sanitation Marketing (TSSM) rural sanitation programme, developed a methodology to assess and monitor eight different components of the enabling environment:

- policy, strategy, and direction;
- institutional arrangements;
- programme methodology;
- implementation capacity;
- availability of products and services;
- financing and incentives;
- cost-effective implementation;
- monitoring and evaluation.

Through monitoring the results per component, a simple and visual overview can be generated and progress tracked easily (see Figure 6.2).

The WSP study found strong support for the hypothesis that countries with a stronger enabling environment made most progress in terms of their large-scale rural sanitation programmes (Rosensweig et al., 2012). In a broader discussion about the application of this assessment, Perez (2013) noted that the monitoring process became very much part of the progress, and that those (state) governments that had clearly committed themselves to the process were also those that made most progress in terms of their rural sanitation programmes. However, it was also apparent that a high score on the monitoring and evaluation component by itself was not an indicator

BEHAVIOUR, SUSTAINABILITY, AND INCLUSION

2007 BASELINE	INDIA-HP	INDIA-MP	INDONESIA	TANZANIA
Policy, strategy, and direction	Medium	Low	Medium	Low
Institutional arrangements	High	Medium	Low	Low
Program methodology	Medium	Low	Low	Low
Implementation capacity	Medium	Low	Low	Low
Availability of products and services	Low	Low	Low	Low
Financing and incentives	High	High	Low	Low
Cost-effective implementation	Low	Low	Low	Low
Monitoring and evaluation	Low	Low	Low	Low

2010 ENDLINE	INDIA-HP	INDIA-MP	INDONESIA	TANZANIA
Policy, strategy, and direction	High	Low	High	Low
Institutional arrangements	High	Medium	Medium	Medium
Program methodology	High	Low	High	Medium
Implementation capacity	High	Medium	High	Medium
Availability of products and services	High	Low	High	Medium
Financing and incentives	High	High	Medium	Low
Cost-effective implementation	Medium	Low	Medium	Low
Monitoring and evaluation	High	Medium	High	Low

Legend:
- Needs improvement
- Progress made, but still not high performing
- Performing at a high level

Figure 6.2 Example of baseline and endline assessments for rural sanitation in Himachal Pradesh and Madhya Pradesh in India, Indonesia, and Tanzania
Source: Perez, 2013.

of success. A general observation was that monitoring costs money. In the TSSM programme, a programme with a strong evidence-gathering objective, a third of the budget was reserved for monitoring and evaluation. This is a key consideration for any government or service provider committing itself to long-term monitoring.

Behavioural outcomes

Coming at it from the opposite side of the spectrum, increasingly sanitation and hygiene are understood to be functions of people's behaviour. The key outcome of many sanitation and hygiene interventions is now defined as eliminating open defecation, and thereby changing individual and collective behaviours towards a situation where everybody uses a safe toilet and habitually practises key hygiene behaviours. This focuses monitoring on *behavioural outcomes* of sanitation and hygiene interventions and services over time.

As explained by Jelena Vujcic of the University at Buffalo, the typical monitoring approach has traditionally been concerned with inputs, processes, and outputs, but has left outcomes and impacts to evaluation (Vujcic, 2013). Whereas measuring impact (health, environmental, social, etc.) is still very much in the realm of evaluation, now that measuring behaviour has become more relevant to understanding whether or not programmes are meeting their objectives, behavioural outcomes have to be part of the monitoring spectrum and cannot be circumvented any longer. But this means monitoring population-level effects rather than programme-level effects. It means aiming

Box 6.1 Monitoring hand-washing behaviour change

When measuring human behaviour, there are three general types of indicators:
1. self-reported behaviour;
2. proxy indicators;
3. observed behaviour.

Each comes with a set of strengths and limitations:

Self-reported behaviour is a common indicator to use, as it is relatively simple to collect data and requires minimal training. However, there is good evidence that behaviour tends to be over-reported. One study showed that only a small portion of those who said they washed their hands with soap at critical times (such as after using the toilet) were observed to do so in direct observation.

Proxy indicators of behaviour, such as the presence of a hand-washing station near the place of defecation or the presence of water and soap or ash at the hand-washing station, give clues about that behaviour. While they cannot validate the actual behaviour (e.g. how often a person washes their hands, how often they use soap, and at what times), they are quick and relatively simple to collect.

Importantly, Orlando Hernandez of the organization FHI 360 explains that the proxy indicators relating to the presence of a hand-washing station and soap and water have been validated through direct observation of hand-washing behaviour, and there is emerging evidence linking the proxies, via behaviour change, to health impact (Hernandez et al., 2012).

Another additional benefit of using proxy indicators is that they are often already measured through large national surveys such as the demographic health survey (DHS) and the multiple indicator cluster survey (MICS). These provide large data sets that make it possible to infer behaviour change from the proxy indicator. They also allow for comparisons of hand-washing facilities against key socio-economic indicators, such as income and education level, and for comparisons between years within the same region or country and between regions and countries.

Ann Thomas of UNICEF stresses the link between wealth and hand washing. When disaggregating the data on households with access to a place for hand washing by wealth quintile, it appears that 50 per cent of the households with access are part of the richest segment, while in the poorest segment only 5 per cent have access. This is important information for the targeting of hand-washing promotion interventions. Thomas encourages WASH sector players to do more with country surveys, stating that they have a wealth of information from surveys that can be used to do this kind of analysis (Thomas and Bevan, 2013).

Direct observation of behaviour is the best monitoring method available at the moment. This is a direct observation of, for example, hand-washing behaviour where an observer is placed in the household or school for several hours and records whether hands are being washed and what materials are being used at specific critical times. This is a very detail-rich method, but it is also very resource intensive. It takes time and well-trained staff to carry it out, and some studies have shown that people react to the presence of the observer.

As discussed by Orlando Hernandez, there is growing evidence to limit hand-washing promotion to two potential junctures: before handling food and after contact with faeces (defecation or cleaning a child's bottom after defecation). Focusing direct observation on these two junctures would increase the feasibility of data collection. It could also stimulate harmonization between hand-washing promotion projects (Hernandez et al., 2012).

In conclusion, monitoring behaviour change at scale is feasible!

The use of proxy indicators at scale is feasible, and the use of proxy indicators and data from large surveys such as the DHS and the MICS can provide a better understanding of hand-washing practices on the ground and potentially what influences these practices. This in turn can help improve programming.

In addition, direct observations, while difficult to scale, can be used as a complementary tool, by using representative subsets of the target population to supplement the use of proxy indicators. Lastly, using a partnership approach where different partners combine their monitoring efforts can provide support for larger-scale data collection and analysis.

to get a complete picture of what programmes actually do and how well they serve or reach the people they are intended to reach. And it makes monitoring much more personal.

A key consideration with regard to sanitation and hygiene behaviour change is the risk that, in a similar way in which sanitation was often overlooked compared with water supply in broader WASH programmes, the strong sector focus on CLTS/CATS and the related ODF status may lead to a neglect of key hygiene behaviours other than the use of a latrine, such as hand washing with soap or ash at critical times.

To further complicate matters with regard to monitoring hand-washing behaviour change, the context in which hand-washing promotion takes place is highly diverse. Typically, programmes focus on household-level promotion, school-based promotion, and/or communal practice. It is common for hand-washing promotion to be nested within programmes that have wider overarching goals, for example WASH programmes, CLTS, nutrition programmes, disease prevention programmes, and so on. This requires smart monitoring, but it also presents an important opportunity to gather monitoring data on hand-washing behaviour and behaviour change within these various programme contexts. And it is important to have feasible methods to do this. Box 6.1 describes some key methodologies for monitoring hand washing with soap, and the advantages and drawbacks of each of them.

Community approaches to total sanitation

As mentioned above, the reigning paradigm for (rural) sanitation promotion currently is total sanitation. In many respects, CLTS and CATS have been the most successful approaches ever in realizing large-scale sanitation behaviour change. Introduced in the late 1990s in Bangladesh, more than 35 countries in Africa now implement some form of CATS (Thomas and Bevan, 2013), as do more than 15 countries in Asia. As illustrated by Figure 6.3, the number of people living in an ODF environment has increased almost exponentially since the introduction of CLTS.

At the same time, though, the sustainability of behaviours affected by CATS, the broader impact of such approaches on community health, well-being, and further development, and the extent to which these approaches lead to access to and use of high-quality or improved latrines are still under discussion. Part of the challenge lies in monitoring these largely qualitative aspects.

Amsalu Negussie highlights some common monitoring challenges. Like many programmes of this kind, the Plan International Pan-Africa CLTS programme has both numerical targets (e.g. the number of communities and schools triggered, the number becoming ODF, and how many people gain access to improved sanitation) and broader objectives that need to be measured (Negussie, 2013). The broader objectives include reduced child morbidity and mortality, empowered communities, and a scaled-up CLTS approach – all very difficult to measure and to attribute. Whereas people using improved latrines can be observed and counted fairly systematically, it is much more complex to assess whether a community, its people, or certain vulnerable groups have been

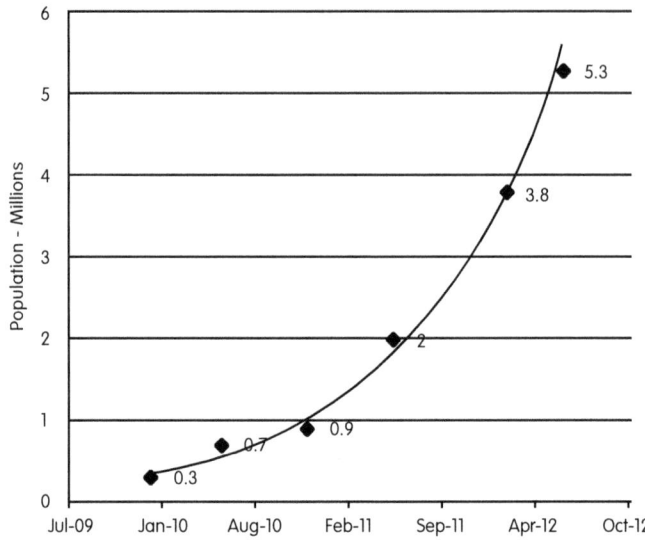

Figure 6.3 ODF population in the West and Central African region, mid-2012
Source: Thomas and Bevan, 2013.

empowered through the process; it is also very context specific and difficult to do at scale. Negussie remarks that monitoring these broader outcomes of CLTS is 'impossible', as CLTS is only one factor among many impacting on a healthy living environment.

Taking a pragmatic approach, work carried out by Thomas and Bevan (2013) analysed national ODF protocols from across Africa to gain more insight into the determinants for success and sustainability of ODF. A protocol is 'an accepted or established code of procedure', usually a national-level, government-led document. ODF protocols are important as they can:

- validate the national CLTS strategy as part of the larger sector strategy;
- harmonize approaches nationally – streamline processes, and agree on key programming principles and philosophy across the sector, i.e. subsidies, rewards, recognition, definition, etc.;
- be a step towards improved sanitation and other outcomes – as part of a broader sector strategy;
- be an opportunity to link monitoring to sustainability at various steps.

As remarked by Ann Thomas, an ODF protocol may in fact trigger the development of a national sanitation policy, as was the case in Somalia. Figure 6.4 illustrates the content of an ODF protocol.

The protocol analysis gathered some important lessons from the country experiences. For example, it was found that the ODF protocol could be leveraged for outcomes beyond ODF, such as hand washing with soap, safe

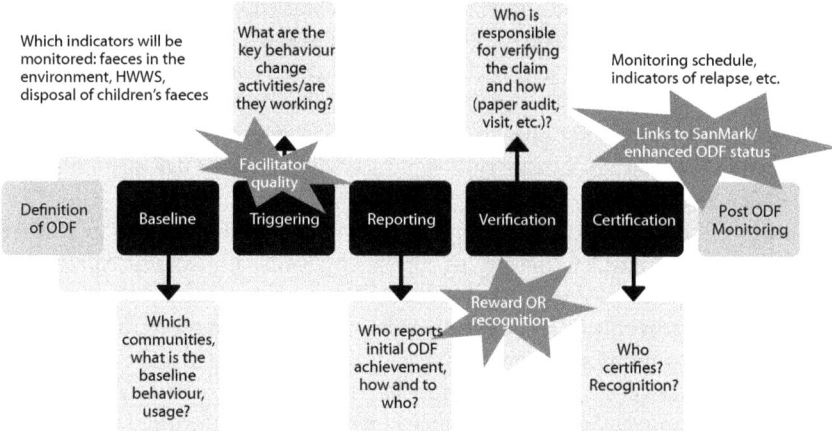

Figure 6.4 An ODF protocol
Source: Thomas and Bevan, 2013.

disposal of children's faeces, or maintaining a clean environment around the toilet. To this effect, many countries have developed a second-tier ODF, sometimes called 'ODF++' or total sanitation, incorporating these additional indicators. This supports the sustainability of the ODF status, as ODF becomes only the first step in a longer-term process towards the main outcomes of total sanitation and sustainable behaviour change.

Other lessons included the following: the focus should be on recognition rather than rewards; deliberate time lags should be included between ODF declaration, certification, and validation of outcomes beyond ODF; and follow-up visits or continued monitoring need to be considered, included and budgeted for.

With regards to monitoring, experience with the national protocols shows that it is important to include process indicators such as testimonies of women and the quality of facilitation by natural leaders, as well as output indicators.

A general observation was that countries displaying better collaboration also showed better progress at scale. Nigeria, for example, organizes an annual CLTS round table to review progress, discuss challenges and lessons learned, and recognize different actors by giving awards to the best natural leader, the best-performing local government area, and so on. This strengthens relations between the stakeholders and also creates a sense of healthy competition.

In CATS, the way in which progress towards the outcome of reaching ODF is tracked and the people tracking it become key parts of ensuring ODF. In this respect, CATS has become a breeding ground for participatory monitoring approaches, including monitoring by natural leaders, WASH committees, children's committees, women's groups, and more.

Natural leaders are often considered key elements in the successful triggering of CLTS and achievement of ODF. The quality of their facilitation can greatly influence the outcome, and they are important stakeholders and actors in the monitoring process. Recognizing this role, Plan Malawi has supported natural leaders to form networks at regional, district, and village levels, in order to exchange information and to validate monitoring data from other districts. Dan Kapatuka shows that empowering natural leaders to take a lead in their own sanitation matters can be one way of ensuring post-ODF sustainability (Kapatuka, 2013).

However, one question with regards to working through natural leaders concerns the voluntary nature of their engagement. Many experiences using volunteers to follow up and monitor their own or other communities' progress have proven not to be sustainable; volunteers have eventually either demanded remuneration or employment, or their enthusiasm and engagement have faded over time. A key question is: what will happen to monitoring when programme staff leave the area, and when project funding stops? What about sustainability? As discussed further in Chapter 3 (Danert, 2014), the key to sustainability in this respect seems to be that monitoring, as part of the broader commitments and protocols for successful CLTS and post-ODF programming, needs to be inherently government-owned or government-led. This is discussed in another example from Malawi, in Box 6.2 (Kennedy and Meek, 2013).

Cost-effectiveness of hygiene interventions

While there is widespread acceptance of the key purpose of sanitation and hygiene interventions in terms of ensuring behavioural outcomes and health and development impact, in a sector where funds are limited, human resources scarce, and priorities abundant, it is essential that the interventions carried out do not only result in the intended outputs and outcomes, but are also cost-effective and evidenced to be the most appropriate and relevant under the circumstances.

Like rural sanitation, hygiene practices are viewed as a private responsibility. However, public resources are used to trigger household investments in hygiene. The link between funds and outcomes is less clear. Hygiene promotion – i.e. the planned approach to preventing sanitation-related diseases through the widespread adoption of safe hygiene practices (Peal and van der Voorden, 2010) – has public and private costs and benefits. The suggested principle is that public funds (taxes and transfers) should be used to maximize public benefits, while private funds (tariffs) for things such as soap and individual latrines should be used for private benefits.

Developing a credible evidence base on the cost-effectiveness of hygiene promotion is important to advocate for continued and improved investment in hygiene promotion, and for strengthening knowledge in the sector on the kinds of interventions that are effective. The potential impact of cost-effectiveness studies to date has been diluted by the use of different methodologies, indicators, and approaches. Little has been done to synthesize

Box 6.2 Block system planning and monitoring in Malawi

In Malawi, Engineers Without Borders Canada has been working with local government staff in Salima and Zomba districts on 'extension agent' reorganization for CLTS implementation and monitoring (Kennedy and Meek, 2013). Through an approach called 'block monitoring', district-level CLTS and hygiene promotion activities are integrated directly into everyday health centre work. This is done without specific project funding and using the existing resources of health extension services.

Health surveillance assistants (HSAs) are grouped into 'blocks' that cover numerous villages; this contrasts with the traditional approach of a lone agent assigned to only a few villages. The block HSAs jointly create plans for CLTS triggering, follow-up visits, and monitoring and tracking of their CLTS activities. But, more importantly, CLTS activities are integrated into regular planning, alongside office work, patient visits, outreach clinics, and other work. Simple matrix-based plans are written jointly and progress tracked.

The main successes are:

- streamlined training of HSAs;
- prioritizing CLTS monitoring activities;
- understanding the impact of CLTS activities on extension agent workloads overall;
- increased accountability;
- monitoring CLTS activities using the block system at the field and district level.

Table 6.1 Example of a block planning sheet

Day		Blessings	Ona	Noel	Lucy	Charles	Comments
M/16	Activity	Triggering	Triggering	Triggering	Triggering	Triggering	High attendance at triggering – promising flames
	Location	Madalo	Madalo	Madalo	Madalo	Madalo	
T/17	Activity	Jiggers follow-up	Jiggers follow-up	CLTS follow-up	CLTS follow-up	CLTS follow-up	Jiggers at Madalo – needs another follow-up
	Location	Madalo	Madalo	Chibwana	Chibwana	Chibwana	
W/18	Activity	W. chlorination	W. chlorination	W. chlorination	W. chlorination	W. chlorination	Unclean borehole at Chisomo – asked VHC to clean
	Location	Madalo	Chisomo	Chimwemwe	Chimwemwe	Malato	
T/19	Activity	Outreach clinic	Outreach clinic	Outreach clinic	Outreach clinic	Outreach clinic	
	Location	Madalo	Madalo	Madalo	Chimwemwe	Chimwemwe	
F/20	Activity	Office work	Office work	Office work	CLTS follow-up	CLTS follow-up	Lucy and Charles did not follow up because of rain – went to HC instead
	Location	HC	HC	HC	Madalo	Madalo	

Source: Kennedy and Meek, 2013: 9.

However, there are also challenges. The system is designed to be championed by one person at the health centre. Until the system is rolled out on a larger scale, with the district environmental health officer holding the health centre accountable for reporting, there is a risk of system breakdown if the responsible person leaves the health centre or is unable to go to the centre for other reasons, such as a transfer or fuel shortage. In these situations, the expectations in the health centre were set but the follow-up planning and scheduling did not take place (Kennedy and Meek, 2013).

or pull together common indicators and findings to generate a broad evidence base, or to conduct multi-country studies using consistent or comparable indicators and methodologies (Potter et al., 2011).

As a sideline to its WASHCost programme, IRC developed a methodology to monitor the cost-effectiveness of hygiene interventions. So far, IRC has tested it in Ghana, Burkina Faso, and Mozambique, to establish whether hygiene interventions are effective and at what cost. While findings were mixed and the methodology will need further sharpening, it can be helpful in justifying why and how to invest in hygiene promotion. Policy makers want to know the answers to the following:

- Why invest in hygiene promotion?
- What works, where, and why?
- How much is enough?
- How do we know that inputs are achieving outcomes?

Hygiene behaviour changes need to be measurable in order to monitor (and manage) and to demonstrate effectiveness. Three indicators were looked at:

1. faecal contamination and use of latrines;
2. hand washing with soap or substitute after defecation and before handling food;
3. the source of drinking water and management of drinking water at the household level.

For each of these indicators, five different service levels were established, as summarized in Figure 6.5.

In developing this methodology, the developers had to face the key question: is hygiene promotion a service or an intervention? Hygiene promotion can be seen as a public or environmental health function and therefore as part of a service led (ideally) by public or environmental health departments, as in the example from Malawi, or by the sanitation provider or utility.

However, water and/or sanitation infrastructure-related hygiene promotion is usually an 'intervention' that happens in project cycles. These interventions are rarely planned, managed, and/or implemented in an integrated manner in cooperation with broader public and environmental health services.

Focusing on what was reasonable within existing sector constraints, the methodology was developed to concentrate on hygiene interventions, rather than on service levels. Nevertheless, some initial findings showed direct use of the methodology by programme managers and decision makers in the public domain.

For example, the Mozambique study (Potter et al., 2013) found that an investment of US$5 per person per year resulted in a 5 per cent increase in basic latrine use; a 28 per cent increase in basic hand washing; and a 57 per cent increase in basic drinking water management. In Burkina Faso, the study helped flag that certain interventions seemed less effective than others in terms of moving people up service levels (Nansi, 2013).

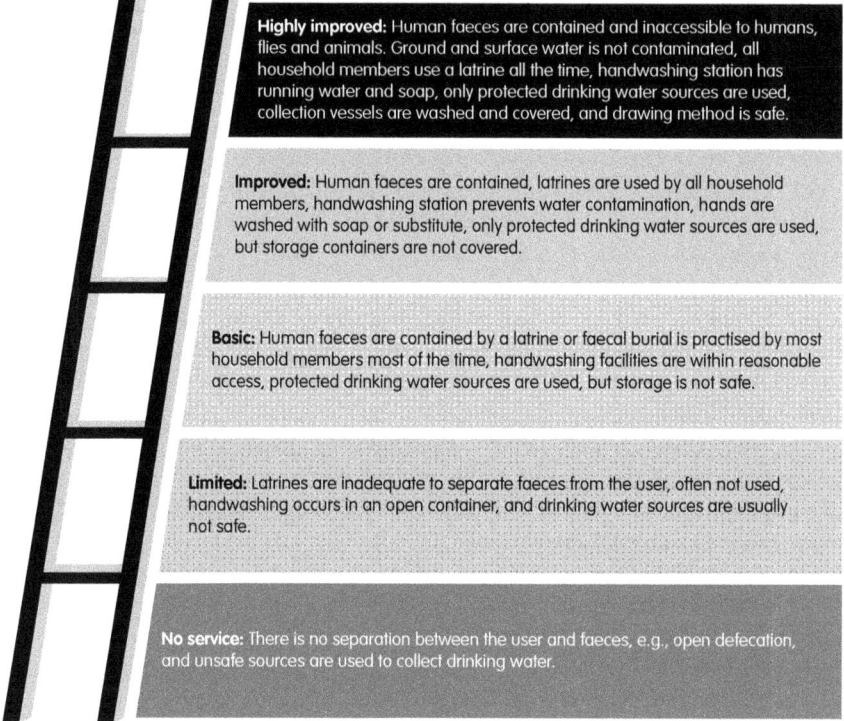

Figure 6.5 Summarized hygiene effectiveness ladder

Source: McInytre et al., 2014: 62, borrowed from Potter et al., 2011.

Overall, though, the three country studies of the WASHCost project showed that higher expenditure does not necessarily lead to higher impact. Much of this has to do with the relevance of the approach or intervention for that particular setting or target population – something the next section will address in more depth.

Equity and the right to water and sanitation

In many cases, efforts to achieve the MDGs have meant that programmes have targeted the proverbial low-hanging fruit of the wealthier or more easily accessible segments of society, thereby widening disparities and reinforcing inequalities. But the world can never reach total sanitation, and countries and communities will never accrue the full health and wider developmental benefits from improved sanitation and hygiene practices, without a focus on equity. Equity is essential to sustain behaviour change practices at scale.

Equity involves recognizing that people are different and require specific support and measures to overcome the particular context-specific impediments that stand in the way of their being able to access and use services sustainably, in this case safe sanitation and hygiene practices (Patkar and Gosling, 2011). For this to happen, 'equity will need to be woven into the fabric of every investment, every supervision mission, every reward and every audit' (Patkar and Gosling, 2011: 1).

For example, while many programmes have historically taken the household to be the 'lowest-level unit' in terms of monitoring, it is important to go beyond this and monitor access and use with a true equity and inclusion lens, in terms of both who is *being* monitored and who is *doing* the monitoring. This means unpacking who in a household, community, region, or country is able to (or unable to) access and use sanitation facilities in a safe, dignified, and convenient manner; or use adequate water and soap for washing hands, bathing, or managing menstrual flows. For people who are disabled from birth or due to an accident or old age, it means adjusting services so that they are convenient and can be used at all times.

Applying an equity lens involves *aspiration* – to universal access and use, and to linked benefits and sharing of responsibilities – and *recognition* – 'business as usual' will exclude the same groups and will reduce sustainability practices (Patkar and Gosling, 2011).

But, remarks Patkar, in trying to reach this goal of universal access, the sector has applied a generic, almost neutral, approach to service delivery that ignores the diversity and reality of human needs. This has resulted in the de facto exclusion of everyone who does not fit into this antiseptic mould of toilet and hand-washing facilities. For example, how can we speak of appropriate facilities if the needs of women are not taken into account?

Patkar argues that the solution is quite simple: respect and be explicit about difference, do not use jargon, redefine success and how it is measured, and be clear about what is meant by the following three principles:

1. Apply a human lifecycle approach – infancy, childhood, puberty, child birth, menopause, and old age.
2. Apply three universal equity parameters – age, gender, and physical ability.
3. Apply context-specific parameters – location, occupation, ethnicity, class, caste, religion, geopolitical, geographical, and geological parameters.

Programmes and service providers need to ask themselves some key questions:

- Who is left out and why?
- Who does not use the services, when, and why?
- Who cannot practice, when, and why?
- Who cleans and maintains the services, at what cost, and for whom?
- Who is unable to maintain, rebuild, upgrade, or invest, and why?
- Who benefits and who does not?

An inability to answer these questions most likely means that certain groups of people are excluded from the services provided. For sustained behaviour change at scale, the sector cannot afford to exclude those who cannot use safe sanitation facilities or practice safe hygiene behaviour.

> **Box 6.3 The human right to water and sanitation: what to measure?**
>
> The United Nations General Assembly formally recognized the rights to water and sanitation by supporting the resolution initiated by Bolivia on 28 July 2010. Resolution 64/292 acknowledges that *clean drinking water and sanitation are integral to the realization of all human right.*
>
> In September 2010, the United Nations Human right Council adopted the resolution on human right and access to safe drinking water and sanitation, *affirming that the rights to water and sanitation are part of existing international law.* This therefore confirmed that these rights are legally binding upon states.
>
> The human right to sanitation and hygiene require the sector to take a look at how it monitors – reminding all actors that service delivery cannot fall back on old excuses.
>
> Ten per cent of the world's population is disabled or physically challenged, yet they make up more than 40 per cent of the 2.5 billion people without access to safe sanitation.
>
> Until recently, menstrual hygiene management has been ignored as a priority issue, but at least half the 2.5 billion are women and girls. Some 350 million women and girls are menstruating at any given time, and this recurs every month for five to six days. This makes 3,500 days over a lifetime.
>
> **Some key principles**
>
> *Equity* requires the correction of unjust differences. In WASH, equity requires a focus on marginalized groups, e.g. the poorest of the poor, including the rural and the urban poor.
>
> *Non-discrimination* refers to the legal principle of non-discrimination, which prohibits less favourable treatment of individuals or groups based on ethnicity, sex, religion, or other status. In the WASH context, non-discrimination requires well-targeted and carefully tailored interventions to ensure that no group suffers less favourable treatment or impact.
>
> *Equality* is the legally binding obligation to ensure that everyone – regardless of status, race, sex, class, caste, or other factors – enjoys equal enjoyment of their rights. In the WASH context, equality necessitates progressive improvements to close gaps between those who have access at the level of an adequate standard of living and those who have not.
>
> *Universality* is the foundational principle that all human beings have equal rights as human beings. In the WASH context, universality requires that services are provided to everyone – including those who are hardest to reach.
>
> So what would success look like, and what goals should the sector monitor against?
>
> - The bottom of the pyramid shows measurable and consistent use and practice.
> - Women and girls attend to menstrual hygiene needs with dignity and safety.
> - Those with physical challenges practise sanitation and hygiene with comfort.
> - Children and older people use and practise behaviours with convenience and comfort.
>
> *Source:* JMP Working Group on Equity and Non-Discrimination, 2012.

Monitoring for inclusion, quality, and sustainability

More and more organizations are attempting to facilitate better monitoring by developing tools or methodologies that aim to address the complexity of sanitation and hygiene interventions and services within one monitoring system and set of indicators. They seek to include the full range of stakeholders involved; assessments of the quality and inclusiveness of the outcomes; financial, technical, and social sustainability considerations; and so on. An example of such an aggregate approach is the Household Water Treatment and Safe Storage Toolkit, which allows users to choose from 20 harmonized, field-tested, and reviewed indicators that focus on behaviour change factors such as user aspirations and social norms; economic factors such as cost-effectiveness and willingness to pay; and the quality of implementation, i.e. process monitoring relating to the amount of time spent with users, user fidelity to a product, etc. (Rowe, 2013).

At the same time, many such frameworks or tools have combined planning and monitoring and evaluation uses: one example is the Technology Applicability Framework tool (Coulibaly, 2013), a participatory evaluation tool that identifies blockages likely to impact on the overall sustainability, scalability, and performance of a specific WASH technology. The framework has underscored the importance of not only counting numbers of outputs with respect to new technologies, but also assessing the 'softer' elements of technology development such as how well the technology can be accepted and inserted into local markets and supply chains, and its social and environmental implications.

A key challenge faced by the sector is the need to turn the complicated web of actors, outcomes, indicators, data collection methodologies, and frameworks for analysis into a monitoring system that is useful, affordable, reliable, and scalable.

According to Kumar and Singh (2013), a robust and effective monitoring system:

- collects information on critical indicators at scale;
- is timely;
- is cost-effective;
- ensures the quality of the data collected;
- can be undertaken periodically;
- feeds back into programme management and enables course correction.

The examples below illustrate some of the challenges and successes of programmes that have attempted to build such robust and effective monitoring systems that incorporate the range of equity, quality, and sustainability elements – each one taking a different angle.

Inclusiveness at scale in BRAC WASH. Sijbesma and Ahmed (2013) show that it is possible to include hard-to-reach groups on a large scale. The BRAC WASH programme in Bangladesh (WASH II) has recently finished its first round of annual monitoring, and findings show the positive effects of reaching out to vulnerable groups. All household data collected is disaggregated by poverty levels, and toilet usage is disaggregated by gender and age. This makes it easy to track those who are left out, and progress to date shows that the programme is fairly successful in reaching the ultra-poor, the poor, and the non-poor equally.

The first phase of the programme (WASH I) monitored inputs and outputs. It was clear that WASH II also needed *performance* monitoring, to assess how well toilets are used; how well VWCs (village WASH committees) continue to perform; to what extent women are integrated in planning and management; and so on. To this end, the programme used a qualitative information system (QIS).

Developed in the late 1990s by IRC and WSP, QIS is a quantified qualitative assessment methodology that aims to replace surveys, which are extractive and inform only central management and donors, not the users, the VWCs, or the field workers. QIS provides the possibility of using participatory monitoring at scale, combining statistical rigor for accountability with the opportunity to share knowledge for local development (Sijbesma and Ahmed, 2013). QIS:

- visualizes for all participants where they perform well and where they can improve ('climb the sanitation ladder');
- produces statistics that inform management and donors on the progress of the whole programme;
- allows a comparison of results over time and between locations.

QIS uses adapted Likert scales. Participants score on a scale from 0 to 4, where 0 is the lowest and 4 the highest score. Participants can see their level and can climb from 0 ('nothing to show') to 4 ('the ideal'). The scores can be analysed statistically.

For WASH II, a performance monitoring framework was developed with 15 indicators for households, schools, and VWCs. For each of these indicators a scale was developed, and teams consisting of one male and one female collect data by asking participants to score themselves. Collected data is entered directly into a smartphone, aiding quality assurance and the reliability of data. Where relevant, data collectors verify scores through observation; for example, the hand-washing indicator is measured by using the proxy indicator of 'presence of a hand-washing facility in or near the toilet'.

Table 6.2 The 15 headline indicators used by WASH II

VWC	1. Safe and protected drinking water source
	2. Performance of VWC
	3. Women's participation
Households	4. Safe and protected main drinking water source
	5. Drinking water management from source to cup
	6. Sanitary and hygienic household latrine
	7. Who uses the latrine
	8. When are latrines used
	9. Hand-washing provisions after defecation
	10. Sludge management when latrine pit is full
Schools	11. Sanitary and hygienic school toilets
	12. Student brigade
	13. Menstrual hygiene management
	14. Performance of school WASH committee
Rural sanitation centre (RSC)	15. Performance of RSC

After having sampled more than 8,000 households in over 100 unions,[2] experience with the QIS as a monitoring instrument has generally been positive. Initially, there were some problems, because both villagers and field staff saw a low score as very negative. Once they understood that the scales are ladders to climb over time and that low (or lower) scores are a guide to where and how to progress, participants really liked the ladders and the possibility of seeing where they were. They also appreciated the low time demands (around 40 minutes per session); the QIS was quicker than a questionnaire interview. In the future, they will also be able to compare their patterns with those in neighbouring locations, when they can access a map with geo-referenced data using Integrated Collaboration and Rapid Emergency Support Services (iCRESS) (Sijbesma and Ahmed, 2013).

Strengthening outcome monitoring in rural sanitation. Discussing the example of the nationwide Total Sanitation Campaign (TSC) in India, Kumar and Singh (2013) confirm the importance of strengthening outcome monitoring. Rooted in the failures of conventional approaches – which were based on the assumption that once infrastructure is provided, behaviour change will automatically follow – recent trends in the rural sanitation sector in India have identified sustainable behaviour change as the key outcome of a successful sanitation programme. But the focus on behaviour change in rural programmes poses specific challenges for monitoring sector progress:

- While monitoring infrastructure is a one-off activity with cross-checks over longer time periods, monitoring behaviour is a constant activity that requires frequent cross-checks over relatively shorter time spans.
- The cost of monitoring, in terms of effort, time, and money, can be significant when done at scale and at high frequency.
- Sample surveys make data available on programme outcomes, but this is often too late to make a mid-course correction.
- Quality control is also an issue when such monitoring is done at scale. Results, if they are controversial, can end up being challenged on methodological fronts.

The TSC has been plagued by a weak monitoring system, illustrated by the absence of a system to track toilet usage and sustainability, a focus on tracking inputs (e.g. money spent) and toilets constructed, and one-off assessments of community-wide ODF.

As a result, official TSC data is not always considered reliable and has been shown to misrepresent reality. For example, whereas TSC routine data on toilet construction showed that 55 per cent of households had access, independent district-level and household surveys based on household surveys of usage showed a (forecast) level of 14.6 per cent.

In order to produce more reliable figures on toilet usage and sustainability, WSP collaborated with the government of India to develop the outcome tracker – a mobile app – with a focus on critical indicators such as poverty status, household access to a toilet, sanitation behaviour of each member of the household, types of child faeces disposal, and materials for hand washing. In addition, respondents were photographed with their toilets (where available), geo-tags added, and responses compiled in real time in a management information system, all in a bid to increase accuracy and to allow for easy access to the data and comparability over time.

The pilot was initiated in two blocks (sub-districts) – Rajgir block in Nalanda district of Bihar, one of the poorest states in India, and Kandaghat block in Solan district in Himachal Pradesh, a state that has traditionally performed well in terms of economic and human development indicators. The pilot covered the entire rural population of the two blocks, which is around 23,000 households. In both blocks, experiences were mainly positive.

In mobile monitoring, generally less is more, and the total number of indicators or questions needs to be limited. The pilot in India, as in many other areas, found various advantages to using mobile phones: relatively low average unit cost per record; speed; real-time data transfer; reduced error rates due to electronic data entry; quality assurance through date or time stamps; and increased credibility through geo-tagging and photographs. Efforts to scale up and fine-tune the module, including by adding customizable questions for household and institutional sanitation, are currently ongoing. Overall, mobile monitoring has the potential to support baseline, routine, or any other data collection, as well as the ability to support large-scale surveys.

Applying market-based perspectives. Currently, numerous organizations are focusing on markets, businesses, and the private sector as key agents for bringing about positive, sustainable change to fragmented sanitation service chains throughout the world (Schaub-Jones, 2011). These approaches have varying names, from *sanitation marketing* to *sanitation as a business*, but the strategies are rather similar: they use markets and the incentives that motivate the actors that support them to implement sanitation models that are scalable and sustainable and do not require long-term support from outside aid.

One element underlying this shift is the fact that many programmes are searching to ensure post-ODF sustainability and movement up the proverbial 'sanitation ladder', on the premise that once people's demand for a certain service has been created or strengthened, in an ideal scenario the market will provide access to such services, thereby creating choice and competition and providing services or infrastructure at a price level that matches the demand and households' willingness to pay. What is more, there is a growing acknowledgement of the key role that local sanitation service providers, primarily the private sector and local businesses, can play in sustainably supporting the *entire* sanitation service chain, from household infrastructure (e.g. toilets) to sludge management (e.g. pit and septic tank emptying) to treatment.

In market-based approaches specifically, sanitation sustainability is predicated on the assumption that the market will provide the correct incentives to foster and extend relationships between consumer and provider, households and businesses, and that the sanitation benefits and impacts so sought after by the sanitation sector will be implemented and maintained naturally by a healthy market environment. This implies a new type of monitoring – one that maintains a household-level picture as far as outcomes are concerned, but also incorporates assessments at the level of business, the enabling environment, and the programme in order to paint a more holistic picture of market health.

As discussed by Sparkman, Water for People has been working since 2008 to support businesses along the sanitation chain, to help them identify viable financing opportunities, minimize subsidies, and generally strengthen their position and capacities to deliver sustainable services (Sparkman, 2013). In order to monitor this type of programme, the organization developed a monitoring strategy that focuses on three levels:

- *Level one: household – level of sanitation service access.* Based on the concept of service levels developed under the IRC-managed WASHCost project, households are scored on different indicators via surveys and observations, including their level of access to and use of a facility, the state of infrastructure, sludge management, user satisfaction, and ease of maintenance.
- *Level two: business or service provider and/or finance institution.* For each business, the following information is collected annually: number of pits emptied; income from emptying pits, septic tanks, or drums; number of low-income areas reached; staff utilization; transport costs for sludge; dumping costs; wages paid; latrines constructed; value of latrines; and investment made in the business. The following information is collected monthly: number of latrines; number and size of loans taken out; number of orders for latrines; and amount of loan paid back by customers.
- *Level three: enabling environment – the bigger picture.* This evaluates components of the overall sanitation market 'ecosystem' and how well different market functions are being carried out and sustained. For each of the actors carrying out certain roles, sustainability is assessed by looking at motivation, incentives, and capacity.

Monitoring the sanitation market ecosystem is complex. Some key lessons from Water for People's work include the following:

- It is nearly impossible to analyse the sanitation ecosystem objectively, and so any scores or assessments will always have some level of subjectivity. The important aspect is the participatory *process* of monitoring the ecosystem itself, and taking the time to reflect on what elements are key to sustaining sanitation, who is responsible for them, and how well they are currently being implemented.

- Household monitoring still provides the key outcome to track; that is, access to and usage of sanitation services across the entire chain. However, unless they understand the bigger picture – including businesses, service providers, government, finance, etc. – aid organizations will not be able to gain a true sense of how sustainable their interventions are, and how likely it is that they will be able to exit the process at some point. In other words, without understanding the service providers themselves, their incentives, satisfaction, capacity, and viability in the sanitation sector, it will be difficult to tell how likely it is that they will continue offering services.

By Sparkman's admission, this is work in progress and is more a proposed *strategy* for monitoring rather than a final product. Sustaining this kind of monitoring would require direct involvement of government, a manageable number of indicators, and, particularly, clarity on who would pay the long-term bill. Eventually, though, this kind of monitoring and iterative reflection has huge potential to contribute to sustainable service delivery models, and the sought-after exit of external aid organizations.

Conclusion

Sanitation and hygiene are messy and complicated fields that are difficult to monitor, as is illustrated by the broad range of monitoring methodologies, angles, indicators, and approaches highlighted in this chapter. However, despite the complexities, a number of recurring common themes and findings can be identified.

For one, it is clear that large data gaps still exist on effectiveness, practices, behaviour, inclusion, needs, costs, and cost-effectiveness. Besides this lack of data, there is also a lack of comparability: governments, agencies, donors, NGOs, and service providers use different methodologies, definitions, indicators, and data sources. This makes it difficult to harmonize and systematize monitoring at a national scale or to use data to improve sanitation and hygiene.

At the same time, too much data is collected that goes unanalysed and unused (Norman and Franceys, 2013). This may be because data is collected only for donor-reporting purposes without establishing proper mechanisms to feed lessons and information back into the planning and programming cycle of (local) government. However, it is also because data is collected by different sectors, programmes, and ministries and the various stakeholders are either not aware of or not clear about how this data could be used for their programmes. For example, programmes do not often think to include or compare their data to the data of national-level surveys such as the MICS and the DHS.

Secondly, there is broad agreement that government needs to be in the driving seat – both in terms of ensuring that there is the right environment for programmes and services to be delivered at scale, and in terms of continuous monitoring, data collection, and analysis. This is particularly apparent at the local level, where local government institutions have to play a lead role in providing the environment for successful programme implementation and service delivery, planning, oversight and monitoring, quality assurance, and follow-up.

Thirdly, in order to ensure sustainability and continued service delivery, better systems need to be developed to allow continuous monitoring, follow-up, and regular revisiting of previously collected data in the long term. This is evident in the challenge to ensure post-ODF sustainability of behaviour change and to support the move towards improved sanitation. But it is also a key element in the service delivery discourse. The enabling environment under which services have to be delivered is highly changeable and requires continuous monitoring in order to ensure viable and sustainable service delivery, by the public sector or by the private sector.

Fourthly, behaviour is now considered key, as is the requirement to measure behavioural outcomes rather than programme outputs. At the most basic level, this means a move from assessing whether a household has a toilet to assessing whether all people in the household use this toilet, at all times and unimpeded. At a broader level, this may include assessing behaviours of service providers and consumer sentiment towards new technologies and services.

Fifthly, there is an increased understanding that no development goal of universal coverage will ever be met if inequity and the exclusion of vulnerable groups are not addressed. More programmes now attempt to collect disaggregated data, responding to the huge need for better identification of the poorest and most marginalized groups and for transparent targeting of investments. The post-2015 sanitation and hygiene goals developed under the auspices of JMP include targets and indicators to systematically measure any progressive reduction in inequalities over time (JMP, 2012). Overall, though, a systematic application of an equity lens to service delivery, programme implementation, and monitoring is a long way off.

In summary, good monitoring systems, methodologies, or processes in sanitation and hygiene:

- focus on outcomes, in addition to inputs and outputs;
- are ideally government-owned, if not government-led;
- are harmonized across projects;
- provide data that is actively used rather than simply collected, for example by providing real-time access to data;
- reach across sector borders, for example by showing cross-linkages between sanitation and nutrition, or hand washing and education;
- are inclusive by design – asking the right questions and measuring the right targets;
- combine methodologies to improve the reliability and quality of findings, for example by using both proxy indicators and direct observation;
- facilitate dialogue and reflection – often the process is as important as the outcome.

Endnotes

1. The authors would like to acknowledge valuable inputs and comments on this and previous versions of this paper from David Sparkman, Archana Patkar, Marielle Snel, and Joseph Pearce, and have gratefully built on the papers and presentations prepared by a range of sector partners, all included in the References at the end of this chapter.
2. Unions are the smallest rural administrative and local government units in Bangladesh.

References

Coulibaly, Y.C. (2013) 'Using the Technology Applicability Framework (TAF) tool for urine dry diverting toilet (UDDT): technology evaluation and recommendations for sustainability in Burkina Faso', paper presented at the IRC Symposium 2013: Monitoring WASH Services Delivery, Addis Ababa, Ethiopia, 9–11 April.

Danert, K. (2014) 'Messy, varied and growing: country-led monitoring of rural water supplies', in T. Schouten and S. Smits (eds), *From Infrastructure to Services: Trends in Monitoring Sustainable Water, Sanitation and Hygiene Services*, pp. 39–62, Rugby: Practical Action Publishing.

Hernandez, O., Devine, J., Karver, J., Chase, C. and Coombes, Y. (2012) *Measuring the Behavioral Determinants of Handwashing with Soap*, Washington DC: Water and Sanitation Program of the World Bank.

JMP (2012) *Proposal for Consolidated Drinking Water, Sanitation and Hygiene Targets, Indicators and Definitions*, Geneva: Joint Monitoring Programme (JMP) of the World Health Organization (WHO) and UNICEF.

JMP Working Group on Equity and Non-Discrimination (2012) *JMP Working Group on Equity and Non-Discrimination Final Report*, Geneva and New York NY: World Health Organization and UNICEF Joint Monitoring Programme (JMP) for Water Supply and Sanitation.

Kapatuka, D. (2013) 'Natural leaders energising change in villages to attain and sustain open defecation free status: a case study of Plan Malawi impact areas – Mulanje and Lilongwe districts (traditional authorities Juma and Njewa)', paper presented at the IRC Symposium 2013: Monitoring WASH Services Delivery, Addis Ababa, Ethiopia, 9–11 April.

Kennedy, M. and Meek, A. (2013) 'Extension agent reorganization into a "block" system for CLTS: implementation and monitoring in Salima and Zomba Districts, Malawi', paper presented at the IRC Symposium 2013: Monitoring WASH Services Delivery, Addis Ababa, Ethiopia, 9–11 April.

Kumar, A. and Singh, U. (2013) 'You manage what you measure: using a mobile to web MIS to strengthen outcome monitoring in rural sanitation', paper presented at the IRC Symposium 2013: Monitoring WASH Services Delivery, Addis Ababa, Ethiopia, 9–11 April.

McIntyre, P., Casella, D., Fonseca, C. and Burr, P. (2014) *Priceless! Uncovering the Real Costs of Water and Sanitation*, The Hague: IRC.

Nansi, J.H. (2013) 'Results from the hygiene cost effectiveness study in Burkina Faso', PowerPoint presentation at the IRC Symposium 2013: Monitoring WASH Services Delivery, Addis Ababa, Ethiopia, 9–11 April.

Negussie, A. (2013) 'Monitoring CLTS across Africa: experiences from Plan's Pan-Africa programme strategy', PowerPoint presentation at the IRC Symposium 2013: Monitoring WASH Services Delivery, Addis Ababa, Ethiopia, 9–11 April.

Norman, R. and Franceys, R. (2013) 'Monitoring: fit for purpose?', PowerPoint presentation at the IRC Symposium 2013: Monitoring WASH Services Delivery, Addis Ababa, Ethiopia, 9–11 April.

Patkar, A. and Gosling, L. (2011) *Equity and Inclusion in Sanitation and Hygiene in Africa: A Regional Synthesis Paper*, Geneva and London: Water Supply and Sanitation Collaborative Council and WaterAid.

Peal, E. and van der Voorden, C. (2010) *Hygiene and Sanitation Software: An Overview of Approaches*, Geneva: Water Supply and Sanitation Collaborative Council.

Perez, E. (2013) 'Monitoring policy and sector national reform to accelerate and sustain access to improved sanitation', PowerPoint presentation at the IRC Symposium 2013: Monitoring WASH Services Delivery, Addis Ababa, Ethiopia, 9–11 April.

Potter, A., Klutse, A., Snehalatha, M., Batchelor, C., Uandela, A., Naafs, A., Fonseca, C. and Moriarty, P. (2011) *Assessing Sanitation Service Levels*, WASHCost Global Working Paper 3, 2nd edition, The Hague: IRC.

Potter, A., Zita, J., Naafs, A. and Uandela, A. (2013) 'Costs and effectiveness of hygiene promotion within an integrated WASH capacity building project in Mozambique', PowerPoint presentation at the IRC Symposium 2013: Monitoring WASH Services Delivery, Addis Ababa, Ethiopia, 9–11 April.

Rosensweig, F., Perez, E. and Robinson, A. (2012) *Policy and Sector Reform to Accelerate Access to Improved Rural Sanitation*, Washington DC: Water and Sanitation Program of the World Bank.

Rowe, R. (2013) 'WHO and UNICEF toolkit for monitoring and evaluating household water treatment and safe storage', PowerPoint presentation at the IRC Symposium 2013: Monitoring WASH Services Delivery, Addis Ababa, Ethiopia, 9–11 April.

Schaub-Jones, D. (2011) 'Market-based approaches to water and sanitation: the role of entrepreneurship', *Waterlines* 30 (1): 5–20.

Sijbesma, C. and Ahmed, M. (2013) 'Participatory performance monitoring of sanitation and hygiene services at scale in Bangladesh', paper presented at the IRC Symposium 2013: Monitoring WASH Services Delivery, Addis Ababa, Ethiopia, 9–11 April.

Sparkman, D. (2012) 'More than just counting toilets: the complexities of monitoring for sustainability in sanitation', *Waterlines* 31 (4): 260–71.

— (2013) 'From beneficiaries to businesses to the big picture: monitoring for sustainability in market-based approaches to sanitation', paper presented at the IRC Symposium 2013: Monitoring WASH Services Delivery, Addis Ababa, Ethiopia, 9–11 April.

Thomas, A. and Bevan, J. (2013) 'Developing and monitoring protocol for the elimination of open defecation in sub-Saharan Africa', PowerPoint presentation at the IRC Symposium 2013: Monitoring WASH Services Delivery, Addis Ababa, Ethiopia, 9–11 April.

Verhagen, J. and Carrasco, M. (2013) *Full-chain Sanitation Services that Last: Non-sewered Sanitation Services*, The Hague: IRC.

Vujcic, J. (2013) 'Monitoring handwashing behavior', PowerPoint presentation at the IRC Symposium 2013: Monitoring WASH Services Delivery, Addis Ababa, Ethiopia, 9–11 April.

About the authors

Carolien van der Voorden is Senior Programme Officer at the Water Supply and Sanitation Collaborative Council (WSSCC) and is in charge of WSSCC's work on behavioural change. Carolien van der Voorden serves as the focal point for the development of national-level strategic plans for WSSCC priority countries.

Ingeborg Krukkert is Programme Officer at IRC and sanitation and hygiene expert with a special focus on the South Asian region. Ingeborg Krukkert leads IRC's collaborative WASH initiatives with BRAC in Bangladesh.

CHAPTER 7

Small steps towards building national–regional–global coherence in monitoring WASH

Piers Cross

The global system of water, sanitation, and hygiene (WASH) monitoring lacks coherence. There are large numbers of monitoring initiatives, yet there are major gaps in data collection, analysis, and reporting. Despite the enormity of the challenge, there is reason for optimism. Some countries have taken the initiative to promote a convergence of user and provider data. Regional monitoring instruments are under development in Africa and South Asia reporting on regional political commitments; they should seek consistency with national and global systems. Global instruments such as the Joint Monitoring Programme and UN-Water Global Analysis and Assessment of Sanitation and Drinking-Water (GLAAS) have made significant advances and are well positioned to adapt to the post-millennium development goal environment; they should align with global accountability frameworks, such as the political accountability being built into Sanitation and Water for All (SWA).

Keywords: Joint Monitoring Programme (JMP), Global Assessment and Analysis of Sanitation and Drinking-Water (GLAAS), sector review, provider data, fit for purpose

Introduction

The water, sanitation, and hygiene (WASH) sector is experiencing strong demand for better data and good analysis. This desire is fuelled by: a focus on measurable results from aid; the competition for resources (requiring detailed evidence of inputs, outputs, outcomes, and impacts); the increasing complexity of WASH issues; the multiplicity of and growth in sector agencies; growing links with other sectors (such as climate change, human right, water resource management, and health); a desire to achieve better value for money from WASH investments; and better information and communication technology (ICT), which provides easier data collection and new opportunities to use data. This chapter will provide an overview of the state of global, regional, and country sector monitoring. It will explore key challenges, presenting main advances, lessons learned, and key innovations. Against a backdrop of haphazard monitoring initiatives, the storyline of this chapter focuses on the small steps made and new ideas emerging to improve the coherence and overall architecture of WASH monitoring.

The global monitoring landscape

The number of monitoring initiatives has grown significantly in recent years and many of the established ones are evolving. The landscape is both crowded and fragmented. Duplication occurs both horizontally (across inputs, processes, outputs, and outcomes) and vertically (local, national, regional, and global). The demand for sector information has increased (frequently driven by donor needs) and, when a gap is perceived, new and often parallel systems are added. Coordination is weak, so parallel systems go unchallenged. Looking towards the future, the WASH monitoring landscape is going to get even more complex with new issues, new data monitoring initiatives, and new collection methods that will generate large volumes of data.

Key monitoring initiatives at the global level include the UNICEF/World Health Organization (WHO) Joint Monitoring Programme (JMP), which measures outputs, and the UN-Water Global Analysis and Assessment of Sanitation and Drinking-Water (GLAAS), which measures inputs. These are discussed in more detail below. Another important global database that collects data from water utilities, but is not fully integrated into the global monitoring framework, is the International Benchmarking Network for Water and Sanitation (IBNET) managed by the World Bank.

At a regional level, regional sanitation meetings (AfricaSan for Africa, LatinoSan for Latin America, EASAN for East Asia, and the South Asian Conference on Sanitation (SACOSAN)), which were initiated with the first AfricaSan meeting in 2002, are evolving in different ways and at different paces into regional advocacy and monitoring processes to track the implementation of action plans and commitments (such as the eThekwini commitments[1]). Regional political bodies such as the African Union (AU), the African Ministers' Council on Water (AMCOW) and, in South Asia, the South Asian Association for Regional Cooperation (SAARC) have also initiated regional monitoring activities in the water and sanitation sector.

Most countries undertake national monitoring, but its effectiveness varies considerably. A key problem in national sector data is that service provider data often differs from user data (from household surveys). This hinders the understanding of the state of the sector and, as a result, the design of effective policies and interventions. A number of agencies have developed analytical tools for the WASH sector but generic approaches have not been agreed.

Cross and Brocklehurst (2013) argue that the current landscape has evolved as a result of a lack of alignment of global and national monitoring. Much of the emphasis has been on creating regional and global products, rather than on supporting national-level monitoring as the bedrock on which to build national processes, and providing results upwards to global monitoring platforms. A further weakness is that, even when the data generated for global reports includes information of relevance at national level, this is seldom fed back into country-level planning. Lack of feedback loops is a generic problem that limits incentives to provide quality information at all levels.

The challenge is to provide a supportive framework that ensures that this information is consistent, relevant, and reliable and that it leads to action. The poor response to global and regional monitoring from national level is because there is little incentive to share information. The case for why global monitoring is necessary is not clearly made nor appreciated at national levels (and frequently sub-national to national levels). Overburdened monitoring officers often receive extensive requests from a myriad of agencies for data at national level. No resources are made available to support the costs of extracting the required information.

Similarly, the incentives to share information between agencies are slim. Global and national agencies are discouraged from sharing information, since they often compete for resources by demonstrating their exclusive access to information. The global information system is unregulated, and there is little attempt to assess what is a reasonable burden for national agencies to bear in providing data for regional and global monitoring systems. What are their obligations? What can they expect in return? What might this additional data collection reasonably cost and who should pay?

Advances in communications and information management technology introduce a new era of possibilities for sector monitoring. Water point mapping using geographic information systems (GIS), database set-up and management, mobile-to-web data transfers, and new modes of information dissemination have all transformed concepts of what is now possible, compared with the early days of sector monitoring.

The amount of WASH data collected and the number of reports written in the WASH sector have increased exponentially. Luyendijk and Bostoen (2013) show the increase in the number of indicators and the frequency of JMP reports in recent decades. Rachel Norman's research (Norman and Franceys, 2013) identified 45 study types generating WASH data sets. We are awash with WASH data, but use little of it.

A problem also exists in that the timing of data collection is not coordinated; for instance, household surveys that provide data for the JMP are carried out every three to five years, while the JMP is issued every two years. Sector analytical tools, such as the Country Status Overviews (CSOs) and the WASH Bottleneck Analysis Tool (BAT), are not carried out consistently and are not linked to the biennial GLAAS report, for which such analysis is very useful (and there is no future commitment to continue CSOs). Moreover, there are few benchmarks as to what monitoring should cost and what would be optimal to spend on monitoring.

Country-level issues and trends

Are existing country WASH monitoring systems fit for purpose?

Rachel Norman (Norman and Franceys, 2013) describes the enormity of the task of bringing order to country WASH monitoring. Norman's research in Uganda and Kenya – countries generally regarded as having better than average monitoring systems – shows the large number of sector databases available. Only 8 per cent of 293 sector data records identified for Uganda are used in analysis. Only 9 per cent of 166 sector data records in Kenya have any cost information. Not only is there a large number of databases, but the volume of entries is also increasing. Norman's research shows that less than half the data gathered has a clear purpose, very little data is gathered on water and sanitation system functionality, and little data refers to costs. While there is an increasing number of indicators being reported against, there is an indication that only a small proportion of the data being collected is being analysed or reported. While there are attempts to reduce the numbers of key indicators used in joint sector reviews, in both Uganda (which has 10 'golden' indicators) and Kenya (which has nine), some of these super-indicators are ratios or composite indicators and are made up of more than one type of data point. Norman shows that there is a plethora of international and national agencies collecting sector data, but it is unclear the extent to which these various forms of data are captured in national records. Combining the data extracted from the documents and data records, Norman shows that in Kenya 60 per cent of 1,404 indicators were reported against once (i.e. were unique, showing a very wide spread of indicators in Kenya), and in Uganda 18 per cent of the 5,644 indicators were reported against once (which shows a substantially improved focus). Figure 7.1 shows the increase in data collected and reported in these two countries over time.

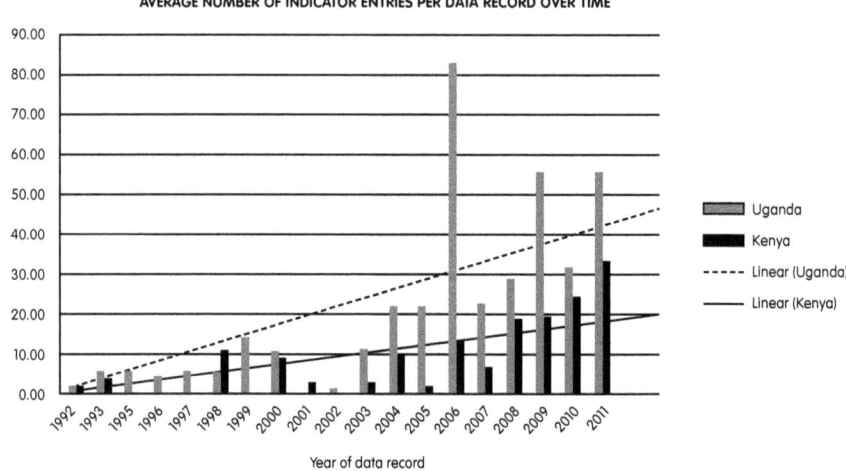

Figure 7.1 Average number of indicators identified across all data sources in Uganda and Kenya

Source: Norman and Franceys, 2013: 6.

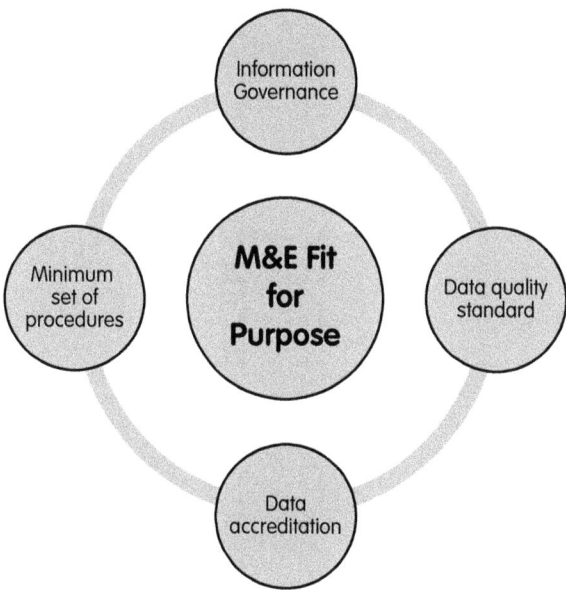

Figure 7.2 Key factors influencing monitoring systems
Source: Norman and Franceys, 2013: 19.

Norman goes on to argue that the country monitoring systems she studied were not necessarily fit for purpose. The sector will be able to improve its performance only if it has a much more credible monitoring system with verifiable results. As illustrated in Figure 7.2, key factors that need to be considered to make monitoring systems fit for purpose are: information governance (clear roles and responsibilities), data quality standards, data accreditation, and an established minimum set of monitoring procedures (so the focus is on essentials for decision making rather than what is nice to know).

Examples of coherence and convergence in national-level monitoring

Many developing countries are faced with apparently contradictory data on levels of access to water and sanitation. These can often be explained by different data sources or different definitions. Household surveys measuring actual usage often give higher coverage figures (because they do not take into account walking distance and other qualifiers attached to national definitions of service access). The JMP also reflects linear regression (a trend line) from recent surveys and not the results from a specific survey. On the other hand, data from service providers (measuring water points or taps) often relies on service coverage assumptions (e.g. 250 persons per borehole) or does not take into account facilities that are dysfunctional.

Multi-stakeholder dialogue and national leadership can help bring more convergence to national-level data. Several countries have taken this

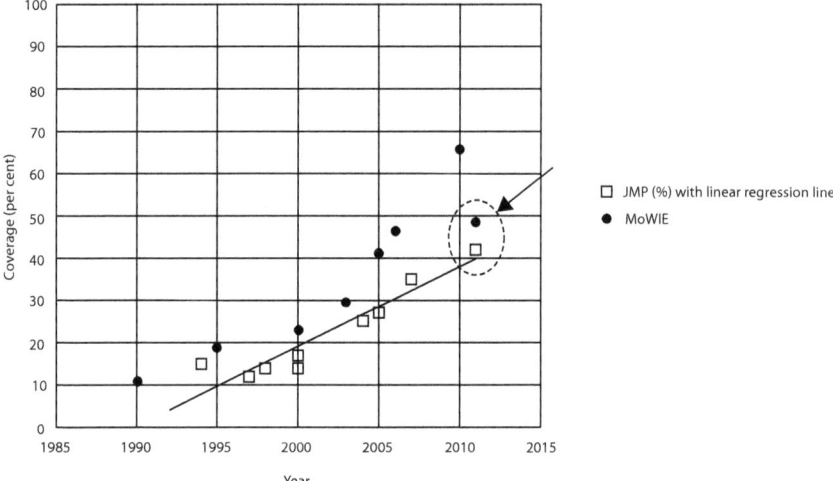

Figure 7.3 Convergence in Ethiopia's rural water coverage figures
Source: Butterworth, 2013: 4.

initiative, Ethiopia being among the most impressive (Butterworth, 2013). Two key national data sets – Ministry of Water, Irrigation and Energy (MoWIE) provider data and JMP data, based on a trend analysis of household surveys undertaken by the Central Statistical Agency – showed rural water coverage figures that differed by up to 30 per cent in 2010. From 2012, Ethiopia's lead agency undertook a national WASH inventory (NWI) that collected provider and user data and applied service standard norms (such as what in Ethiopia is regarded as an acceptable distance to walk to collect water). A concerted national dialogue between stakeholders in Ethiopia resulted in improvements in household survey data and, as a result, the latest JMP recorded a higher figure (39 per cent for 2011) while the NWI led to a downward revision of MoWIE results (to 49 per cent), leaving just a 10 per cent access figure difference (see Figure 7.3). The closer convergence of these figures and a better understanding of what each figure is measuring have given policy makers and Ethiopia's leadership clarity on the scale of the challenge the country faces to achieve the national target of universal access.

A key dialogue in building national convergence in monitoring data is the one between the lead sector agencies and national statistical organizations. Agreement between national provider and user data will automatically reflect a closer coherence between global, regional, and country data.

Deepening country WASH analyses

Many countries have undertaken sector assessments and a number of global agencies have developed methodologies and deepened approaches to country sector analyses. These include CSOs as used in Africa (and their derivatives in Asia and Latin America) introduced by the Water and Sanitation Program (WSP) of the World Bank and the WASH BAT developed by UNICEF. National sector analyses can: pinpoint bottlenecks or areas of weaker performance; identify strategic areas where focus is needed to resolve problems; track progress against agreed strategies and plans; and mobilize partner support for key areas. Their impact is sector-wide and not only focused on analysis of a specific project. Quality sector reviews give decision makers insights into whether policies are working and sector reforms are on course, what is needed to sustain services, and what is the financing gap. Sector analyses can feed into sector reviews, such as joint sector review meetings, and regularly take stock of sector progress or assist in budget submissions.

CSOs, SDAs and MAPAS. CSOs benchmark service delivery pathways and identify issues that might be inhibiting progress. Applied to each sub-sector of a country, they score progress in three areas: enabling service delivery; developing services; and sustaining services (AMCOW, 2011). The methodology has evolved since WSP Africa first applied CSOs in 2006, and, in collaboration with AMCOW and other partners, plans are in place to have CSOs completed in all 54 countries in Africa by 2016. The methodology has also been extended by WSP to Latin America (where it is called Monitoreo de los Avances del País en Agua Potable y Saneamiento (MAPAS) or Monitoring of Country Progress in Drinking Water and Sanitation), and South Asia and South East Asia (as sector development analyses or SDAs).

Dominick De Waal (2013) shows how CSOs have evolved in response to these different regional priorities. In Latin America, the infrastructure built in the 1970s and 1980s is reaching the end of its lifespan, so sector investment requirements for replacement of capital stock are more than 50 per cent of the total requirements in all countries. A key issue emerging from MAPAS is that countries have no reserve mechanisms in place, putting at risk the progress in coverage achieved during the past two decades. The costing model has been adapted to show the relative effects of new service development versus replacement of existing capital stock. The concept of the 'medium-term scenario' has been introduced; this compares the current situation with a second scorecard showing the expected results, recognizing existing efforts to improve sector performance.

Many countries in South East Asia are experiencing a major shift in rural water service delivery levels: from point source wells to piped network systems. SDAs in South East Asia have been adapted to focus on decision options in this transition. There has been considerable focus in SDAs in the region on the core challenge of addressing open defecation, and indicators have been added to address equity, city-wide faecal sludge management, and key water resource issues.

WASH BATs. Multiple constraints in the WASH sector make it difficult to assess the causes of problems. WASH BATs (Hutton et al., 2013) have been developed by UNICEF as a facilitated process and software application, to identify not only priority problems but also how to solve them. WASH BATs are arguably quicker and easier to use than CSOs. CSOs are developed over several months, commonly use external agents for verification, and incorporate a multi-stakeholder analysis, all measures that arguably lead to a more accurate and comprehensive sector analysis.

Like CSOs, WASH BATs provide a rational, evidence-based approach for formulating a financing strategy and understanding impacts of choices. But they can also track progress in bottleneck removal over time. WASH BATs have developed a modular approach, so lead agencies can select modules in which they want to apply a WASH BAT. There is a module for each of the following sub-sectors: national, sub-national, service provider, community, or household; and/or urban water, rural water, urban sanitation, or rural sanitation.

In each sub-sector, WASH BATs score the enabling factors, identify bottlenecks (their causes and activities to remove them), evaluate costs and the costs of solutions, prioritize activities, and assess the impact on sector coverage. WASH BATs do not benchmark service performance and do not estimate the funding gap to reach targets. Having gone through pilot implementation, based on country demand and UNICEF and partner capacity, WASH BATs are now poised for an extensive roll-out as a flexible instrument that national agencies can use to analyse and indicate solutions to sector problems.

Sustainability analysis. A third country-level analytical tool focuses specifically on the sustainability of rural water services (Harvey, 2013). Sustainability of rural water systems is a key challenge and this tool, developed with UNICEF support, sets out to provide a tool for government-sector agencies to identify sustainability issues and provide the basis for rural water service sustainability improvement plans. The tool is flexible and can be reviewed and adapted to the local context.

The tool analyses and scores many sustainability factors, including: policy-level factors (programmatic approach, service delivery approach); management (community management, local government management, private sector management options); finance (sustainable financing, realistic cost recovery); community (operation and maintenance, equity); technology choices (whether the desired service levels are provided); and supply chains (procurement, integration). The approach is based on a user-friendly, issue-specific tool rather than a sector-wide tool.

Alignment of different country analytic tools. These different tools raise two alignment questions:

- Do we need all these different approaches, or could we standardized them in one tool?
- Should a clear connection be made with GLAAS country monitoring?

On the first question, agencies' vested interests in developing these analytic tools discourage collaboration. On the other hand, competition between agencies is a stimulus to improve analytic tools. Each of the tools discussed above has different merits. The choice of tool matters less than the fact that countries are seeking to deepen their own analysis of the state of the sector and solve problems. All tools increase national capacity to manage large-scale programmes seeking to achieve sustainable service delivery.

On the second question, full harmonization between in-depth national analyses and gathering country-level GLAAS information is probably not realistic, but there is scope for improvement:

- WSP, UNICEF, and other agencies supporting country-level capacity development should increase their collaboration and should advise countries on the applicability of different analytical options and not duplicate country applications. Through better collaboration, a larger number of countries could benefit by having stronger country sector analysis.
- These agencies should increase collaboration between themselves and with GLAAS to standardize parameters so that the data is consistent between the different approaches.
- All countries should be encouraged to apply at least one of the available tools to deepen their understanding of the national state of the sector every two to three years and to gain more insight into the factors shaping or limiting progress.
- GLAAS could focus its limited country support in countries where no recent country-level sector analysis has been undertaken.

Regional issues and trends

Aligning regional monitoring

Some regions are developing monitoring systems to track progress against regional political commitments.

In **Africa**, Vodounhessi and Mbaziira (2013) describe progress in the development of a pan-African AMCOW-led monitoring process to report on progress against the Sharm el-Sheikh commitments in the water sector made by African heads of state. An ambitious monitoring system has been planned, addressing seven areas of commitment to water development on the continent. The system plans to aggregate national government and regional water data. The AU issued its first continental African water report in 2012 summarizing this monitoring information. The data in the first report is limited and reflects only a 41 per cent response rate, but plans are in place to develop a monitoring process as a source of evidence for sector advocacy. The AU is conscious of alignment issues and has created a strong multi-stakeholder task force to support development of this regional monitoring system.

South Asian countries attending SACOSAN committed in 2006 that an inter-country working group would be responsible for harmonized monitoring of country progress towards agreed targets in sanitation and hygiene. SACOSAN monitoring has focused on access, but also functionality, equity, health, education, and financial allocations. In April 2012, health ministers in the SAARC agreed that a common monitoring framework should include access to safe sanitation and drinking water.

Archana Patkar (2013) in her work on regional sanitation and hygiene monitoring, presenting snapshots of the eight countries in the sub-region, points to the huge variability in issues and capacity across the region. Afghanistan, for example, has less focus on sanitation and hygiene and faces a tremendous challenge with respect to capacity and monitoring. Bhutan has ambitious targets of universal access. India, with a population of over 1.2 billion people, is making massive sector investments and has a distinctly different set of sector challenges from other countries in the region. By contrast, the Maldives, with a population of 200,000, faces the acute environmental challenges of a small island. Patkar argues that while South Asian regional data and targets are broadly aligned with global and national figures (there is a common SACOSAN focus on universality of access, reduction in disparities, participation, and social audits), countries have distinct challenges and the programme and monitoring focus will continue to differ between the countries of the region.

Divergent contexts, divergent theories of change

Complementing this, De Waal (2013) links the evolution of country and regional sector analyses to their contexts, arguing that divergent methods reflect both different regional contexts and different theories of change. De Waal argues that each region has a core sector problem on which decision makers focus and which should also be the core for analysis. He depicts the theory of change at the core of regions as follows:

- *Africa*. Accelerating improved access requires donors to work with and through country systems (budget support, public sector financial management, decentralized delivery).
- *East Asia*. Better health and faster economic growth require piped water supply.
- *Latin America*. Reaching sustainable universal access is threatened by water resource constraints and climate change.
- *South Asia*. Better health is contingent on 100 per cent of faecal sludge produced being collected, transported, and treated.

This implies that not all regions, nor necessarily all countries within regions, are interested in analysing or monitoring the same range of issues, and that much of the data on institutional processes is not really suited to global aggregation.

Global monitoring

Aligning global monitoring

The UNICEF/WHO JMP has been the sector's path-breaking global monitoring initiative. Launched in 1990 to measure sector performance, following the International Drinking Water Supply and Sanitation Decade, it has become the UN-mandated tool for measuring progress towards the water and sanitation millennium development goals (MDGs). The JMP, now based on data from nationally representative household surveys, measures WASH access, i.e. sector outputs. Rolf Luyendijk and Didier Allély-Fermé (2013) and Rolf Luyendijk and Kristof Bostoen (2013) reflect on what has been learned and what remains to be done to strengthen the global architecture of global WASH monitoring.

The JMP has evolved into an impressive global monitoring instrument. The decision to rely on household surveys undertaken by national statistics organizations has meant that JMP data reflects household views and derives its data from nationally accredited sources. Piggy-backing off these surveys makes the JMP highly cost-effective. The JMP's strengths are: its accuracy and quality controls; the fact that its data is independently verifiable; that it analyses country data; the transparency of its analysis; its focus on a limited set of data points on service access data; and its clear primary audience of country sector leaders and agencies interested in MDG achievement.

In recent years, the JMP has significantly improved its communications and ability to mine its data. The JMP now can provide thematic analysis, regional analyses, and in-depth country analysis for different WASH sub-sectors. Increasingly there is a focus on using JMP analyses as a trigger to regional and national action. The JMP has improved the frequency and user-friendliness of its reporting and gives a clearer explanation of why its data and trend analysis are likely to differ from national provider data and what can be done to improve convergence of these data points. Use of household surveys for monitoring access might enable measurement against locally defined human right issues. Water quality remains a key output item not yet captured in global monitoring.

UN-Water Global Analysis and Assessment of Sanitation and Drinking-Water

An important new entrant to the WASH monitoring scene has been GLAAS, implemented by WHO, which issued its first full report in 2010 (Swann, 2013). A further GLAAS report was issued in 2012 (WHO, 2012) and the 2014 report is in preparation. As opposed to the JMP, GLAAS measures 'inputs' to sector performance, including governance, implementation and institutional arrangements, monitoring, human resources, and finance. GLAAS's origins lie in the UNDP *Human Development Report* (2006), which analysed the political and policy weaknesses in the sector and led to the British government's proposal to streamline global support to the water sector through 'five ones' (one global report to monitor progress; one high-level global meeting to decide on action; each country to have one national water and sanitation plan; one water and sanitation coordination group; and one lead UN body for water and sanitation at the national level).

So GLAAS (measuring inputs) and the JMP (measuring outputs) have become the critical components of the WASH global monitoring framework. GLAAS's vision is to produce a regular global report summarizing trends in the key factors that determine sector performance, enabling comparison between countries and catalysing in-country monitoring. GLAAS is designed as a key source of information for the biennial Sanitation and Water for All (SWA) high-level meeting (HLM).

In contrast to the JMP, which uses the data from household surveys, GLAAS relies on data that needs to be collected and collated at country level by sector agencies. The response rate to the early GLAAS reports has been low and the quality of some of the data questionable and difficult to verify. But the number of countries engaging with GLAAS is growing and the data collection process for GLAAS 2014 is making a conscious effort to learn from earlier reports. GLAAS measures some critical drivers for success in the sector that are not captured elsewhere, including finance and human resources.

Approaches to future global monitoring

Looking to the future, the JMP and GLAAS are developing a focus and complementarity that have the makings of a far more structured and strategic global monitoring framework. If WHO and UNICEF, running GLAAS and the JMP, can retain focus on a small set of comparable data points over time and across countries, they appear well positioned to adapt to post-2015 monitoring in support of global targets. These targets appear likely to address universal access, improved school and health coverage, elimination of open defecation, improved faecal sludge management, and reduced inequities in service access. A key challenge will be the selection of a few key useful indicators in these areas.

A fundamental sharpening in global monitoring design would include the formalization of a clear accountability framework and global monitoring that would enable global decision making. The strength of country and sub-national (service provider or local government) monitoring is that the accountable authorities are responsible for monitoring and reporting on sector progress. Global agencies leading sector monitoring have no similar accountability. The emergence of SWA and regular HLMs as a forum for global commitments and to provide a framework for global stewardship of the sector offers the beginning of a global accountability framework. To realize this framework, the SWA partnership needs to further broaden its membership, and, where possible, high-level commitments and monitoring of these commitments should be aligned with the sector's main global monitoring instruments.

Global agencies should redouble their efforts to facilitate dialogue at regional and national levels in order to improve understanding of what different instruments measure and to encourage convergence of data points. These processes should seek to triangulate household survey data, service provider data, and 'third source' data, including citizen reporting, social audits, and regulator and consumer data.

The focus on improving the WASH evidence base has led to the growth of global research studies. Generous research grants have deepened global understanding of many WASH topics, including health impact, climate change, lifecycle costs, sustainability, community-led total sanitation, sanitation marketing, hygiene behaviour change, and many other topics. The essential findings of these studies need to be given more prominence in global learning exchanges and greater effort is needed to make this knowledge available in a form in which it can be understood and used by local decision makers.

Trade-offs in global monitoring architecture

De Waal (2013) points to several trade-offs that need to be made in moving to a more effective global monitoring system. Firstly, he makes a distinction between '**light political tracking versus in-depth analytical**'. More sophisticated methodologies are increasing the complexity of monitoring. The global monitoring system might be reformed by applying in-depth analytical tools only in specific contexts led by country demand. On the other hand, global monitoring should be simplified so that it has a 'light touch', collecting comparable data in a few easily monitored areas, preferably 'harvested' from country-led processes.

A second and related distinction is between '**global consistency versus country relevance**'. A useful distinction to make is that global and regional data should remain comparable across countries and regions and through time to indicate trends. On the other hand, country monitoring should focus on the critical concerns and issues in that context. So, for example, monitoring donor coordination is not relevant in a country where there are no donors. This distinction implies that country analysis need not be standardized across countries, whereas global monitoring needs strict standardization. Global consistency is irrelevant if the data items are of no interest to countries.

A third trade-off is that between '**participatory processes versus audits**'. Participatory approaches such as CSOs can leverage a variety of perspectives and create more country interest. On the other hand, where governments have shown limited willingness to work with development partners, country analytical tools may have a lesser catalytic effect. In these situations, harder tools such as audits may have more impact.

Finally, there is a distinction between **micro (fast) learning versus macro (slow) learning**. The learning process from global tools such as the JMP takes several years, allowing course corrections only every few years. On the other hand, country analytic learning can have an immediate impact, can strengthen country processes, and can be timed, for example to influence specific budget and other policy decisions.

150 FROM INFRASTRUCTURE TO SERVICES

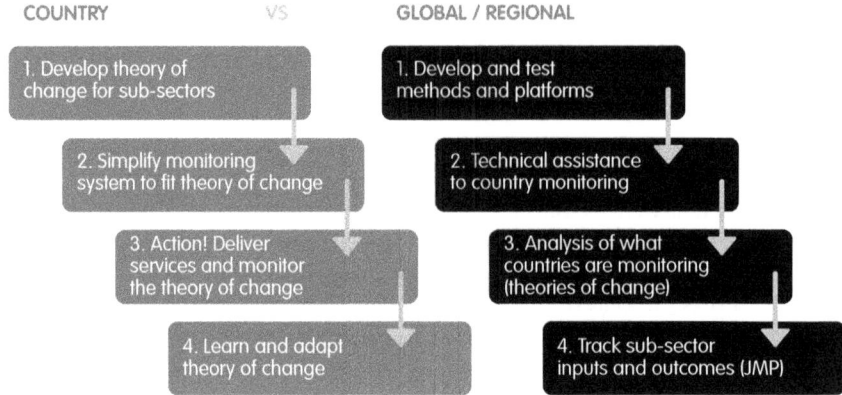

Figure 7.4 Roles in WASH monitoring
Source: De Waal, 2013: 10.

These trade-offs led De Waal to suggest that the global monitoring system might work towards discrete roles and different monitoring strategies at country and global or regional levels, as illustrated in Figure 7.4. De Waal argues that it is difficult for an approach to undertake both these columns of activities.

Developing a shared monitoring framework through Sanitation and Water for All

The emergence of SWA provides a timely platform to better align global, regional, and national monitoring. The sector is well positioned to develop a shared global monitoring framework as described in Brocklehurst (2012). Brocklehurst describes the components of such a shared framework to be:

- 'a shared vision of the **goals and principles** of monitoring;
- an inventory of the **key monitoring initiatives** that make up the framework;
- a menu of the **types of monitoring** (water resources, infrastructure, financial flows, human resources, functionality, equity outcomes, impacts etc.) which avoids gaps and optimizes complementarities;
- a **range of methods** used for data collection and analysis, including new methods supported by mobile technology, and joint efforts to scale up innovation;
- a set of agreed, **common standards** for monitoring information;
- **shared use of monitoring information** to improve transparency, strengthen accountability for results achieved and advocate for the sector, both within countries and globally' (Brocklehurst, 2012).

SWA has created a task team on the global monitoring framework to increase its support to harmonizing global monitoring and improving global, regional, and national alignment. As a partnership, SWA is seeking to:

- facilitate consensus on a shared global monitoring framework across the entire sector, and increase coordination of monitoring between development stakeholders that are SWA partners;
- support efforts to find new and improved ways to monitor challenging aspects, such as measuring hygiene, or tracking financing from all sources;
- support efforts to strengthen national and sub-national monitoring and analysis of sector bottlenecks;
- facilitate the development of a shared set of standards for monitoring data;
- support countries to use the results of monitoring to strengthen sector processes, particularly planning;
- encourage donor partners to use credible financial flow and disaggregated access data to better target assistance and assess investment effectiveness;
- use monitoring information to raise the profile and political prioritization of the sector, and advocate for WASH in global monitoring initiatives, in particular in post-2015 monitoring.

A greater level of cohesion and collaboration could ultimately lead to agreement within the sector on one global agency to undertake sector monitoring and one agency to take on a regulatory function in global monitoring. This function could include encouraging monitoring according to agreed standards, benchmarking and reporting on the quality of monitoring, facilitating coordination across agencies, tracking the burden put on national agencies by global and regional initiatives, and balancing the costs and benefits of data sharing. While ambitious, this step would ensure that the concept of a shared monitoring framework became an operational reality.

Conclusions

Monitoring in the WASH sector is crowded and poorly coordinated and there is little consistency or quality control of sector data. Much valuable data is collected but not used fully, and there is considerable duplication of effort. Lack of alignment between global, regional, and national monitoring is a significant challenge.

What are the challenges at the different levels and what are the promising ways forward to tackle them?

Country level

Strengthening national and sub-national monitoring will undoubtedly give the greatest and most direct return to improving sector data and monitoring systems. Effective national-level monitoring is imperative, as it is the basis for sub-national, national, and global decision making.

Countries have highly diverse sector problems. Country monitoring systems should be designed to respond to country-specific theories of change and problem frames and be encouraged to focus resources on a few local objectives. In order to make monitoring 'fit for purpose', WASH monitoring at country level (and at all other levels) needs a set of minimum procedures to avoid monitoring systems capturing everything just because they can thanks to advances in ICT. Instead, country sector monitoring should focus on a much shorter list of what is 'sufficient to know', as opposed to what would be 'nice to know'.

Countries should be encouraged to build coherent national monitoring systems with the following characteristics: strong information governance with clear roles and responsibilities and with its foundations in national legislation and regulation; standard processes; a standard set of definitions and parameters (measuring the same things in the same way); and a system to validate data and accredit data collectors.

Systems should have incentives consciously built into their design so that data collection is directly linked to decisions. Feedback mechanisms need to be a standard component of all monitoring processes.

There are encouraging examples of countries taking the initiative to promote convergence of data points from different sources through multi-stakeholder dialogue and political will.

The sector has several tested country sector and thematic analytical tools that can deepen country sector analysis. Stronger collaboration is needed between the agencies that have developed these tools, and they should agree to try not to duplicate country applications but to seek the widest country support, so that a larger number of countries benefit by having stronger country sector analysis. All countries should be encouraged to apply at least one of the available tools to deepen their understanding of the national state of the sector, to identify and address key bottlenecks, and to gain more insight into the factors shaping or limiting progress.

Regional level

Regional monitoring instruments are under development in Africa and South Asia to report on regional political commitments. This is a welcome addition to better inform regional leaders, but carries risks of introducing further incongruities and spending additional resources on monitoring with limited impact.

Regions are diverse, have different theories of change, and need different priorities in monitoring. Regional monitoring systems should have a 'light touch' and build on country priorities without imposing monitoring on a range of indicators of little importance at country level. Regional monitoring systems need to reach out to both national and global systems to retain the integrity of the whole global monitoring system.

Global level

The WASH sector's key global instruments – the JMP for access data and GLAAS for information on inputs – have made significant advances in their focus and strategy. They monitor complementary issues. Arguably both processes might be housed in a single, well-resourced entity, but their contents and approach are necessarily different. Both the JMP and GLAAS are preparing major reports in 2014 and are well positioned to adapt to the post-MDG environment.

The range of global data collected needs to be highly selective, to be comparable spatially and over time, and to minimize the burden it places on national agencies. The JMP has already effectively achieved this through its use of household surveys and 'harmonization' through the introduction of standardized questions. GLAAS is at an earlier stage of development, but the signs are encouraging that its scope and number of indicators are being streamlined.

GLAAS should continue dialogue with agencies supporting country-level analytic processes, such as CSOs and WASH BATs, and encourage them to include a GLAAS common core data set. However, it should not attempt full alignment between country data sets of country sector analyses. GLAAS should remain 'light touch' and focused. GLAAS could focus its limited country support in countries where no recent country-level sector analysis has been undertaken, and, in other countries, it could harvest data from data sets created by existing analyses.

The global monitoring system should align with a global accountability framework. SWA represents an important and growing grouping of JMP and GLAAS clients. Without burdening the JMP and GLAAS with further bureaucratic management, they should be encouraged to be accountable to a global platform, such as SWA, which represents all sector stakeholders and interacts with the sector's global leadership in the HLM.

The emergence of SWA provides a timely platform to better align global, regional, and national monitoring. The sector is well positioned to develop a shared global monitoring framework: SWA has created a task force on the global monitoring framework with a mandate to work towards a shared WASH monitoring framework.

A greater level of cohesion and collaboration could ultimately lead to agreement within the sector on one global agency to undertake sector monitoring and one agency to take on a regulatory function in global monitoring.

Endnotes

1. Ministers at the 2008 AfricaSan meeting committed to 11 key commitments to improve sanitation investment and performance in their countries.

References

AMCOW (2011) *Pathways to Progress: Transitioning to Country-led Service Delivery Pathways to Meet Africa's Water Supply and Sanitation Targets. AMCOW's Country Status Overview Regional Synthesis Report*, Washington DC: Water and Sanitation Program of the World Bank.

Brocklehurst, C. (2012) 'Towards a shared global monitoring framework: defining a role for Sanitation and Water for All', background paper prepared for the SWA Partnership Meeting, Johannesburg, South Africa, 12–14 November.

Butterworth, J. (2013) 'Why different methods generate different numbers: case study from Ethiopia', paper presented at the IRC Symposium 2013: Monitoring WASH Services Delivery, Addis Ababa, Ethiopia, 9–11 April.

Cross, P. and Brocklehurst, C. (2013), 'Building coherence in global–regional–national monitoring', keynote paper presented at the IRC Symposium 2013: Monitoring WASH Services Delivery, Addis Ababa, Ethiopia, 9–11 April.

De Waal, D. (2013) 'CSOs, MAPAS and SDAs: different contexts, divergent theories of change', PowerPoint presentation at the IRC Symposium 2013: Monitoring WASH Services Delivery, Addis Ababa, Ethiopia, 9–11 April.

Harvey, P. (2013) 'Applying sustainability analysis to rural water services', paper presented at the IRC Symposium 2013: Monitoring WASH Services Delivery, Addis Ababa, Ethiopia, 9–11 April.

Hutton, G., Trevett, A. and Harvey, P. (2013) 'The WASH Bottleneck Analysis Tool (BAT)', paper presented at the IRC Symposium 2013: Monitoring WASH Services Delivery, Addis Ababa, Ethiopia, 9–11 April.

Luyendijk, R. and Allély-Fermé, D. (2013) 'Next generation of global approaches to WASH monitoring', PowerPoint presentation at the IRC Symposium 2013: Monitoring WASH Services Delivery, Addis Ababa, Ethiopia, 9–11 April.

Luyendijk, R. and Bostoen, K. (2013) 'Global monitoring's forgotten history: typewriter to smartphone in five decades', PowerPoint presentation at the IRC Symposium 2013: Monitoring WASH Services Delivery, Addis Ababa, Ethiopia, 9–11 April.

Norman, R. and Franceys, R. (2013) 'Monitoring: fit for purpose?', PowerPoint presentation at the IRC Symposium 2013: Monitoring WASH Services Delivery, Addis Ababa, Ethiopia, 9–11 April.

Patkar, A. (2013) 'South Asia and sanitation monitoring', PowerPoint presentation at the IRC Symposium 2013: Monitoring WASH Services Delivery, Addis Ababa, Ethiopia, 9–11 April.

Swann, P. (2013) 'The role of UN-Water GLAAS in monitoring WASH', PowerPoint presentation at the IRC Symposium 2013: Monitoring WASH Services Delivery, Addis Ababa, Ethiopia, 9–11 April.

UNDP (2006) *Beyond Scarcity: Power, Poverty and the Global Water Crisis. Human Development Report 2006*, New York NY: United Nations Development Programme (UNDP).

Vodounhessi, A., and Mbaziira, R. (2013) 'The pan-African M&E as high level advocacy tool for accelerating achievement of water and sanitation goal in Africa', PowerPoint presentation at the IRC Symposium 2013: Monitoring WASH Services Delivery, Addis Ababa, Ethiopia, 9–11 April.

WHO (2012) *UN-Water Global Annual Assessment of Sanitation and Drinking-Water (GLAAS) 2012 Report: The Challenge of Extending and Sustaining Services*, Geneva: World Health Organization (WHO).

About the author

Piers Cross, a South African, is a leading international spokesperson and strategist in water supply and sanitation. Piers Cross worked for over 20 years with the World Bank, including as global manager of the Water and Sanitation Program. He supports several agencies on advisory, policy, and evaluation assignments. Piers Cross was recently inducted into the World Toilet Organization's Hall of Fame for his dedicated services to global sanitation and he is a member of IRC's supervisory board.

CHAPTER 8
Setting the priorities

Ton Schouten and Stef Smits

The chapters of this book cover a broad spectrum of monitoring initiatives – from global monitoring to monitoring at the level of local government, from country-led monitoring to project monitoring, and from monitoring water service delivery to monitoring sanitation and hygiene. The great opportunities of new information and communication technologies (ICTs) have been explained and assessed. Constraints and opportunities have been identified for all these levels and sub-sectors. The question for this chapter is whether these ongoing monitoring initiatives are contributing to sustainable water, sanitation, and hygiene (WASH) service delivery, and to lasting water and sanitation for everyone.

Keywords: government leadership, repeated data collection, coordination, performance monitoring, service levels

A genuine drive to monitor more and better

There is a genuine drive to monitor and to make monitoring better and stronger. At all levels and by all stakeholders.

- Governments see the need to have data about the performance of water and sanitation services to be able to plan and manage these services better. The last couple of years have seen the first country-wide inventories of data at scale, for example in Ethiopia, Liberia, and Ghana (Hailu Debela, 2013; Koroma, 2013; Adank et al., 2013).
- Development partners are more critical about the value of their investments; this is driven by reports of high levels of non-functionality of infrastructure and by political debates in the home countries demanding value for (aid) money. Monitoring is a tool for development partners to assess the value of their investments. Some development partners have included sustainability clauses in arrangements with implementing agencies; these oblige agencies to assure sustainability of investments for a period of 10 years (Lockwood, 2014).

- With the end of the millennium development goals (MDGs) in sight, the international community is defining the development goals and targets for beyond 2015 – and consequently the monitoring indicators to measure whether the targets are met. New targets will need new monitoring indicators and possibly new ways to measure the indicators (Luyendijk and Allély-Fermé, 2013).
- ICT has enabled much faster and more efficient data collection and attractive visual ways to report on data. ICT has caused a rush of data collection, not only for monitoring project results but also for national-scale mapping of WASH services and their functionality (Pearce et al., 2014).
- There is a shift in thinking on what exactly needs to be monitored. Over the last 20 to 30 years, the focus has been on monitoring access to WASH services driven by the desire to provide water and sanitation to as many people as possible and as fast as possible. Coverage has gone up and more people have gained access to water supply and sanitation; this means that there is more infrastructure on the ground and more infrastructure to be maintained. Information on the high levels of non-functionality of infrastructure has therefore caused concerns and the call for a much greater emphasis on the sustainability of infrastructure; monitoring should provide data not only on access but also on the sustainability of services provided (Adank et al., 2013).
- Triggered by the endorsement of the United Nations of the human right to water and sanitation and by research projects of international organizations such as IRC, the attention is shifting from monitoring the supply of infrastructure to monitoring the delivery of water and sanitation services (De Albuquerque, 2012; Moriarty et al., 2010). From a service delivery perspective, monitoring needs to show the level of service people receive and are entitled to receive: the amount of water, the quality of that water, and the reliability and accessibility of their water supply. For sanitation, taking a service delivery perspective means not only counting the number of toilets built but monitoring the use of those toilets, hygienic behaviour, and the disposal of faecal sludge (Potter et al., 2011). For both water and sanitation, the supply-driven notion of functionality of infrastructure is shifting to the notion of the service that people are entitled to receive.

Haphazard monitoring initiatives

Are these monitoring initiatives and the shifting perspectives on what it is that needs to be monitored contributing to more sustainable WASH services? There is not a great deal of evidence as yet that a service delivery approach, new ICT, the sustainable development goals (SDGs) for beyond 2015, sustainability clauses, and the recent national inventories are resulting in more sustainable services. It is too early to see changes on the ground. And monitoring on its own will not result in more sustainable services. There are other building blocks that need to be taken into account, although having the information on what exactly is provided on the ground is a crucial first step to start solving problems and improving the planning of service delivery (Lockwood and Smits, 2011). What are the challenges that will need to be tackled to make monitoring contribute to more sustainable services?

Most of the recent initiatives are happening in a rather haphazard way. Some are driven by the opportunities of new ICT; some are driven by the elaboration of the post-2015 SDGs; and some are driven by the interests of development partners to assess the value of their investments. The interests in monitoring are diverse and accountability goes to a variety of stakeholders, from political leadership in countries and regions to taxpayers and to customers.

- Even though some countries have taken the initiative to start collecting data on their WASH services, often with the support of development partners, these initial efforts are not repeated. This means that changes over time in the quality of services are not being measured, although this is at the heart of good monitoring, i.e. monitoring to improve the planning and financing of WASH service delivery (Dickinson and Bostoen, 2013).
- Many aid agencies deploy their own monitoring systems for their own projects, as they need to provide accountability to funders at home, be they taxpayers or donors. The result is a multiplicity of project-monitoring systems, which most of the time are not linked to each other or to country monitoring systems, and which usually do not support the development of country monitoring systems (Lockwood, 2014).
- Too often data collection has become a goal in itself, a technical exercise facilitated by political motives and new ICT, while the analysis and use of the data are disregarded.
- Too often the purpose of collecting data is not clear, resulting in databases that are not used for corrective action or decision making. Data is collected from the perspective of 'nice or interesting to know', not from the perspective of 'must know' – i.e. necessary in order to improve services, to repair and correct them, to make a profit, or to be accountable to customers (Norman and Franceys, 2013).
- ICT offers great opportunities for fast and efficient data collection. However, it is too easily forgotten that ICT builds on the same difficult processes that have hampered sector progress so far, and, by itself, ICT cannot improve these processes or the capacities to use the data. Good governance of WASH services includes good governance of monitoring: clear accountability lines, clear purpose and ownership of monitoring, incentives for data collection, systems and processes to analyse and use data, finance and capacity to collect data repeatedly, and finance to act upon the data (Pearce et al., 2014).

- Much of the emphasis on monitoring over the last 20 to 30 years has been on creating global data systems such as the Joint Monitoring Programme (JMP) and Global Analysis and Assessment of Sanitation and Drinking-Water (GLAAS). Country-level monitoring based on service provider data has lagged behind and data used by global monitoring systems is seldom used in countries (Cross, 2014).
- Monitoring sanitation remains a challenge. Most stakeholders acknowledge that counting toilets is not sufficient to understand whether people live healthier lives. Community-led total sanitation (CLTS) has given a boost to short-term change in people's hygienic behaviour and 'open defecation-free' (ODF) is a great indicator to monitor the sustainability of CLTS-triggered changes. But sanitation has not yet penetrated national and local government monitoring systems, which do not measure broader aspects of hygienic behaviour such as hand washing. Monitoring the enabling environment of sanitation and hygiene is an even bigger challenge, for example monitoring private sanitation businesses and the disposal of waste (Van der Voorden and Krukkert, 2014).
- The focus of the WASH sector over the last 20 years has been on providing access – this is understandable, with so many people lacking access to services – and monitoring has focused on the finance for new infrastructure. Now that sustainability is becoming a driver of WASH sector development, financing for infrastructure operation and maintenance, for support to providers, and for repairs and replacement needs to be monitored as well. Systems for monitoring the lifecycle costs of service delivery have not yet been fully developed, which is not surprising given that there is also a lack of systems for budgeting and financing the lifecycle of service delivery (Fonseca, 2014).

Setting the priorities: strengthening local government monitoring

These are some of the challenges of the current monitoring initiatives and their changing perspective – a move towards monitoring the sustainability of services as well as access to services. What is needed to overcome these challenges, and what is needed to make monitoring contribute to more sustainable WASH services? Throughout this book the benchmark for assessing whether monitoring initiatives are contributing to sustainable services has been whether these initiatives contribute to stronger country-led systems, and in particular to stronger monitoring systems at the level of local government. Different stakeholders – governments, development partners, projects, citizens, and others – have different interests and need different data to account for policies and investments. However, they should all put greater effort into strengthening country-led monitoring and monitoring at local government level. Global monitoring, project monitoring, ICT, and government monitoring should strengthen monitoring systems at the level where services are provided; that is, local government. Ultimately (local) government has the mandate and is in the position to deliver and regulate lasting services to customers beyond projects, and it will need systems to monitor whether those services are provided in accordance with the norms and standards of national policy. The priority should be to collect and use data at local government level so that remedial action can be taken; this action could be repairing a broken pump, planning and financing service delivery, instructing service providers to correct mistakes and improve their performance, etc. Such data will be aggregated to national level to inform national government, direct national finance, regulate providers and local authorities, target aid money, and adapt policies and regulation.

The conclusion of this book is a call to action.

- A call to national governments to take ownership of their monitoring systems, to strengthen the capacities and processes for monitoring at local government level, to take leadership in defining the norms and standards for services that need to be delivered and thus monitored, and to coordinate stakeholders and enable them to align their project-monitoring systems with government-led monitoring systems.
- A call to the developers of ICT to strengthen their technologies to allow for repeated data collection and data analysis, and to adapt their ICT to the capacities and data needs of local government.
- A call to development partners to support governments in strengthening national monitoring systems, capacities, and processes, and to set budgets to facilitate monitoring at local government level. This is in addition to development partners conducting the monitoring they need to provide accountability to taxpayers at home.
- A call to international non-governmental organizations to cooperate with local government and strengthen its ability to monitor service delivery in its jurisdiction, and to invest in monitoring systems at local government level besides having the monitoring systems necessary to be accountable to home constituencies.
- A call to all stakeholders to start monitoring actual services delivered, focusing on the norms and standards for water quality, quantity, accessibility, and reliability defined in national policies for those services.
- A call to global monitoring systems to support strengthened monitoring capacities of governments, particularly those relating to the monitoring of actual services delivered, as well as monitoring using household surveys.
- A call to all stakeholders for patience and long-term engagement. Developing and sustaining a monitoring system from the bottom up takes a lot of time for trial and error and each country will need to follow its own particular journey. Uganda needed 15 years to collect the data for its 11 'golden' indicators and to have a water and sanitation atlas and the institutions and processes (such as the joint technical review) that were required to analyse and use the data. Uganda proves that, in the end, long-term engagement pays off. National data is being used by all stakeholders and informs decisions at all levels.

The call to action does not mean that existing monitoring systems should cease to exist. There is a need for the international community to monitor the MDGs and SDGs; service providers will need to have their own systems to monitor whether customers pay and whether their costs are recovered; development partners need data for accountability to home constituencies. All stakeholders have their rightful purposes for collecting data, whether they are to safeguard international norms and standards, to have a sound business, or to be accountable to taxpayers. Monitoring should be driven by the interests of different stakeholder groups. However, looking at the missing link – the imbalance in the array of monitoring initiatives and the potential for monitoring to contribute to delivering sustainable WASH services – priority should be given to strengthening the monitoring systems and capacities of local government. Opportunities and potential are at the door, and that door can be opened by ICT, ongoing decentralization, human right for WASH, and above all the realization that a shift is needed from monitoring access to monitoring services, and from aid dependency to country ownership.

References

Adank, M., Smits, S., Bey, V., Verhoeven, J. and Pezon, C. (2013) 'Development and use of service delivery indicators for monitoring rural water services in Ghana, Uganda, Burkina Faso, Colombia, Honduras, Paraguay, El Salvador', paper presented at the IRC Symposium 2013: Monitoring WASH Services Delivery, Addis Ababa, Ethiopia, 9–11 April.

Cross, P. (2014) 'Small steps towards building global–regional–national coherence in monitoring WASH', in T. Schouten and S. Smits (eds), *From Infrastructure to Services: Trends in Monitoring Sustainable Water, Sanitation and Hygiene Services,* pp. 137–156, Rugby: Practical Action Publishing.

De Albuquerque, C. (2012) *On the Right Track: Good Practices in Realising the Rights to Water and Sanitation*, Lisbon: Regulatory Authority for Water and Waste Services (ERSAR).

Dickinson, N. and Bostoen, K. (2013) *ICT for Monitoring Rural Water Services: From Smartphones to Cloud Computing*, Triple-S Working Paper, The Hague: IRC.

Fonseca, C. (2014) 'Making the invisible visible: monitoring the costs and finance needed for sustainable WASH service delivery', in T. Schouten and S. Smits (eds), *From Infrastructure to Services: Trends in Monitoring Sustainable Water, Sanitation and Hygiene Services,* pp. 21–38, Rugby: Practical Action Publishing.

Hailu Debela, T. (2013) 'Monitoring water supplies and sanitation in Ethiopia', PowerPoint presentation at the IRC Symposium 2013: Monitoring WASH Services Delivery, Addis Ababa, Ethiopia, 9–11 April.

Koroma, A. (2013) 'Monitoring wash services: the Liberia story', PowerPoint presentation at the IRC Symposium 2013: Monitoring WASH Services Delivery, Addis Ababa, Ethiopia, 9–11 April.

Lockwood, H. (2014) 'Transforming accountability and project monitoring for stronger national WASH sectors', in T. Schouten and S. Smits (eds), *From Infrastructure to Services: Trends in Monitoring Sustainable Water, Sanitation and Hygiene Services*, pp. 63–84, Rugby: Practical Action Publishing.

Lockwood, H. and Smits, S. (2011) *Supporting Rural Water Supply: Moving Towards a Service Delivery Approach*, Rugby: Practical Action Publishing.

Luyendijk, R. and Allély-Fermé, D. (2013) 'Next generation of global approaches to WASH monitoring', PowerPoint presentation at the IRC Symposium 2013: Monitoring WASH Services Delivery, Addis Ababa, Ethiopia, 9–11 April.

Moriarty, P., Batchelor, C., Fonseca, C., Klutse, A., Naafs, A., Nyarko, A., Pezon, K., Potter, A., Reddy, R. and Snehalatha, M. (2010) *Ladders and Levels for Assessing and Costing Water Service Delivery*, WASHCost Global Working Paper 2, The Hague: IRC.

Norman, R. and Franceys, R. (2013) 'Monitoring: fit for purpose?', PowerPoint presentation by Rachel Norman at the IRC Symposium 2013: Monitoring WASH Services Delivery, Addis Ababa, Ethiopia, 9–11 April.

Pearce, J., Dickinson, N. and Welle, K. (2014) 'Technology, data, and people: opportunities and pitfalls of using ICT to monitor sustainable WASH service delivery', in T. Schouten and S. Smits (eds), *From Infrastructure to Services: Trends in Monitoring Sustainable Water, Sanitation and Hygiene Services*, pp. 85–108, Rugby: Practical Action Publishing.

Potter, A., Klutse, A., Snehalatha, M., Batchelor, C., Uandela, A., Naafs, A., Fonseca, C. and Moriarty, P. (2011) *Assessing Sanitation Service Levels*, WASHCost Global Working Paper 3, 2nd edition, The Hague: IRC.

Van der Voorden, C. and Krukkert, I. (2014) 'Behaviour, sustainability, and inclusion: trends, themes, and lessons in monitoring sanitation and hygiene', in T. Schouten and S. Smits (eds), *From Infrastructure to Services: Trends in Monitoring Sustainable Water, Sanitation and Hygiene Services*, pp. 109–136, Rugby: Practical Action Publishing.

Index

Access-based data management 91
access to WASH
    definition 47
    equity and 123–5
    indicators, examples of 46, 58
    in Liberia 95
    progress in 87, 158
    widespread monitoring of 2, 158
accountability
    development partners, issues for 64, 69, 157, 159
    governments, issues for 66–8, 74
    increased demand for 2, 157
    project and country-led monitoring, coordination of and 64, 67–9, 79, 159
    as reason for monitoring 66
affordability, measurement of 33–4
Afghanistan, challenges for 146
Africa
    regional monitoring in 145, 146
    sanitation and hygiene programs in 117–19
    sector-level approaches in 70, 81
    see also specific country
African Development Bank (AfDB) 70, 81
African Union 145
Ahmed, M. 126–8
aid agencies *see* development partners; *specific agency*
Akvo Field Level Operations Watch (FLOW) 78, 88, 89, 95, 101
algorithms 14
Asia
    South Asia, regional monitoring in 146
    South East Asia, sector development analyses in 143
asset management 32
Australian Government Department of Foreign Affairs and Trade (DFAT) 74–5, 78, 97
automated data collection 89, 92, 93–4, 102–3

Bangladesh, BRAC WASH monitoring in 126–8
behaviour monitoring in sanitation and hygiene 112, 115–17, 126–9, 132
Bevan, J. 118–19
block monitoring, in Malawi 121
Bolivia, smartphone data collection in 65

BRAC
    ICT support services 103–4
    monitoring in Bangladesh 126–8
Burr, Peter 31

capital expenditure, definition 24
challenges for monitoring *see* monitoring: challenges and issues for
CLTS *see* Plan International Pan-Africa CLTS program
collaboration and monitoring *see* sector-level monitoring
Colombia, data collection structure in 13
community approaches to sanitation and hygiene 110, 111, 117–20, 121
community roles in monitoring 44–5, 51
cost-effectiveness monitoring 120, 122–3
costs and financing, monitoring of 21–35
    affordability and financial sustainability indicators 33–4
    challenges for 24, 28–9, 32
    current state of 22
    importance of 21–2
    sources of funding 23–4
    studies on 29–31
costs of monitoring 15, 16, 73, 104
country-led monitoring 39–58
    case studies 41–2, 43–4, 49–56, 142
    challenges for 39, 40, 66–7, 138
    community roles in 44–5
    global monitoring and 149–50
    importance of 11
    indicators for 45–9, 57
    information flow in 42–4
    leadership of 42, 56, 66–7, 79, 141, 161
    messy reality of 41–2
    project monitoring, combination with (*see* project monitoring)
    recommendations for 3, 56–7, 141, 145, 152
    Sanitation and Water for All (SWA) 150–1
    use of term 42
    see also sector-level monitoring
coverage, definition 47
criteria, definition 13
CSOs (country status overviews) 6, 143, 144

Danish aid agency (DANIDA) 82
data collection
    case studies 88–9, 94–9
    challenges for 85, 86, 93–4

INDEX

household surveys 141, 147, 148
sector-level monitoring, divergent data in 138, 139, 141–2, 148
by volunteers 45, 120
see also mobile technology
data processing 13–15
data storage 103
De Waal, D. 146
development partners, support of for sector-level monitoring 67–81
  accountability issues 64, 69, 157, 159
  examples 43–4, 70, 71–3, 76–9, 95–9, 128–9
  recommendations 80–1, 161
  strategies for 74–5
  types of collaboration 9–11
  vicious cycle of accountability 64, 69
direct observation, indicators based on 116, 127, 129
disability and access 123–5
Dutch government development agency (DGIS) 71–2, 73, 78

East-Timor *see* Timor-Leste
enabling environment 6, 7, 75, 114–15
Engineers Without Borders Canada 50, 73, 121
equality and WASH 125
equity and WASH 123–5
  indicators for 46
Ethiopia
  cost and finance monitoring in 25, 29–30
  indicators and reporting in 81
  monitoring journey 55–6, 142
  perverse incentives in 47
Excel-based data management 91, 100, 103–4

feature phones 89, 90, 97
Franceys, Richard 32
FrontlineSMS 88, 89, 90, 98
functionality indicators 46

Ghana
  cost and finance monitoring in 31
  ICT usability in 100, 102
  service delivery indicators in 78
  water services ladders, use of 48
GLAAS (Global Analysis and Assessment of Sanitation and Drinking-Water) 26, 147–8, 153
global monitoring
  challenges for 138–9
  current state of 138–9, 147–8
  recommendations and considerations for 148–51, 153
  Sanitation and Water for All (SWA) 150–1

governance 8–10, 16, 66–7
government-led monitoring 42, 131–2
  see also country-led monitoring; local government; national government
Grundfos Lifelink 93

hand-washing 116, 117
handpumps, smart technology for 93–4
Honduras, monitoring in 79, 81
household contributions to WASH services 23–4
household surveys 141, 147, 148
hygiene effectiveness ladder 123

ICT (information and communication technology)
  benefits of 2, 86
  case studies 88–9, 94–6, 96–9
  challenges for 98–9, 104
  definition 85–6
  design considerations 99–105, 126
  for management and analysis 91–2
  see also mobile technology
impact monitoring 8
'improved drinking water sources,' definition 58
India 128–9, 146
indicators
  for access 46, 58
  for behaviour change in sanitation and hygiene 116, 122, 127
  for country-led monitoring 45–9, 57
  definition 13
  examples of 46
  increasing number of 48, 139, 140
  perverse incentives and 47
  recommendations for 57
indices, definition 14
Indonesia, management information system setup in 78
information systems 13–15
innovation *see* ICT; trends in monitoring
input monitoring 2, 7, 147–8
institution-based monitoring 10
international law, recognition of right to water and sanitation 125
inventories *see* water point mapping
IRC
  cost-effectiveness monitoring 122–3
  lifecycle costs approach 24, 30
  qualitative information system (QIS) 127–8
  water services monitoring in Ghana 100

Joint Monitoring Programme (JMP) 2, 62, 132, 141–2, 147–8
joint sector reviews 43

INDEX 167

Kenya 41, 140
Kumar, A. 126, 128–9

Latin America
  challenges for WASH 146
  common monitoring systems in 81
  service delivery monitoring in 143
leadership, in country-led monitoring 42, 56, 66–7, 79, 141, 161
Liberia
  data collection in 88–9, 94–6
  monitoring journey 55
  see also data collection: case studies; monitoring journeys: case studies
lifecycle costs 24, 25
local governments, role in monitoring
  importance of 16, 119–20, 132
  recommendations 160–2

M4Water 88, 89
Madagascar, indicator definition issues 48
Malawi
  block monitoring in 121
  indicators used 46
  monitoring journey 51–2
  need for affordable monitoring 73
  water point mapping in 51
Maldives, challenges for 146
MAPAS (Monitoreo de los Avances del País en Agua Potable y Saneamiento) 143–4
market based solutions 129–31
measurement of data 13–14
menstrual hygiene management 125
mobile technology 14, 45, 87–91
  feature phones 89, 90, 97
  smartphones 65, 89, 90, 127, 129
  SMS 45, 90, 93–4, 97, 98
    automated data collection 89, 92, 93–4, 102–3
    FrontlineSMS 88, 89, 90, 98
MoMo 89, 93
monitoring
  areas and types 4–11
  challenges and issues for
    capacity and resources 16, 66–7
    for cost and finance monitoring 24, 28–9, 32
    cost of 16, 73, 104
    for country-led monitoring 39, 40, 66–7, 138
    for data collection 85, 86, 93–4
    governance 8–10, 16, 66–7
    in ICT 98–9, 104
    intra-institutional collaboration 64, 66–9, 71, 72–4, 138–9, 159
    political issues 32, 47
    in rural areas 40–1, 52, 66
  using information 1–2, 12, 15, 131, 159
  trends (*see* trends in monitoring)
monitoring cultures and journeys 49–56
monitoring cycles *see* project cycles
Monitoring Sustainable WASH Symposium 77, 79
Mozambique 30–1, 122
mWater.co 89

national governments, role in monitoring 2, 42, 56, 79, 161
NGOs
  in country-led monitoring 43–4
  finance monitoring and 25
  see also development partners; *specific NGO*
Nicaragua, SIASAR initiative in 79
Nigeria, sanitation and hygiene programs in 117–19
non-discrimination, definition 125
Norman, Rachel 140
Nyarko, Kwabena 31

observation, indicators based on 116, 127, 129
Open Data Kit (ODK) 89
open defecation-free (ODF) environments 115, 117, 118–20
outcome monitoring
  in sanitation and hygiene 112, 115–17, 126–9, 132
  scope of 7–8
output monitoring 7 *see also* Joint Monitoring Programme (JMP)
Oxford University, smart handpumps piloting by 93–4

Panama, SIASAR initiative in 79
parameters, definition 13
Paris Declaration 2, 39, 63, 68
Patkar, Archana 146
performance monitoring *see* outcome monitoring
perverse incentives 8–9, 47, 69
Plan International Pan-Africa CLTS program 117–18
private sector in sanitation and hygiene 129–31
programme design 104–5
project cycles
  ICT within 88
  monitoring of 5
  steps and phases 11–12, 58
project monitoring
  advantages of 63, 64, 65
  country-led monitoring, combination with

challenges 67–9, 71–4, 76, 131
  examples 70, 71–2, 76–9
  recommendations 79–81
 definition and types 9, 64–5
 disadvantages
  accountability issues 64, 66–7, 69, 159
  narrow focus of 63, 64
  power of development partner 66, 69
  short-term nature of 63, 64, 71, 159
proxy indicators 116

qualitative information system (QIS) 127–8

recurrent expenditure, definition 24
regional monitoring 145–0, 150–1, 152
relational databases 91
results monitoring 5, 65
rural communities, challenges of
  for monitoring 40–1, 52, 66
  for WASH sector 87

SACOSAN 146
sanitation and hygiene
  behavioural outcomes, monitoring of 112, 115–17, 126–9, 132
  benefits of monitoring 109–10
  case studies 126–9
  community approaches 110, 111, 117–20, 121
  cost-effectiveness, monitoring of 120, 122–3
  enabling environment and 114–15
  market based solutions 129–31
  recommendations for monitoring 126, 132
  right to 123–5
  trends in monitoring 109–13
Sanitation and Water for All (SWA) 150–1
sanitation ladder 110–11
sanitation marketing 129–31
scores, definition 14
sector development analyses (SDAs) 143
sector-level monitoring
  data divergence in 138, 139, 141–2, 148
  definition 10
  intra-institutional collaboration
   challenges for 64, 66–9, 71, 72–4, 138–9, 159
   examples 43–4, 70, 71–3, 76–9, 95–9, 128–9
   recommendations 80–1, 161
   strategies for 74–5
   types of collaboration 9–11
  see also country-led monitoring; global monitoring; regional monitoring
SeeSaw 90
self-reported behaviour as indicator 116, 127–8

service delivery monitoring 6, 110, 143
SIASAR (Sistema de Información de Agua y Saneamiento Rural) 14, 79
Sierra Leone 56
Sijbesma, C. 126–8
Singh, U. 126, 128–9
smart handpumps 93–4
smartphones 65, 89, 90, 127, 129
SMS 45, 90, 93–4, 97, 98
  automated data collection 89, 92, 93–4, 102–3
  FrontlineSMS 88, 89, 90, 98
South Africa
  data collection in 45
  indicators used 48
  monitoring journey 52, 53
  use of SMS in 45
South America see Latin America
South Asia, regional monitoring in 146
South East Asia, sector development analyses in 143
spreadsheet-enabled mapping 91
stakeholders, disconnects between 8–9
sustainability
  of sanitation and hygiene behaviours 113, 130, 132
  of sanitation and hygiene monitoring 120
  of WASH services 33–4, 144, 158–60

tariffs, for financing 23–4, 120
taxes, for financing 23, 120
technology see ICT
Technology Applicability Framework tool 126
Thailand, monitoring in 45, 52, 54
Thomas, A. 118–19
3Ts (tariffs, taxes, and transfers) 23–4
Timor-Leste
  cost and finance monitoring in 25
  data collection in 96–9
  ICT use in 102
  monitoring journey 54–5
  service monitoring in 46
TrackFin initiative (GLAAS) 26
transfers, for financing 23, 34, 120
trends in monitoring 1–2
  accountability, increased demand for 2, 157
  government leadership, increased focus on 15–16, 79, 131–2
  ICT developments 2, 65, 85, 86, 87, 106, 139
  market solutions, support for 129–31
  in sanitation and hygiene monitoring 109–13
  sector-level monitoring, shift towards 15, 63–4, 113

shift to community approaches 110, 111, 117
sustainability, greater emphasis on 2, 158, 160
volume of monitoring and data, increase in 138, 139, 140

Uganda
  cost and finance monitoring in 26–7, 30
  data collection structure 13
  indicators used 46, 48
  information flow in 43–4
  inter-institutional cooperation 10
  monitoring journey 50, 161
  publicising of performance reports 45
  sector monitoring in 72, 82
  use of SMS in 14
  volume of data in 140
UK, cost and finance monitoring in 32
UK Department for International Development (DFID) 50
UNICEF
  Joint Monitoring Programme (JMP) 2, 62, 132, 141–2, 147–8
  in Liberia 78, 95
  in Mozambique 78
  sustainability analysis support 144
  WASH BATs 143–4
United Nations, recognition of right to water and sanitation 125
United States Agency for International Development (USAID) 72

universality, definition 125
'use of water supply,' definition 47

volunteers, role in monitoring 45, 120

WASH Advocates study (WASH in Schools) 76, 77
Water For People (WFP) 65, 71, 130–1
water ladders 7–8, 48
Water Missions International 93, 101
Water Point Mapper 88, 89, 100
water point mapping 5–6, 51, 56, 89
water quality 2, 46, 54, 147
WaterAid 29–30, 30–1, 51 *see also* Water Point Mapper
WellDone 93
West Africa, monitoring in 44, 45
World Bank programmes 78 *see also* WSP (Water and Sanitation Program)
World Health Organisation (WHO)
  GLAAS (Global Analysis and Assessment of Sanitation and Drinking-Water) 26, 147–8, 153
  Joint Monitoring Programme (JMP) 2, 62, 132, 141–2, 147–8
WSP (Water and Sanitation Program)
  qualitative information system (QIS) 127–8
  rural sanitation programme 114, 128
  Total Sanitation and Sanitation Marketing program 114
  water point mapping in Liberia 95

www.ingramcontent.com/pod-product-compliance
Ingram Content Group UK Ltd.
Pitfield, Milton Keynes, MK11 3LW, UK
UKHW021636230326
11407UKWH00015B/38